Practicing Islam

Central Eurasia in Context Series
Douglas Northrop, Editor

Practicing Islam

Knowledge, Experience, and Social Navigation in Kyrgyzstan

David W. Montgomery

University of Pittsburgh Press

Portions of Chapter 5 include a reworking of material previously published as David W. Montgomery, 2014. "Towards a Theory of the Rough Ground: Merging the Policy and Ethnographic Frames of Religion in the Kyrgyz Republic." *Religion, State & Society* 42 (1): 23–45. The author appreciates the journal's permission to reuse some of this material.

All photographs in this book were taken by David W. Montgomery.

Published by the University of Pittsburgh Press, Pittsburgh, Pa., 15260

Library of Congress Cataloging-in-Publication Data

Names: Montgomery, David W., 1968– author.
Title: Practicing Islam: Knowledge, Experience, and Social Navigation in Kyrgyzstan / David W. Montgomery.
Description: Pittsburgh : University of Pittsburgh Press, 2016. | Series: Central Eurasia in context series | Includes bibliographical references and index.
Identifiers: LCCN 2016039767 | ISBN 9780822964285 (pbk.)
Subjects: LCSH: Islam—Kyrgyzstan. | Kyrgyzstan—Religious life and customs.
Classification: LCC BP63.K96 M66 2016 | DDC 297.095843—dc23
LC record available at https://lccn.loc.gov/2016039767

For my parents, Luke and Dee Montgomery
*All things of meaning have origin
and most begin at home*

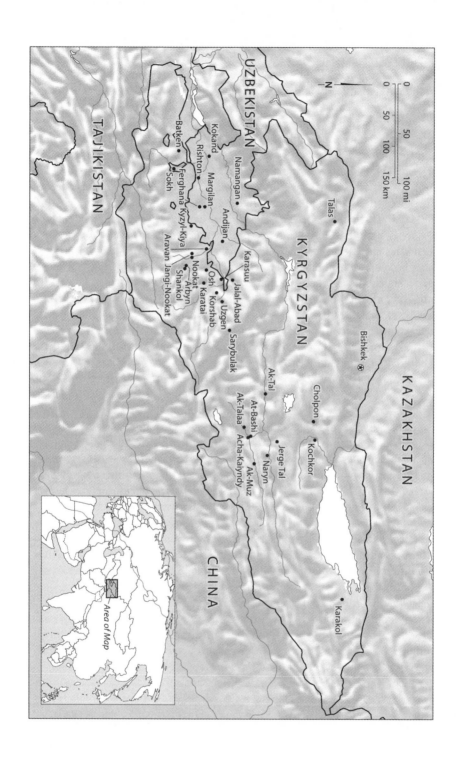

Whichever way the ship steers its course, there will always be seen ahead of it the flow of the waves it cleaves. To the men in the ship the movement of those waves will be the only motion perceptible.

It is only by watching closely, moment by moment, the movement of that flow, and comparing it with the movement of the ship, that we are convinced that every moment that flowing by of the waves is due to the forward movement of the ship, and that we have been led into error by the fact that we are ourselves moving too.

Leo Tolstoy, *War and Peace*

Out of timber so crooked as that from which man is made nothing entirely straight can be built.

Immanuel Kant, "Idee zu einer allgemeinen Geschichte in welbürgerlicher Absicht"

Contents

Preface

Music, states of happiness, mythology, faces scored by time, certain twilights, certain places, all want to tell us something, or told us something we should not have missed, or are about to tell us something. This imminence of a revelation that does not take place is, perhaps, the esthetic fact.

Jorge Luis Borges, *A Personal Anthology*

There are no religions that are false.

Emile Durkheim, *The Elementary Forms of Religious Life*

The problem in talking about religion is that there are so many abstractions associated with it that people, in reality, rarely talk about religion, even when the topic is religion. Evoking religion in politics is not a theological discourse on religion but something quite different, even in Islam, where politics is not viewed as separate from religion. The talk of politics in religion, however, places those who agree or disagree in separate playgrounds of differently constructed imaginations.

These imaginative worlds are deeply rooted in the world of experience. A world of sharing bread, of raising children and burying loved ones, of arguments with strangers and conflicts with neighbors—in short, a world of the everyday. The everyday, filled with the spectacularness of the seemingly unspectacular. The everyday is at once routine and always around, yet it is also responsive to extraordinary events and contributes to the making of a meaningful life. This book addresses how meaningful existence is created through people developing the narrative of a religious and cultural self and how this in turn allows one to navigate the social self.

The idea of being critical about religious knowledge came to me through a reflective experience of trying to make sense of my own lived reality relative to stories I was hearing in Kyrgyzstan during my first visit in 1999. That summer, the emergence of the Islamic Movement of Uzbekistan (IMU) as an armed group that wanted to overthrow the Uzbek government and ostensibly establish an Islamic government in the Ferghana Valley created a lot of anxiety, optimism, and fear. I heard claims that the IMU was going to "bring the good life" of employment and higher wages while ushering in a new morality and the end of corruption. There were claims of entire villages supporting the them and that in return the IMU purchased livestock and supplies at above market rate.

In 2000, I spoke with some villagers who said the IMU brought about an increase in religious awareness and higher numbers of worshippers at the local mosque. There was a general understanding by outsiders (meaning nonlocals as well as internationals) that this increase was connected to the ideology of the IMU, which advocated a return to traditionalism, claiming the time of the Prophet Muhammad as the most enlightened and just period of civilization. In conversations with some mosque goers, I noticed the difference between older and younger members. Some of the elders talked about the increase of mosque attendance in economic terms—meaning that people saw material benefit to be gained that may have been a natural corollary of the IMU allegedly purchasing goods at prices above market value. Some of the younger men saw it as the proper reorientation of the village toward a more orthopraxic rendering of Islam.

In both cases, the issue was less about an ideological conviction that brought people to action but rather an ideology that was developed after going to mosque. And the explanations given by both groups of men seemed closely connected to their experiences—the elders looking at things in economic terms and the youth wanting to be different. There is often, however, a tendency to assume more about religion than should be assumed. And this appeared to be one such instance, because what was assumed was that all the men now going to mosque had accepted the ideology of the IMU and of traditionalist Islam, and were thus complicit in supporting a militant overthrow of the government. It is not true, of course. Ideologies come later and one needs only to think of one's own experience to be aware of this.

As children, we come to recognize that which marks the significance of a particular holiday or family gathering. One such aspect is prayer, which to a child may not hold much meaning. But it separates those who pray from those who do not, and it connects a group of similar people who also pray at holidays or family gatherings. To a child, prayer means a cessation of play and the requirement of seriousness and reverence, for which children rarely long.

The development of religious ideology has an uneventful origin. One may join a particular religious community because one was invited, because friends are members of that community, because business opportunities are enhanced by such an association, or a number of equally benign reasons. Of course religious development is more complex than friends, invitations, holiday prayers, and business relations, but the point is that often it is not ideology that first brings someone to a particular religious tradition. It is usually not until later that the meaning of prayers and words is appreciated. And it is not until much later (if ever) that differences of doctrine are understood. But it is often the case that, early in their development, children are introduced and to some extent predisposed to accepting certain (religious) behaviors and actions as normative.

It is a similar situation with those who were seen as supporting the IMU with increased attendance at mosque. It was not an acceptance of ideology, but an act better explained in pragmatic terms such as wanting to be seen acting a particular way, not wanting to be the one who does not go to mosque, and establishing another layer of connectedness for social and economic relationships. There is no doubt that an ideology can be developed quickly and many who went to mosque did find affinity for what they were taught. It thus seemed that a first step toward understanding religion and religious development was to look at what was taught. To look at how people came to know what they claim to know. And that search is tied to experiences that extend beyond formalized religious education.

—⁓—

This book is about the nature of, and need for, practice—practice in the sense of doing. As such, and as the book's subtitle implies, the general argument I am making is about the relationship of knowledge, experience, and social navigation to our engagement in the world. The world in which we all live is messy, imprecise, and contradictory, yet somehow we manage to get through—bruised and broken at times, but we manage—and ascribe meaning to the process.

We do not interact in the world alone and while origins of ideas are at times difficult to pinpoint because of the evolving process through which we make sense of the world, my engagement with the concepts of knowledge, experience, and social navigation has antecedents in my own engagement with the works of others. The use and conceptualization of "knowledge" and the framework of an anthropology of knowledge that I use is heavily influenced by the work of Fredrik Barth.

To some extent, this book can be seen as a partial response to a challenge he gave a graduate class in the fall of 2002: that we "see the world of others as being valued through a lens of knowledge." There, we discussed his proscriptive essay "An Anthropology of Knowledge" (Barth 2002), which sets forth a theoretical agenda for understanding the interconnected, mutually determining components of knowledge: its social organization, corpus, and medium. "Knowledge" is a slippery beast and dividing it into components to understand its constituent parts is where I begin (Chapters 2–4). Barth is less concerned with this, arguing rightly, I believe, "that these three faces of knowledge appear together precisely in the particulars of action in every event of the application of knowledge, in every transaction in knowledge, in every performance" (Barth 2002, 3). This is the framework of analysis that he wishes us to explore, and the synthesis that I attempt in the later parts of the book (Chapter 5 and Conclusion). On the whole, this book attempts to provide a concrete example of how to apply a framework of knowledge and argues its utility to more fully understand variation and change in Islam in Kyrgyzstan.

Seeing the relationship between Islam and everyday life in Central Asia within the ethnographic context is perhaps the most obvious contribution of this work. It builds from the work of some very good colleagues working on the region, but it is presented here as more of a generalist theoretical argument—emerging out of interactions with my interlocutors—of how we can look at religion and knowledge, with Kyrgyzstan being the case that tells that story.

One question that emerges regards the extent to which the discussion of Kyrgyzstan herein is unique—how does Islam in Kyrgyzstan differ from Islam elsewhere? There are differences, to be sure, but part of what I try to show is that there are differences even within Kyrgyzstan and within particular communities that may seem homogenous. This ubiquity of difference is found everywhere.[1] And so while in some instances Kyrgyz Muslims are different from Muslims in Indonesia, Egypt, or anywhere else, the focus is not their exceptionality so much as the way they navigate their social environments to normalize and live within the restrictions and potentialities of their everyday lives. These are some aspects of generalizability that make Kyrgyzstan of interest beyond Central Asia.

A recurring theme throughout, generalizability relates to a theoretical concern of how to theorize movement and change. Theorizing is often understood to describe the paths from point A to point B in a concise, often linear and deliberate fashion, though of course life never proceeds in straight lines—it is fraught with confusion, opportunity, serendipity, and all sorts of things way outside of our control. (Theorists know this, of course, but structure requires simplification.) How we as actors deal with the ongoing challenges of life is what I refer to as "social navigation"—an imprecise concept intended to capture both movement and the ever-present correctives one engages in to realign life toward a particular direction.[2]

Getting by in the world is socially navigating the world, and it entails a good deal of uncertainty and ambiguity that has to be dealt with somehow. This is one function of Islam—and while I focus on Islam and religion in this book, the argument is not unique to Islam; one could apply it more broadly to any context in which we have to get by—that it provides people with a complete vision for understanding and living within the world. This is not to say that it solves all problems, but there is a rich framework that people draw upon to make sense of their environments. They do not do so exclusively, but in collaboration with other conceptual framings of the world. The book explores a multiplicity of ways people engage with Islam and use it to negotiate, give meaning to, and make sense of their worlds.

This social navigation is done within a framework of knowledge. When one navigates one's environment, one does so based on what one "knows" and the contingencies inherent to that knowing. Knowledge is a very amorphous concept and the challenge is how one makes sense of it in a way that can be "seen." Breaking down knowledge into the components of "social organization," "corpus," and "medium" begins to make observing the concept of knowledge—and the context of social navigation—analytically more manageable. Experience, in the sense that John Dewey talks about, is central to this.

Following Barth, I argue that knowledge is a more appropriate tool than simply culture for understanding social navigation. One reason for this is that it helps minimize the risk of essentialism and overgeneralization inherent to engaging with the concept of culture while at the same time acknowledging the need to continue seeing culture as a generative aspect of both knowledge and meaning creation. There are many pieces that go into making our "knowing" that are not fully captured in "culture," but also, importantly, I think we value knowledge differently—more—than culture. The hope behind approaching the subject through a lens of knowledge is that we value the worldview and lifeworld of the subject and all its particularities more than if we come at it from culture alone. Knowledge includes culture, but not only culture. And while the case of Kyrgyzstan may be unique in terms of content, the theoretical framework/argument for understanding the tools used in socially navigating life is not specific to it.

Here I should note that a good deal of research looks at cognitive theories of knowledge and religion. Much of this is elaborate and sophisticated—and I reference some of it throughout—but reducing religion to scientific explanation, in my view, misses the essence of religion as an explanatory way of life. Most often, those advancing cognitive theories do so through a lens that favors a secularist or nonreligious agenda, couched within the constructs of science and scientific language. These are different answers to different questions. To understand religion and social navigation, we need to look beyond science and theoretical abstractions and look to the messiness of everyday life—how even in the midst of suffering, meaning is found and life goes on. This is not my story, at least not only, but that of my interlocutors talking about religion and getting by in the everyday, a story that highlights what these cognitive theories overlook: poetry and the poetics of life. Aristotle understood this; despite relevant insights, reducing life to neuronal stimulation risks obfuscating this point.

The approach I take to exploring religion suggests not only an orienting methodology but also a frame of relevance; that is, the goal is to provide a way of seeing Islam and religion—really everyday life—in a way one can make sense of. The focus is on *everyday* knowledge rather than *doctrinal* knowledge, because people do not live within the sphere of doctrinal knowledge, or at least nowhere near the same extent. Knowledge often is seen to reside with elites, especially intellectual elites, but the more ubiquitous and important task is to better understand the known/lifeworld of nonelites.

———*∿∿*———

The various experiences that are so foundational to becoming aware of how to interact in the world are tied up in the stories that people live. Central here is a community of people who know each other, know about each other, or imagine about each other. In *Spoon River Anthology* Edgar Lee Masters shows through free verse how the various stories of everyday people create an image of the place in which they live (Masters 1992). It is in that sense that I introduce, in varying depth, nearly thirty of my interlocutors. (The List of Interlocutors [Table A.1] will help the reader navigate through this.) The convention within anthropology is to focus more attention on fewer interlocutors and afford the reader a sense of really knowing the person. Perhaps that does make for easier reading, but in art as in life, the details and passing comments in the background give color and context to situation. The network of all my interlocutors is dynamic and at various times draws from the stories of people whom they know well and those whom they barely know, if at all. Some characters the reader may wish to know more about, but that too represents one of the unresolved tensions of knowing and being part of a community: all knowledge is always incomplete.

Acknowledgments

I make the case throughout this book that it is largely through *doing* that we come to *knowing*. In my years of working on this project, it has also become abundantly clear that it is the network of relations that allows us to socially navigate our doing in meaningful ways; even solitude is not managed alone.

Within the context of relations, I have come to know a lot about the generous spirit of my colleagues and friends. I have been constantly amazed by the time and friendship that so many have offered to improve my writing, to make my thinking clearer, and to lighten my days. The number deserving thanks exceeds the many that are mentioned—and some names from the field are absent to protect their identities—but that only highlights how much of a collective endeavor the meaningful aspects of life can be.

I have received assistance from the Institute on Culture, Religion and World Affairs at Boston University; the Institute for the Study of Conflict, Ideology, and Policy at Boston University; the East-West Center for Research and Intercultural Dialogue at the American University in Central Asia; the Aigine Cultural Research Center; the Kroc Institute for International Peace Studies at the University of Notre Dame; and the Center for Russian and East European Studies at the University of Pittsburgh. Some of the initial research for this work was supported in part by a grant from the International Research & Exchanges Board (IREX) with funds provided by the National Endowment for the Humanities, the U.S. Department of State (Title VIII Program), and the IREX Scholar Support Fund. The significance of such funding cannot be overstated, for it provided me the opportunity to conduct long-term ethnographic research in Kyrgyzstan and Uzbekistan. None of these organizations is responsible for the views expressed in this work, but hopefully all will find some validation of their support.

At a personal level, it is friends and colleagues who have made this work possible. Of those connected to the Central Asia region, I express appreciation here to only a representative few of a large list: Laura Adams, Medina Aitieva, Gulnara Aitpaeva, Noor Borbieva, Ted Callahan, John Heathershaw, Alex Horsby, Melitta Jakab, Junus Karimov, Abdujabbor Kayumov, Alisher Khamidov, Cheng-Un Stephen Lam, Morgan Liu, Mukharram Maksudova, Eric McGlinchey, Jennifer Murtazashvili, Madeleine Reeves, Carrie O'Rourke, John Schoeberlein, and Farhod Yuldashev. Sasha and Sveta Titov; Volodia,

Ludmila, Sergei, and Nina Fransov; Rysbai Sarybayev; and Jamilya Nurkulova deserve special mention.

My thinking on the issues of knowledge, experience, and social navigation has been influenced by a number of mentors who have been generous with their support. Fredrik Barth encouraged me to pursue an anthropology of knowledge while Michael Jackson encouraged me to think of theory in terms of social navigation. Adam Seligman, whose influence can be seen throughout my work, pushed me to appreciate the significance of experience as an analytical frame, while Thomas Barfield, Robert Weller, and Thomas Luckmann joined him in setting standards for critical thinking that I aspire to meet. Nelia Ponte helped with the figures used while Irina Burns greatly improved the readability of the text. And Douglas Northrop and Peter Kracht were supportive of this project reaching publication. To all I am grateful.

Last, and more personally, I thank my family for their unfailing support. My sister, Jennifer, and her husband, Nathan, with my niece and nephew, Lauren and Reed, have reminded me of the impact family has on our own becoming. My wife, Sarah, has shown how love and generosity of spirit enrich life itself. And my parents, Luke and Dee Montgomery—to whom this book is dedicated and to whom I trace the beginnings of my knowing and appreciation of the world—made possible so much of what I hold important in life. My gratitude for their impact on my life cannot be overstated; may the efforts put forth in this work be a small token of my appreciation.

Of course, all standard caveats and disclaimers apply: the errors and shortcomings of this work are my own; any successes are due to the influence of my companions in this project. Thank you. It is with humbleness and deep gratitude that I acknowledge the contributions of so many to my understanding of the importance of others in making the everyday meaningful.

ACKNOWLEDGMENTS

Note on Transliteration and Spelling of Personal and Geographical Names

This work uses the standard version of the Library of Congress system for transliterating Russian names and works cited. Exceptions to this rule are personal and geographical names that have accepted English spellings; for example, Leo Tolstoy instead of Lev Tolstoi. The spelling issue becomes more complex with Central Asian personal and geographical names, which have changed since the collapse of the Soviet Union and are no longer russified; for example, Andijan instead of Andizhan, Almaty instead of Alma-Ata, Akayev instead of Akaev. The issue is complicated by the more recent trend to transliterate Central Asian personal and geographical names directly from the Central Asian languages and not from the Russian. Thus, Andijan becomes Andijon, etc. Given the timeframes within which this research was conducted, this work uses *Merriam-Webster's Geographical Dictionary* (1997, 3rd ed.), *Merriam-Webster's Bibliographical Dictionary* (1995), and *Merriam-Webster's Collegiate Dictionary* (2003, 11th ed.). As such, I use Andijan, etc., throughout this book.

Practicing Islam

Introduction

An Anthropology of Knowledge and Life "in the Field"

> "It's a strange image," he said, "and strange prisoners you're telling of."
> "They're like us," I said. "For in the first place, do you suppose such men would
> have seen anything of themselves and one another other than the shadows cast
> by the fire on the side of the cave facing them?"
>
> **Plato,** *The Republic*

> Knowledge about a thing is not the thing itself. You remember what Al-
> Ghazzali told us in the Lecture on Mysticism—that to understand the causes
> of drunkenness, as a physician understands them, is not to be drunk.
>
> **William James,** *The Varieties of Religious Experience*

Religion is what it does. What it *does*, however, is contentious terrain. Contentious not only because it is the actual doing, the expression in action of something inward and at times collective, that challenges community, but also because what religion does involves a great deal of interpretive ambiguity that eludes neat categorization. Getting at what someone believes is generally studied—both informally and academically—by reconciling what one says with observations of what one does. Assessing internal states of meaning is complicated, but essential to navigating the demands of sociality.

It is the relationship between doing and knowing, between action and social navigation that is of concern here. Knowing what it is to be Kyrgyz, Muslim, and/or a Kyrgyz Muslim is formed through the events out of which an individual tries to make sense and meaning of experience. Being Muslim involves some aspect of doing, some part of repetition that frames a particular meaning of Islam. Thus, this book is not a manual of practices, but rather a claim that through the art of doing and the training of practice, Islam is imbued with meaning and creates an environment for community and contestation. Addressing the relationship between meaning and lived experience of Islam in Central Asia—and how events, opportunities, and potentialities create the context from which knowing emerges—sets up the moral distinctiveness of interpreting what religion does.

Introductions to religion generally center on works. Theology is important to the religious, but goes unnoticed except when it gets explicitly tied to action. The pillars of (Sunni) Islam—*shahadah* (declaration of faith), *salat* (prayer), *sawm* (fasting), *zakat* (alms-giving), *hajj* (pilgrimage to Mecca)—are markers of the causal (and casual) association of one's religiousness with the public expression, in one sense, of Islam.[1] It is thus action and environment that become central to making sense of what a religion does.

Of the five pillars of Islam, keeping the fast during Ramadan is perhaps the most dramatic for a traveler to a Muslim country. Friday prayers, of course, are an event and sometimes a statement (though less of a statement about religiosity than many infer) about religious prayer in numbers, but when a community collectively keeps the fast, restaurants are often closed or at least empty during the day, and reopen in full as the sun sets and the fast is broken. The streets fill with excitement as people commune over the evening meal and exuberance emerges from the quiet of the day.

This can be seen in Muslim communities throughout the world, but the picture must not be overly essentialized. In 2004, on a typical Wednesday afternoon during Ramadan in Bishkek, Kyrgyzstan, I went for a walk to get a feel for the activity on the streets.[2] A few hundred men were hurrying to the main mosque for afternoon prayers; just behind the mosque, a man was having a quick lunch outside before going to meet others for prayers at the mosque; and at a restaurant one block away, there was a normal-sized crowd where some women joked about having smaller portions to "work their way into" the fast while a table of men in suits toasted Muhammad with vodka.

To what extent these actions bring people together and hold meaning for those who partake is interesting, but one has to note variation and be mindful that religious activity is not merely a synonym for religious belief. Any number of influences can be seen as relevant to describing the (occasionally unorthodox) behavior in Bishkek during Ramadan, but here I argue that, among other things, such variation can be best understood through an inquiry into the relationship between *knowledge*—by which I imply a social organization, corpus, and medium of knowledge—and *action*—the expresser and informer of religion.

SEEING THE DOING AS KNOWING

Eleven years after Kyrgyzstan declared its independence in 1991, twelve years after the ethnic violence of the first Osh riots, and four years after the first incursion of armed *jihadis* (Islamic Movement of Uzbekistan, IMU), Murat began to discover what religion meant for him. The same year signified twenty-five years since Murat's birth, one year since his cousin's death, and one year before the birth of his first child. It was also seven years since Murat met his first missionary, five years since his first prostitute, and twelve years since he stole away with his schoolmates to get drunk on his first bottle of vodka (see Montgomery 2007a).

Murat's sense of self—his identity—was not determined by his birth so much as by the community in which he was raised. He was not merely born Muslim and Kyrgyz so much as he became Muslim and Kyrgyz, becoming one of the many possible variations of what that might mean. As he got older, the environment in which he was raised was determined for him. Within that environment, he was brought up within a social structure that allowed a number of social options, determined his present, guided his future, and regulated his behavior. The social structure was not perceived by him as structure so much as a prevailing presence of what people do. And it was early on that he began the process of distinguishing what he *knows* from what he does not know.

There are gradations of certainty in his knowing, but community offers ways of resolving uncertainty. And while neither Murat nor anyone else can be forced to behave or to believe in any particular way, socialization is a process rooted most fundamentally in the actions and interactions of our everyday world. Sometimes significant events that lie beyond the everyday—a revolution, a war or peace, an earthquake, drought or abundance—determine the restrictions of action, and sometimes the political environment—an oppressive regime or a liberal politic—determines them. But the parameters of what he comes to *know* is a combination of events and options situated in a habitat that is immediate and makes sense to Murat throughout the stages of his development.

Murat experienced a lot before he adopted an orthopraxic approach to Islam, and his experiences were formed largely by community and a combination of what he knows and the potentiality of action. Culture plays a role at numerous levels and contributes greatly to society's structure and the social organization of knowledge. But calling it knowledge—something Murat would do; after all, he knows his culture as well as other things he would not call culture—forces one to look at Murat's situation differently.[3] Many would see Murat's adoption of religion as a discrete event, for example, without seeing that his understanding of religion and culture is continuously under construction. The issue then is not what knowledge means, but rather that people are grappling with what it means in relation to their potentialities and the everyday.

—⟶⟶—

Knowledge allows us to interpret.[4] Thus, maneuvering through life, making sense of life, and coming to terms with the profound problems of existence are all accomplished by working through what we have learned and claim as part of what we know. This is not to say that knowledge is located only as part of what is recognized, or that the process of acquiring knowledge is necessarily a formalized or even a cognizant one. The reality of action is that we do not always think it out or at least we do not always hold thought at the most immediate level. Murat's experiences, for example, led to his understanding of, among other things, life and death, sex and politics. Through experience, he recognized the boundedness of his place within his community and began to discover what constitutes the parameters of everyday practice, what can be shared publicly and what must be kept private. The same applies to the worlds of others to be introduced later, who have also experimented with the limits of their actions within the social confines of their respective communities.

Murat shares a myriad of ideas with others. His abbreviated history does not constitute a series of isolated events but rather significant moments that stimulated conversations among close friends and placed the actions he revealed within the approval and disapproval of those around him. He knew to keep his visit to the prostitute from his mother and the more religiously pious, but shared it with his closest schoolmates; this secret not only bound them together but marked him as the most knowledgeable about the sex act. The wrath of his father after he got sick from the vodka he drank with his friends and the praise he got for receiving high marks in tenth grade gave him a strong idea of the expectations others placed upon his behavior. The buzz about the IMU left him with a cautious interest in what the group was allegedly trying to accomplish and, while watching others in his community, led him to begin to discern how the elders practiced Islam and the difference between his classmates who wanted carefree lives and those who began to turn their interests to the strictures of Islam. Though Murat is not as certain as some of his friends and his religious identity remains in flux, the birth of his son brought an increased sense of responsibility for the life he lives.

SEEING THE KNOWING ANTHROPOLOGICALLY

Terms of knowledge and culture are used with a certain looseness. When talking with Murat and others, the justification they articulate for their actions oscillates between statements of cultural certainty—"it is our culture to do it this way"—and discussions about moral certainty—"I know this is right [or wrong]." While the former is a relative claim and the latter a normative claim, my interlocutors do not make these distinctions. Murat, for example, will frequently talk about culture as if it was normative, but he does acknowledge that different cultures exist and that this makes the reasons for doing things relative. As discussed later, this distinction becomes more important when it is an argument between religion and culture. Because culture comes from man, cultural claims may be relative; but religious claims, if taken to be transcendent, must be normative. The distinction between the two is constituted in knowledge.

Anthropology concerns itself with the study of culture and in so doing creates a lexicon and way of defining what is, at some level, an abstract yet recognizable grouping of behaviors. People's motivations for action and inaction, their sense of feeling at home or out of place in the world comes together with what constitutes culture—a vague grouping that at once justifies the parameters of behavior and at the same time limits discussion/criticism by outsiders.[5] Though a reference group constitutes culture and individuals know many things that include culture, knowledge is more than culture.

Culture forms a sense of intuited embeddedness that discourages others from questioning the normative perception of what should be done. As a concept, culture has developed such a self-evident/taken-for-granted character that it runs the risk of turning into something other than an analytical tool for describing and grouping behavior.[6] It becomes enough to explain behavior as culture. But one can identify behaviors, events, and the means of maintaining and institutionalizing power within the realm of culture precisely because the making of meaning drives understandings of culture, and culture is about prioritizing different types of knowledge. Furthermore, both culture and meaning are public (Geertz 1973, 12, 14). Murat makes sense of what he has learned by interacting with his family, friends, and neighbors. His embeddedness in the community in which he lives provides the medium for the creation of significance.

Thus, viewing culture as an aspect of knowledge possessed by individuals gives us an added way of appreciating the complexities of existence and social interaction that Murat and others face on a daily basis. It is what they know, situated in a particular cultural setting, that allows them to derive meaning from their experiences, to distinguish between when they are being taken advantage of in the market or a cultural setting as well as foundations of relationships upon which they can base trust (Seligman 1997, 2000). The goal of this argument is neither to provide an abstraction of knowledge that is purely theoretical and normative in its assertions about what knowledge constitutes, nor to be relativistic. Rather, the idea is to look at how Murat and others construct a net that can hold the events they experience together in a context of meaning and direction.

Such a net is formed by a social organization, a medium, and a corpus of knowledge, none of which exist independent of the others. The social organization is the structural component, the contextualization through which one understands knowledge. The corpus of knowledge is the body, the reservoir, of what is known. And the medium of knowledge is the mode through which what is known can be shared and acquired (Barth 2002).

All knowledge is experienced and from a variety of experiences, meaning is inferred. While all three aspects of knowledge exist in a fluid relationship with each other, there is a complex interrelationship between different aspects of knowledge: verbal language is not merely spoken but is performed, and nondiscursive gestures that may accompany the discursive message may emphasize meaning or entirely negate meaning (see Luckmann 1967). The challenge is to understand how people come to know about their surroundings and how they exchange the messages they use to come to a state of what they say they *know*.[7]

In the case of Murat, he explains why he did not practice religion earlier in his life, as well as why he now practices religion, in part by apologia and in part through discursive justification. This provides both an excuse for growing up in a cultural environment that has religious roots of varying depths

FIGURE I.1. Anthropology of knowledge.

and a reason for succumbing to the pull of at times contradictory calls for action. For example, it is common for Central Asians to refer to Kyrgyz as being less orthopraxic, in an orthodox sense, and Murat could eschew many Islamic obligations by claiming that it is part of his culture not to be regularly observant. When he made his decision to become more religious, his justification for the transformation was marked by a sense of obligation to overcome his predestined past.

The reality, of course, is that each culture has multiple histories that influence the manner in which life is lived and thereby influence the manner of knowing. Discussing history is incomplete without noting the factors and influences beyond the immediate sphere of observation and describing the contexts of existence, which include the social organization, the medium and the corpus of knowledge to be learned, intuited, and appreciated.

It is argued that in addition to offering a grounded understanding of what influences the everyday and the political, approaching behavior though a lens of knowledge addresses the challenge of how to theorize variation and change. An anthropology of knowledge gives form to the pragmatic nature of social navigation and draws attention to the influence of framing in creating categories—for example, a political frame, an ethnographic frame, and a local frame have differing agendas that get reified in and by each other—that influence practice and thus, religious and political change.

EXPLAINING "THE FIELD"

Kyrgyzstan is mountainous—on a clear day, there is nowhere that one can go without seeing mountains. In economic terms, it is considered a poor country and certainly poverty occupies the time of many Kyrgyz. It is jokingly said that a foreigner can be thought to have mastered the Kyrgyz language if he can talk about three things: family, health, and how expensive everything is in the bazaar. In many respects, this captures what is important to many Kyrgyz (and many in the world, more generally). And while there is always a struggle for money, a salary is more likely to be spent right away and shared with extended family rather than saved. Community identification is more important than individualism, and this is seen in discussions of culture and religion (Montgomery 2013b).

Traditionally, and due to the terrain, which always has been a significant factor in people's way of life, most Kyrgyz were nomadic pastoralists. In the mountain areas, this is still an active way of life for some, with schools reminding parents every year that they should wait until after the school year is over before they begin summer migrations in the upper mountain pastures (*jailoo*). In the valleys, most Kyrgyz and other ethnic groups have adopted sedentary lives and cultures. And though the economy remains predominately agricultural, there has been a large influx of migrants to the capital, Bishkek, and further abroad in hopes of securing a better, more lucrative job.

The country is a republic administratively divided into seven *oblasts* (Kyrgyz: province)—Batken, Chuy, Jalal-Abad, Naryn, Osh, Talas, and Issyk Kul—and one city, Bishkek. The Ala-Too mountain range separates the northern part of the country from the south and is seen as a marker of differentiation in both culture and economy. The north produces more meat and wool, and some of the large crops in the south are cotton and tobacco. As the first country in the Commonwealth of Independent States to carry out market reforms, Kyrgyzstan became a member of the World Trade Organization in 1998. In the early 1990s, it was perceived as an island of democracy in a relatively nondemocratic region.[8] The presidency of Askar Akayev, however, began a trend toward presidential seizure of power. Nonetheless, there was greater openness to political dissent and that affected the tone of political expression in the country.

While the focus of this work is Kyrgyzstan, Uzbekistan plays a prominent role in the imagination of those living in the southern part of Kyrgyzstan and thus a brief description for comparison is warranted. Uzbekistan is a much drier country, relying on water from Kyrgyzstan and Tajikistan to irrigate its crops, the most profitable of which is cotton. It is more populous, with a population of over 28 million versus Kyrgyzstan's 5.4 million. Over half the Uzbek population lives rurally,[9] in a republic with authoritative presidential rule and administratively divided into twelve *viloyats* (Uzbek: province), the autonomous republic of Karakalpakastan (*Qoraqalpog'iston Respublikasi*), and the capital city of Tashkent. There are significant differences between the regions; my research in Uzbekistan focused largely on the Ferghana Valley viloyats of Ferghana, Kokand, and Namangan.

The Uzbek government controls most businesses and has a record of general disregard for human rights (see Human Rights Watch 2004, 2007, 2011). The standard of living has been in decline and this has influenced people's discussions and perceptions about the differences between Kyrgyzstan and Uzbekistan. The Uzbeks have often felt themselves to be culturally superior to the Kyrgyz; in early 2000 one would hear Uzbeks in both Uzbekistan and Kyrgyzstan articulate this.[10] By 2004 and 2005, however, the discussion had changed, and my interlocutors in Uzbekistan most frequently asked questions about how much better life was in Kyrgyzstan.

Thus, the environment in which I conducted field research between 2004 and 2005 was one where both Kyrgyz and Uzbeks were dissatisfied with their respective governments and wishing for change and better lives. The Kyrgyz were able to articulate this dissatisfaction more publicly, while the situation in Uzbekistan was becoming increasingly oppressive.

—◊◊◊—

Questions of methodology arise early in almost every work, as a means of establishing the author's legitimacy to claims of what is written; to gauge the representative accuracy of the conclusions he has drawn and the relation of observations, assumptions, and the "real world" to each other. My first interactions with Kyrgyz and Uzbeks came during an extended stay between 1999 and 2001, when I lived and worked in the mountain community of Naryn, Kyrgyzstan. During that period, I made trips throughout Kyrgyzstan as well as Uzbekistan. I collected most of the field data for the writing of this book while conducting anthropological field research between 2004 and 2005. During this time, I was based in Osh, Kyrgyzstan, and traveled extensively throughout the Ferghana Valley, a region administratively shared by Kyrgyzstan, Tajikistan, and Uzbekistan. There were follow-up visits to the region in 2006, 2008, 2012, and 2013.

In Naryn I learned what the harshness of mountain life in the winter and the freedom that a nomadic life in the summer entail. The severity of the winters, the scarcity of vegetables, the reality of unemployment; the vastness of mountain pastures, the cleanness of water and air, and the continuance of a traditional way of living created a pride among locals that they were able to live, and even be happy, in an environment that was undesirable and intimidating to Kyrgyz living in less harsh surroundings.

Associated with being Kyrgyz in Naryn was the stereotype that residents lived both a more traditional life and a less Islamic life. The ways of the city were slowest to reach these kinds of villages, and this was also the case with a more syncretic way of practicing religion. During field research carried out between 2004 and 2005 and in 2012, I returned to Naryn oblast to renew acquaintances, collect data, and administer a survey of religious practice. During these later research stays my primary residence was in the Ferghana Valley sections of Kyrgyzstan and Uzbekistan, which represented a different way of life with milder winters, greater population density, and more abundant produce.

My general approach to understanding the lived situation of the Kyrgyz involved the consideration of the environment and an analysis of events in which they lived (see Jackson 2005). The events of the 2005 Kyrgyz putsch and the Andijan massacre, for example, influenced my research plan. While the long-term impact of these events on the lives of locals is ongoing, as it was part of the shared experience of people and was the concern of many, it fit within my focus on the everyday impacts of events in life. The coup led people to express their fears about a possible return to the Osh riots of 1990 (see Tishkov 1995), and after the Andijan killings there was a heightened fear of religious militancy that could spread and lead to uncontrolled violence.

Despite the fears and concerns raised by these events, after a few days the closed stores reopened and people returned to their daily routines. While it is easy to focus on the significance of the Kyrgyz putsch, it cannot be overlooked that a block from the White House (presidential office building) a woman continued selling sunflower seeds, gum, and cigarettes at the corner and traffic continued while people stormed the White House, effectively ousting the Akayev government.[11] And in Andijan, the borders of the city were closed and people were genuinely afraid. But despite caution in discussing the events, people still went to the markets and tried to resume as normal a life as possible.

My research did not just focus on major events like holidays or protests, but was often carried out over endless pots of tea in *chaikhanas* (teahouses) and during meals in people's homes. It was a multisited research project that built on the experience of life in the mountains and sought to complement it with understandings of life in the valley, largely focused on participant-guided interviews and field observations.

In Kyrgyzstan, I carried out quantitative (survey) and qualitative research in Aravan, Arbyn, At-Bashi, Jangi-Nookat (Yangi-Nookat), Karasuu, Kochkor, Korshab, Naryn, Nookat (Eski-Nookat), Osh, and Shangkol. I also conducted qualitative research in Kyrgyzstan in Achakainda, Batken, Bishkek, Ivanovka, Jalal-Abad, Karakol, Talas, Üser, and Uzgen. Due to the tragic political events in Andijan and the general research climate, I was unable to carry out quantitative research in Uzbekistan as I had intended. I focused my qualitative research in Uzbekistan on the communities of Andijan, Ferghana, Kokand, Margilan, Namangan, Oq'Korgon, Rishton, and Sokh.[12] I also carried our research in Bukhara, Samarqand, and Tashkent.

There are a multitude of boundaries that people recognize. Those that influenced the selection of my research sites were based on location, ethnicity, and nationality. The locational differences are those of mountains and valleys as well as the groups that live in between, at the edge of the valley and the base of the mountains. These boundary communities are at times subject to interpretation and a hard delineation is not overly important. Naryn is clearly in the mountains. Andijan is undeniably not in the mountains but rather in the heart of the valley. And Shangkol is at the foothills.

The general frame of reference in regard to these differences is how people make a living; this is what determines whether a given locality is a mountain or valley community. And while it is clearly the environment that determines the mode of living rather than the other way around, it is the mode of living that people use to categorize the environment. Shangkol is a place that makes use of various modes; people say they are from the valley and they also say they are from the mountains. The distinction I try to make is one of local perception as well as geographical observation; that is, if the mountains begin

FIGURE I.2. A boy herding sheep with his brother and uncle along a highway in the mountains, 2006.

FIGURE I.3. Planting spring crops in the valley, 2012.

TABLE I.1. Communities by Geography

Mountain communities	In-between communities	Valley communities
At-Bashi	Arbyn	Andijan
Kochkor	Jangi-Nookat	Aravan
Naryn	Karatai	Ferghana
Sokh	Korshab	Karasuu
	Shangkol	Kokand
		Margillan
		Namangan
		Nookat (Eski-)
		Osh
		Rishton

in someone's backyard and he claims to be in the valley—as is the case with Jangi-Nookat—I classify this as an in-between community.

Much is made of ethnicity, and most of the communities are separated by ethnicity: it is either a Kyrgyz community or an Uzbek community. And even where populations of both ethnic groups live in the same community, they generally live in different neighborhoods, separated by different types of homes and different ways of living. Thus, the selection of my research sites tried to include a range of ethnic groups along the variables of not only geography but also those of ethnic community in order to better understand the differences in what ethnic interaction—or at least the idea of having to share space even if ethnic interaction was often kept at a minimum—meant in the community.

Perhaps the most straightforward delineation of groups was along national boundaries. These boundaries, while an inconvenience for many, have become the political boundaries and are delineated by a map. A map of ethnicity would suggest different boundaries and typological delineations would also yield a different map. A map that divides mountains and valleys would assign the Kyrgyz section of the Ferghana Valley to the broader territory of the valley. And a map of ethnic density would cut further into Kyrgyz territory that would roughly, though not exactly, correspond to the foothills of the mountains. The reality this creates is that there are ethnic Uzbeks who are under the political administration of Kyrgyzstan and some Kyrgyz who are under the political administration of Uzbekistan. And while these two communities may have family connections, different state policies influence how their lives can be lived. Thus, a third border is that of national boundaries.

The sites were selected based on the need to diversify the variables of the populations and also in places where I had established relationships through

TABLE I.2. Communities by Ethnicity

Kyrgyz communities	Mixed communities (Kyrgyz and Uzbek)	Uzbek communities	Tajik communities
Arbyn	Karasuu	Andijan	Rishton
At-Bashi	Korshab	Aravan	Sokh
Kochkor	Nookat (Eski-)	Ferghana	
Naryn	Osh	Jangi-Nookat	
Shangkol		Kokand	
		Margilan	
		Namangan	

TABLE I.3. Communities by National Boundaries

Kyrgyzstan	Kyrgyzstan (along border or strong identification with Uzbekistan)	Uzbekistan	Uzbekistan (along border and strong identification with Tajikistan)
Arbyn	Aravan	Andijan	Rishton
At-Bashi	Jangi-Nookat	Ferghana	Sokh
Karatai	Karasuu	Kokand	
Kochkor	Nookat (Eski-)	Margilan	
Korshab	Osh	Namangan	
Naryn			
Shangkol			

earlier visits to the region. While an arbitrary marking in some respects, the political borders did influence my research; some questions that I could ask in Kyrgyzstan had to be asked differently or avoided in Uzbekistan. Furthermore, the political situation in both countries, but especially Uzbekistan, varied the environment in which discussions on religion could be conducted.

In general, I was concerned with the everyday aspects of life and found that official interviews with religious and intellectual elites often solicited formal and staged responses that were, to some degree, a construction of what people felt I wanted to hear. This is not to say that all official interviews were devoid of honesty, for I believe many of the people I interviewed in these cases no doubt at least wanted to believe what they were saying. But as is the case with formal and recorded conversations, people are more guarded and less spontaneous in their descriptions about what might actually be happening. That, in combination with a face-saving cultural milieu that is more concerned with relaying a pleasing story than a truthful story, led me to rely most heavily on casual conversations and informal interviews in people's homes and common public spaces. These conversations were often an extension of the discourse begun in friendships and developed after months, or years, of cultivating relations in various communities. At all times, interactions with my interlocutors guided the dialogues we shared. These conversations took place in both public and private spaces.

Because my primary concern was how people lived and came to terms with the challenges of everyday life, interacting with the religious and intellectual elites, while at times illuminating, was often a secondary concern. Some of the more enlightening conversations were with taxi drivers, barbers, shepherds, salespersons, teachers, and pensioners over tea, vodka, or traditional meals. And generally, conversations would begin around what were the concerns of their lives and progress toward the role religion played (or did not play) in making sense of a meaningful life.

However, I soon became concerned about the representative nature of the conversations that I was having—after all, despite my best efforts I could be talking with the only twenty people in a village who might feel a particular way!—and decided to administer a survey of religious and cultural practice in the locations where I was conducting field research. The survey consisted of four parts: the first section asked questions designed to understand how people described their practice of religion and culture; the second section asked questions connected to how people learned about religion and culture; the third section looked at the issue of religion and culture's role in the community; and the fourth section asked basic identifying information. The survey contained 189 questions and took between 50 and 90 minutes to administer.

I intended to administer the survey in three locations, corresponding to the regions where I conducted ethnographic research. I planned the administration of the surveys to be done in three stages between May and June 2005. The first and second stages were in Osh and Naryn oblasts in Kyrgyzstan and the third stage was to be administered in Andijan and Ferghana viloyats in Uzbekistan.

The survey was administered in Kyrgyzstan; regrettably, due to the May 2005 political events in Andijan, it was not administered in Uzbekistan. I had done some trials of the survey in Andijan in May, but the situation remained too tense and the population too fearful to permit it to be administered, as this could have placed many people in danger. Despite people's interest in the survey and the information it contained, the risk was too great and honest answers could not be expected. This has forced me to rely more on the qualitative portions of my work in Uzbekistan rather than the quantitative information the survey was designed to provide. I have been able to discuss all of the questions with a number of Uzbeks living in many of the villages where I worked, but the format of those discussions was informal.

TABLE I.4. Communities by Administrative Groupings

Naryn Oblast (Kyrgyzstan)	Osh Oblast (Kyrgyzstan)	Andijan Viloyat (Uzbekistan)	Ferghana Viloyat (Uzbekistan)
At-Bashi	Aravan	Andijan	Ferghana
Kochkor	Arbyn		Kokand
Naryn	Jangi-Nookat		Margilan
	Karasuu		Rishton
	Karatai		Sokh
	Korshab		
	Nookat (Eski-)		
	Osh		
	Shangkol		

When administering the survey, I drew a map of the village or city; a grid placed on it marked Kyrgyz neighborhoods, Uzbek neighborhoods, and mixed neighborhoods. I assigned assistants to each quadrant and instructed them to randomly visit homes and alternate between age and gender of the interviewee. For example, if a middle-aged male was interviewed at the first house on the street, an elderly woman would be a good match to be interviewed at a house seven houses down on the other side of the road or on a different road altogether.

Of the total of 866 surveys administered, 829 were complete. The surveys were administered by assistants whom I had trained, in Kyrgyz, Russian, and Uzbek. All assistants had copies of the surveys in the relevant languages and they were either bi- or trilingual. For the most part, ethnic Kyrgyz were sent to Kyrgyz neighborhoods and ethnic Uzbeks were sent to Uzbek neighborhoods. I accompanied a number of the assistants during the interviews and checked every survey for accuracy, completeness, and irregularities.[13]

We carried out the survey over a short period of time, which helped keep people from talking about "appropriate" answers. The participants were selected randomly with the exception of two populations that I specifically targeted: a group of Hizb-ut Tahrir members and some members of Tablighi Jama'at, who were referred to as the "local Wahhabis."[14] I gave a number of surveys—in Kyrgyz, Russian, and Uzbek—to various Hizb-ut Tahrir members who agreed to have them filled out by their co-religionists. When I went to collect the surveys, however, none had been filled out completely. One individual said they had been too busy campaigning for the upcoming presidential elections. Another implied that they did not know many of the answers and thus did not want to fill it out, presumably because it would show a contradiction between their approach of acting knowledgeable and the actual breadth of their knowledge about Islam. In the case of Tablighi Jama'at, one member offered to help administer the surveys to like believers. When I met him to collect the surveys, however, he said that most of the people he tried to get to fill them out did not approach it with enough seriousness and did not answer them "correctly." He gave me two surveys out of the fifteen I had given him.

In neither instance was this data included in the qualitative analysis because it was direct solicitation aimed at learning more about two particular segments of population. The results of the experience were, however, quite informative in a general sense. Members of both groups were represented in the surveys that were randomly collected, as a number of interviewees verbally identified themselves as belonging to those groups at the conclusion of the survey. In all instances, the survey served as a useful tool to initiate conversation about the relationship between religious and cultural knowledge and practice.

To give an idea of the relationship of the survey to my qualitative research and how it created opportunities, one story from its administration proved quite telling about the broader social relations within my research sites in Kyrgyzstan. I was administering a survey when I received a phone call from the police in a medium-size village in Osh oblast. They had detained two young men who were helping me administer the survey on suspicion that they were distributing Islamist propaganda. I went to the police station with two friends from the village with whom I had been talking and who, I knew, had economic and political connections in the community. As I walked into the police station to explain about the survey and get my assistants out of custody, I was given a long explanation as to why the police responded as they did and how dangerous the Islamist elements were, especially following the Andijan killings. I explained the nature of my research and they offered to help administer surveys, saying that it would be better if I informed them about my research. I promised that at no point would I share the names of anyone with whom I met, including theirs.

Within twenty minutes of leaving the police station, I returned to the village center with my friends as a new black Mercedes Benz pulled up. First exited a bodyguard, whose size and presence was meant to emphasize the importance of the passengers who approached me, their long beards and imported Islamic dress distinguishing them as Muslims with connections outside the community in which they were living. They had heard about my research and had come to talk to me about it, to inquire what I was seeking to learn. They knew I had just returned from the police station and also knew that I did not reveal any names. It was an opportunity for open discussion, continuing over the remaining months of my research, and I found them as interested in my research as the police had been.[15]

This experience points to the interconnectedness of the community and how much everyone knows about each other.[16] Thus, while throughout this work it is the ethnographic context that gives color to the stories of my interlocutors, the survey gives context to the broader demographics of my field sites and provides a sense of the material and emotional environment of the various communities in which they live (see Appendix B).

Practicing Islam

Though the theoretical structure explored in this book is applicable elsewhere, ethnographically it focuses on the Kyrgyz Republic, a former Soviet republic that has received international media attention because of two coups (2005 and 2010), its proximity to Afghanistan, and Western fears commonly associated with rising Islamic activity. Thus, while the book examines how Muslims in Kyrgyzstan socially navigate their lives in direct relation to local potentialities and political agendas commonly controlled by (interactions with) the state, its discussion of knowledge as containing: (1) a *social organization* that accommodates to geography, economy, and political structure; (2) a *medium* that preferences creativeness of oral storytelling or a more rigid textual (Qur'an-centered) interpretation articulated as orthopraxy; and (3) a *corpus of knowledge* that draws upon experiences in schooling, profession, and history, gives it theoretical applicability beyond the particular region.

Viewing culture as an aspect of knowledge possessed by individuals in a community functions as an added way of appreciating the complexity of existence and social interactions. What we know allows us to filter experience and generate meaningful cultural worlds; to engage in both gossip and the division of labor; and to situate events, interactions, and relationships in a meaningful frame (Barth 2002). This does not suggest an abstraction of knowledge that is purely theoretical and normative, or even relativistic, in its argument about what knowledge constitutes. Rather, this approach toward an anthropology of knowledge begins to look at how people construct a net that can hold the happenings of the world and gather them together for the making of meaning.

This net, as suggested earlier, consists of a social organization, a medium, and a corpus of knowledge, none of which exists independently of the others. Chapter 1 continues with an overview of learning and the everyday as it relates to the case of the Kyrgyz Republic. It includes some of the historical background necessary to convey the environment in which my interlocutors live. History was not always at the forefront of their minds, but social memory and awareness of their past are important, formative, and often used to justify who they saw themselves as being.[17]

Chapter 2 begins a more detailed analysis of the anthropology of knowledge, addressing its first component: social organization. Social organization includes state, social, and economic restrictions or potentialities and is the structural component through which knowledge is understood. Chapter 3 examines the corpus of knowledge, which constitutes the body of what is known and includes the frame of reference one develops in a particular trade or profession as well as an educational frame related to one's level and type of schooling. The medium of knowledge—the manner by which what is known can be expressed—is explored in Chapter 4. This includes oral and textual transmission as well as experiential transmission—the doing of an act. Chapter 5 frames the political and moral aspects of understanding, both as interpreted by my interlocutors and as viewed by outside observers; it is a move toward showing how an anthropology of knowledge can be applied, through exploring the context of bias. All the earlier chapters come together to see (how to see) local variation in relation to the biases with which we view all cases. The Conclusion returns to the issue of potentiality and social navigation, which is ever present in the relationship between knowledge and action.

What people know and what people do is contained within the parameters of their potential to know and to do, and this is in no way static. People are always finding ways to navigate the choices and challenges of life, from elders or youth coming to terms with the IMU and increasing orthopraxy, to others trying to make sense of their world and its concomitant obligations. People become Muslims and develop their understanding of what such Muslimness implies through a continuous, practical engagement with their surroundings. In the end, it is not a one-off affair but rather an understanding that is an ongoing practice. They are, after all, always *practicing* Islam.

Chapter 1

Learning Everyday (Islam)

Coping with the demands of everyday life would be exceedingly trying if one could arrive at solutions to problems only by actually performing possible options and suffering the consequences.

Albert Bandura, *Social Learning Theory*

The things I know, anyone can know—but my heart is mine and mine alone.

Johann Wolfgang von Goethe, *The Sorrows of Young Werther*

In a sense, we live in stories. Stories make the abstract more tangible by giving it a face that is both generalizable and unique. Stories are part of our everyday existence; by amusing, intriguing, enlightening, and saddening us they convey a richness of information about the story's subject as well as the storyteller. Stories are a window into what is compelling to people, what motivates them, and what is at stake. Understanding the complexity of everyday lived religious life and the relationship of knowledge transmission and religious expression is a project that can help account for (or at least inform about) variations in religious expression.

The purpose of stories here, as elsewhere, is to get at the everyday. The diversity of religious life in Central Asia can be characterized through stories, and thus I begin with the stories of two people from two different regions of Kyrgyzstan: one from the mountains in Naryn oblast and the other from the Ferghana Valley in Osh oblast. They represent two extremes in their understanding of Islam, but what is important is that both are adamant in considering themselves Muslim despite their different approaches.

In a remote mountain village in Naryn oblast, Tolkun, in her mid-fifties, begins her day by putting prayer beads in the front pocket of her skirt. She then goes to collect dried herbs that she has stored in the kitchen and makes a special tea. It is Thursday and she begins a purification process to prepare for visiting a *mazar* (sacred site). After washing, she recites some verses from the Qur'an. Tolkun has never read the Qur'an, but like everyone in her circle, she assumes that what she recites comes from the Qur'an. She will cook *borsok* (fried bread) because spirits find the scent appealing: "it helps attract the spirits," she explains. And in the late afternoon or evening, depending on her schedule, she makes her way to a nearby mazar—this one is the tomb

FIGURE 1.1. A woman frying borsok; the spirits are thought to enjoy the aroma, 1999.

of someone who, according to lore, lived a just life (the exact story she does not know), though at other times it is a natural spring known to have healing qualities. Once there, she will light some candles, waving them around as she chants, and she will burn some wool. She prays to Allah, calling on the spirits for help, and she regards what she does as the way one should practice Islam. She does not question it.

Tolkun does not believe that women can go to mosque. In fact, there is no mosque in her village and only a handful of the village men attend a mosque in a nearby village. She recognizes that what she does is different from what others in the valley do, but she sees this as their poverty. While she knows that there are other ways to worship in Islam, she is less interested in them; she wants to continue to worship the way her ancestors taught her.

—◦◦◦—

In the Ferghana Valley of Osh oblast, which lies over the mountain a few hundred kilometers southwest of Tolkun, lives Azarmat, a man in his mid-thirties, who wears a white skullcap and a beard that comes to his clavicle. He also reaches for prayer beads in the morning, prays five times a day, and meets regularly—three or four times a week—with a member of the Muslim missionary movement Tablighi Jama'at, who trained in India. Azarmat studies the Qur'an daily with his friends. He reads Arabic poorly and does not understand it, but his ability to recount stories and passages from the Qur'an in a manner that at least appears close to Arabic garners him status in the village as one who is knowledgeable. He is marginally employed, working sometimes at the mosque and sometimes at home in his garden, selling any extra produce in the market. His interpretation of Islam allows for very little variation. He refuses to see Tolkun as anything other than an old woman who is ignorant of Islam. Azarmat's standard reference for Islam is a text (the Qur'an, he will claim) and a tradition influenced by idealizations of Mecca and the structured time he has spent with the Tablighi Jama'at missionary.

These descriptions portray two very different ways of expressing Islam. Most people in Kyrgyzstan, of course, are neither Tolkun nor Azarmat, but a combination of the two in varying degrees. Nonetheless, many still show a propensity for normative categorization—for example, saying that what Azarmat does is Islamic and what Tolkun does is not. This, of course, makes complete sense regardless of one's own faith background. We generally understand the religion of others, either those close to us or those who are completely Other, in normative terms and described with phrasing that is wrapped in a valuated assessment of people's actions—there are good Muslims and bad Muslims; good Christians and bad Christians; good Jews and bad Jews; and so forth. The looseness of good and bad as descriptors varies greatly—sometimes it refers to people's behavior as individuals in the broader public, with a varying connection to their actual religious beliefs, that is, how they act; at other times, it refers to how people act as supposed practitioners of a particular faith community (individuals in a normative collective), that is, orthopraxy.

As practitioners of faith, we acknowledge that there is an ideal; yet we tend to reconcile our place in relation to others and the ideal. We live with amazing levels of ambiguity and contradiction. For example, Azarmat will drink a little vodka with me in private and Tolkun will seek healing from both a physician and the ancestors, suggesting a degree of uncertainty about the effectiveness of what she does. They are certainly not alone in this. We are slower, however, to recognize that everyone else also has religious lives that they constantly (re)negotiate in relation to the demands of life and attempts to live a meaning-ful life. We engage in a constant social navigation that is much less directed, purposeful, or theoretically tidy than we might like. A myriad of competing interests at local and national, as well as personal and public, levels, constantly forces people to make decisions. And they are limited in what they can do by their potential to act in a particular way.

The reality of everyday religious life is complicated and normative descrip-tors inadequately capture the richness of the lived religious world. Returning to the two vignettes suggests the tension of very different types of Muslims in Kyrgyzstan—Azarmat, who views himself as orthodox and Tolkun as het-erodox,[1] and Tolkun, who sees herself as continuing the tradition of Islam in and of Central Asia, which Azarmat, in her view, has surrendered to a for-eign interpretation. Both, however, call themselves Muslim. This "common denominator" gives a false sense of uniformity that leads to conclusions about a population's religious ideology that is oversimplified and can be dangerously inaccurate.

——∿∿——

The descriptions of Tolkun and Azarmat reveal a layer of complexity that is usually absent in descriptions of Central Asia in general and specifically Kyrgyzstan,[2] a country that is described as 75 percent Muslim.[3] A statistic is limited in what it can convey, and the concern is that it is too readily under-stood as representative of the population, rather than the stories of Tolkun and Azarmat—which, of course, is only partly true.[4]

For Tolkun and Azarmat, their way of practicing religion is not a statistic. It begins with an idea of origin and otherworldly rationale for structuring and ordering the world. It can begin a narrative, but origins are seen more as ex-isting pre-origins, as given and without a need of focus. That is, because they are given, one can focus more on the concerns of the present that the past le-gitimates in a cloak of tradition. Tradition, then, becomes the story, or at least negotiating with tradition becomes the story, that concerns people.

Because a narrative of origin already exists, nothing forces Tolkun and Azarmat to concern themselves overly with it; they can turn their attention away from questions of origin and ordering that otherwise might consume them. When one has a vision of creation, one also has a vision of change and a vision of end. Accepting creation, Tolkun and Azarmat focus on life as a series of dynamically guided events. They do not concern themselves much with ideology; rather, they acquired their religion through more tactile means. In other words, religion is more about learning than about systematized ideas of ideology.

The convergence between religion and the familiar in community is comfortable and held in communion. The communion of the community teaches the ideas and the necessary rationale to support what is believed—an entire apparatus/system that is more elaborate than a single belief—and it comes to be believed, or at least held as believed, in the actions one carries out. Most people, including Tolkun and Azarmat, do not come to beliefs on their own, but in relationship with others and the stories that are told.

In Central Asia, as elsewhere in the world, storytelling is an active and vital part of the transmission of culture. We know who we are from the stories we learn and the reactions we get to the stories we tell. At times this is formalized and takes on a standardized narrative form, but at other times people convey stories in gossip overheard on the streets, or construct them from bits of everyday conversation placed in a progression that colors and valuates life.

In one sense, the meanings we derive from life are intimately connected to the process of storytelling. It is in this broad sense that what follows concerns storytelling. It is not a literary analysis of stories, but rather an anthropological analysis of people's everyday stories, with particular attention given to how the poetics of daily existence animate and are animated by the otherworldly conceptions of religion. People's everyday stories *are* their daily existence. The stories are their history, their memory, and their experience.

While religion is often conceptualized as the framework through which one navigates otherworldly concerns, it is intimately rooted in the lived, everyday world, connected in varying degrees to economic health, political outcomes, social interactions, and physical well-being. Furthermore, people frequently use the perception of one's religious adherence to delineate insiders and outsiders and contextualize them in moral terms.

This contextualization creates Others who are both near and far. Tolkun and Azarmat know the neighbors they are close to, with regard to their shared thoughts, but they also know the distance between each other's beliefs. Living with the Other is a challenge faced by all, and the extent to which it is done successfully often serves as a marker of a region's stability. A certain amount of name calling and labeling reifies perceptions of Otherness, and in many senses this tendency is a learned behavior that begins even before the playground politics of adolescence.

The making of the Other, which is ultimately a function of power and differentiation, takes place everywhere and in all aspects of social relations. This discussion mostly addresses otherness in religion, which is both cultural and ontological, yet to some extent it is interpretive and fungible. And while the discussion here predominately concerns Kyrgyzstan, many of the mechanisms of discovering difference, realizing the potentialities of one's actions, and creating a cosmology of meaning can be recognizable in other cultures with other traditions.

Discovery, realization, and creation are linked fundamentally to the acquisition of knowledge and the expression of action, both in the active lived and contemplated world. This includes, for example, the valuated language Tolkun and Azarmat use to categorize each other. Colloquially, distinctions of who is a good or bad religious practitioner stem from a variety of identifying variables that are fluid in their application. The case of Tolkun and Azarmat is clear. More generally, however, an Uzbek may claim that he is a better Muslim than a Kyrgyz on ethnic grounds; a Kyrgyz from the southern part of the country may claim to be a better Muslim than a northerner because of location. The articulation is based on fluid understandings of orthopraxy and orthodoxy applied in ways that coerce behavior or reify aspects of Otherness.

Broadly speaking, two variables come out of the discussion of religion between Tolkun and Azarmat. One connects to ethnicity and the other to location. "Uzbeks are more religious than Kyrgyz," an ethnic claim made by locals, becomes a shorthand that people accept, despite the absence of an objective connection (outside of social structure) between ethnicity and religion.[5] The missionary with whom Azarmat studies is an ethnic Uzbek. And Azarmat, though Kyrgyz, references his being a better Muslim by saying that he is more like an Uzbek than a Kyrgyz. People use ethnicity as a marker for religiosity, but in reality what is characterized by "Uzbeks being more religiously adherent" is a claim about the social environment of learning rather than anything to do with an inherent connection between ethnicity and religiosity.

To further illustrate this point, few Uzbeks live in Naryn oblast, where Tolkun is from; most live in the southern part of Kyrgyzstan, which includes Osh oblast, where Azarmat lives. But the Uzbeks who live in Naryn are much more like Tolkun than Azarmat. They even claim that they are more Kyrgyz than Uzbek, referring to their religious practice and an indication that they accept that a connection exists between ethnicity and religiosity even though they are exceptions to the generalization. The ethnicity claim has explanatory power, however, to the extent that it is connected to a cultural embrace of being Uzbek or Kyrgyz and the social and educational frame this entails, but here I accept it only as a shorthand for generalized behaviors within a social organization.

The variable of location becomes relevant here—mountain and valley, city and village—for it includes a number of variables tied to the social frames of learning, and differences in the political environment of countries such as Kyrgyzstan and Uzbekistan. All these factors influence the individual's religious identity and contribute to persuading or privileging a particular form of religious expression. According to the usual delineation of these variables, those in mountains, generally ethnic Kyrgyz, can afford a higher degree of syncretic understanding of their religious world than valley dwellers of Uzbek ethnicity. Thus, Tolkun considers Azarmat more an Uzbek than a *real* Kyrgyz.[6] Again, it is not so much actual ethnicity that matters as much as what it comes to symbolize. Ethnicity and location become associated in the local explanation of religious difference even when these categories prove to be filled with exceptions. For example, Azarmat is Kyrgyz and Tolkun claims she is as religious as any Uzbek.

While variations within a population are not exceptional, there are surprisingly few divergent conceptions of reality, despite the endless options possible for ordering society. This homogeneity is best explained by looking at how individuals come to know what they claim to know about religion; this, in turn, accounts for the influence that brings about change from one way of thought and practice to another. This is both the culture they tie to their ethnic identity and the location/environment that influences their daily existence. Connecting this to the religious self, while Azarmat and Tolkun acquire knowledge of religion in many forms—written, spoken, ritually observed—their religious understanding is always rooted in a cultural setting. Thus, the environment of practical knowledge (*phronesis*)—mimetic or textual—in which an individual comes of age in learning his or her religious and cultural self has the greatest explanatory value. The role of cultural actors— that is, those who aid in the dissemination of such information—significantly shapes public opinion of who is "good" or "bad" and who needs to be coopted into a particular way of practice, which in turn pressures a particular way of thought. These are the dynamics of a moral and moralizing process.

Thus, how people *learn* about religion and culture influences how they *practice* religion and culture. In reality, ideology matters significantly less than practice, yet discussions about practice generally assume the embrace of a particular ideology. Ideology can justify practice, but since ideologies develop slowly, what matters more is how people come to know what they claim they know about religion and culture; the manner of obtaining knowledge sets up the conditions and parameters of practice.

This understanding of religious practice underscores the need for an anthropology of religious knowledge that takes into account the social structure, corpus, and medium of knowledge and considers it in relationship to the environment in which people exist, their potentiality to act, and their ongoing experience of social navigation. There is diversity in populations, stories, and interpretations. The interpretations of stories influence behavior. How individuals learn these stories influences interpretation. And the relevance of understanding this has implications beyond the purely academic.

With respect to policy relevance, Otherness is intimately connected to an increasing concern about the rise of fundamentalist or re-traditionalist movements. Media or policy makers—for reasons of expediency or limited understanding—frequently generalize and oversimplify the complexity of religion, leaving the impression that militant re-traditionalist Islam is taking over Central Asia.[7] Some re-traditionalist groups are indeed finding support, but it is neither universal nor without complications. This skirts the heart of the issue fundamentally connected to learning's role in guiding behavior, namely, why people believe or practice religion as they do. Glossing over the complexity and ambiguity can lead to policy miscalculations and to missed opportunities for engaging populations in constructive ways that could mitigate the potential for conflict.

There are reasons why people cannot get along and why at some point religious tolerance could shift to the outward expression of intolerance: diversity can be threatening. The social environment in which people learn religion can explain the development of religious practice and thought. An example of this can be seen in the broad differences between Tolkun and Azarmat and how the relations they exemplify can shape the future of religious practice and issues revolving around tolerance and intolerance.

The case of Central Asia provides a unique example of dialogue with change. The Central Asian context is special in the Muslim world because the change is at a stage of infancy when compared to other areas in the world, including Pakistan, Indonesia, and parts of the Middle East, that have deeply rooted traditions of Islam. Central Asian Islam has deep and profound roots, but the period of Soviet rule was successful in diminishing the confidence of Central Asian Muslims in their own interpretation of and knowledge about religious practice (Khalid 2007). It is not until recently that a normative understanding of what it means to be a Muslim started (anew) to develop. In this contact with outside understandings of what proper Islam is, the character of Central Asian Islam is being altered and developed. This too constitutes a way of learning and sets up the parameters for what religion is and what it can become for subsequent generations of Kyrgyz Muslims.

LEARNING AND THE EVERYDAY

Ways of Learning

Knowledge comes in many forms. For example, academia views (and values) knowledge in what is read and heard in a lecture or series of formalized and structured interactions. Having grown up in a farm town in Illinois, however, I had neighbors who can convincingly argue that if one does not know when to plant the crops, one is without knowledge and may very well starve. For my farmer friends, knowledge is practical and may have little to do with knowledge acquired at the university. At times, there is concern that the formalized setting of university learning does not take into account, or not with enough seriousness, the process of basic observation. In this sense, there is little difference between a farmer in Illinois and one in Naryn. Both believe that observing how one teaches is important in order to learn how to teach; or of connecting what a farmer does in a field with a change in weather and thus intuiting an understanding of when to plant the crops.

This study focuses on the local currency of knowledge, not just formalized Western educational learning. My concern with knowledge is broad and connected with what passes for knowledge in any society in general, and specifically in Kyrgyz society. It is the knowledge of the commonplace, the everyday, where people live the reality of their social worlds, rather than the knowledge of theoretical thoughts and ideas (Berger and Luckmann 1966, 15; see also Schutz 1970). Knowledge originates out of a history, a memory about events in a social context that carries with it an inertia of thought. The issue of learning, which precedes knowledge, helps to explain the character of how what passes as knowledge is expressed in practice.

Thus, there is an inseparable relationship between knowledge and learning. And while that relationship is not always readily apparent—sometimes, for example, we know things that we never thought we learned—it is always there. An infant does not understand the world and the extent to which he sees his mother's breast as an extension of himself. Upon recognizing his hunger he learns that the breast has milk to satiate hunger, a process of coming to know how to address the urge of hunger.[8] The infant begins to understand his environment and in reacting appropriately to the norms in which he is expected to act—in having others in mind—he acquires what is understood as knowledge (Rochat 2009). He knows how to get what he wants.

Learning involves a shift of the object of focus from the transitional objects of the nascent self to the world in which we live. As this study develops, it is here that the world's potentiality is recognized and lived. Learning occurs at some location, both physical and temporal. Surroundings do much to inform us about the world, not in a formal sense, but in a sense more basic than informal—the sense of experience. At some point, we are told that ice is cold, but we experience cold, understand it, and then extrapolate other possibilities for what that means—such as whether ice is desirable or undesirable—based on changing needs in concert with a changing environment of possibilities, wants, and desires (Dewey 1916).

In all its methods then, learning involves a series of attempts to socialize the individual, to conform him, to fit him within socially framed norms.[9] Azarmat, in studying with the Tablighi Jama'at missionary, is trying to fit within a different frame of norms than before and certainly one that is different than that of Tolkun. Though specific lessons learned may diverge between contexts because of differences in environment and community structures, the fundamental ways of learning in Central Asia are not radically different from other locations in the world.

In any cultural or geographic context, there are at least three ways of learning, that is, of coming to the field of knowing and the framework of behavior: *directed passive* learning includes lectures guided to inform and focus conversations; *direct participatory* learning includes mimicry with directed instruction; and *indirect participatory* learning involves observing and mimicking without directed instruction. Passive and active self-discovery serve to put together the pieces of these ways of learning. And while people experience these stages of learning, it is important to note the various means through which they acquire information to construct a meaningful life, because, as will be shown, in practice these means lend a different character and reference toward authority and ambiguity. All of these ways of learning involve attempts to socialize and make sense of such things as ethnic and religious labels, as well as environmental and economic constraints or potentialities.

The Issue of Practice

It is out of the relationship of experience to constructions of truth that we arrive at ideas of the proper context of knowledge, of how to distinguish between what is real and what is imagined (Dewey 1910). And it is out of experience that both Tolkun and Azarmat begin to grasp and understand what it is they claim to believe.

Discussions of belief and ideology are, at one level, discussions of intangibles. There is always the possibility that one is lying about what one claims to believe, making belief a marker that is difficult to assess. Furthermore, when comparing the belief of one person to another, what the first believes is at best generalized to the second but not exact—a belief in God does not distinguish a Jew from a Muslim, much as a belief in Jesus does not distinguish a Presbyterian from a Mormon, at least in their own eyes. Even when two Muslims come together at a mosque, there are aspects of their beliefs that can only be generalized—an Ismaili may pray with his Sunni brothers and a Pakistani may circumambulate the Kabbah with a Bosnian while each holds different beliefs when it comes to the specifics.

Because of this intangibility of beliefs, people concern themselves with practice—the way in which beliefs and ideas are acted out. It is true that the only beliefs we have access to are the ones people speak about—and speaking is a practice—but it is in the lived and acted world that things matter. Everything can be tolerated until some action marks a point of division that accentuates difference beyond what can be accepted (Seligman 1999). It is when the nuances are expressed that tensions arise and labels of difference are applied. This is the reason that people's actions are so crucial.

People's beliefs cannot be forced, but conditions can be set up in ways where someone is more likely to believe them (Waldron 1988). This is, in many ways, what learning attempts to do, to socialize individuals to behave in certain ways. And it may be the case that, with enough repetition and with the proper socialization, one may actually come to believe what is done. While the Islamic Movement of Uzbekistan (IMU) supporters described in the Preface may initially go to mosque as a sign of support, their repeated actions may lead them to accept that this is part of what they do and believe as Muslims in their community.

Returning to the issue of learning and what accounts for differences of behavior between groups, I turn to the various means of gaining religious knowledge, which give character to the nature of religious identity, an identity that people often characterize along ethnic lines. Different means of gaining religious knowledge may change the nature of religious identity. I have observed at least three ways of transmitting religious knowledge in Central Asia. First, students who go to the mosque or madrassa to devote their study to the textual interpretation of Islam transmit religious knowledge. These students tend to be staunch in advocating the rightness of their interpretation on textual grounds. A second means is direct participatory, for example, a father teaching his son how to pray as well as instilling an obligatory sense of regularity in the act. A third, closely related form of transmission is indirect participation. These individuals generally advocate the rightness of their practice on cultural grounds. Here, the community conveys knowledge about religion though not necessarily in a way that assists religious understanding. At circumcisions, weddings, and funerals, for example, one may learn how to participate in the ceremonies without knowing the meaning or possessing the acuity to distinguish the religious aspects of the ceremony from those that are purely cultural. This form tends to be less strict in its religious interpretation. Returning to the dynamic mentioned in the Preface between elders at a mosque who described orthodoxy in economic terms and young adults who viewed practice in normative terms, the means by which they respectively come to know religion could be significant.

My concern is largely the realm of everyday practice. Ideas matter, but so do the terms around what people see as proper and improper. And in the above example, the acceptable action was the increased regularity of visits to mosque. The rationale and beliefs behind the action were less important than the acknowledgment of their presence. While there are always disclaimers about those who are not sincere in their actions, implying that they are not believers, it is only in the absence of their attendance, or in the presence of acts deemed inappropriate by the community, that the issue of belief is genuinely questioned.

The Political Context of Place

For those who study Central Asia, the region's political importance is readily apparent. For most, however, Central Asia is a region full of unknowns. The region at once evokes the romance of the Silk Road and (in the modern imagination of the uninformed) an image of a place filled with Islamic militants (see Baran, Starr, and Cornell 2006; Olcott 2007). Central Asia is, of course, more complex and interesting than such stereotypes; it has a diverse population with rich cultures and an active political climate. Significant energy reserves predispose a particular audience toward the region and the study of terrorism attracts others. One of the reasons Central Asia is of theoretical relevance to those whose focus is outside of the region is that it offers a glimpse of states under development as well as the development of a predominantly Islamic religious identity over a broad area. Furthermore, it is undergoing outside influence of competing interpretations of practice and being challenged by increased religious diversity.

To argue the importance of any location in terms of its relevance to the broader world perhaps misplaces the emphasis of relevance or does a disservice to those who strive for a meaningful existence in a place that is most immediately, for them, the home of their world. That being said, the people of the region take great pride in the richness of Central Asia's interactions with the world, which stir feelings of historical relevance.

For the contemporary outsider, historical relevance is a fascination but not a motivation for political or business interests to engage with geography. The collapse of the Soviet Union in 1991 led to the independence of the Central Asian republics. Though the majority of Westerners still did not have a great awareness of what the region had to offer, oil companies were aware of the region's energy resources. Thus, a new "Great Game" started in the rush to exploit the region's resources.[10]

To contextualize the setting of Kyrgyzstan in the region, however, it should be noted that the oil and natural gas reserves associated with the region lie outside its borders. Kazakhstan and Turkmenistan have the most significant oil fields.[11] And while Uzbekistan's fossil fuels contribute significantly to its gross domestic product, cotton remains its most valuable export and the one that drives its economy, keeping students out of school during harvest season.[12]

Kyrgyzstan, similar to Tajikistan, lacks significant oil and gas reserves, though it does have water, which, while more valuable than oil, has not been effective in being assigned a market price that is comparable to oil. Kyrgyzstan has gold and coal reserves, but those impact the economy only moderately and are difficult to access. Many of the mineral resources are in the more remote mountainous areas and thus not cost-efficient for mass export. Hydroelectric power holds significant potential and electricity is exported to the surrounding countries, but on a much smaller scale than the excitement and foreign investment seen in the energy sector of Kazakhstan, for example.

In other words, while Central Asia is frequently associated with its vast energy reserves, Kyrgyzstan generally is not. Instead, Kyrgyzstan has been more recently associated with political instabilities and Islamism. On 24 March 2005, dissatisfaction with the government in power resulted in a coup that forced President Askar Akayev to flee the country, with Kurmanbek Bakiyev becoming his eventual successor. Though termed the *Tulip Revolution*, in an effort to associate it with the political changes of Georgia and Ukraine, the March putsch was more accurately an accidental shift of power that gave the impression that thuggery works. Since then, political dissatisfaction has continued to be expressed through a series of protests (often financially supported by individuals involved in the dispute) that have included storming the Parliament building, the courts, and, in 2010, a second coup that saw Bakiyev replaced by Roza Otunbayeva and widespread violence in Osh.[13]

It is a climate of dissatisfaction that continues to pervade Kyrgyz politics, a desire for immediate change and a struggle for power among both opportunists and leaders genuine in their desire to govern. But a structure of patronage has also resulted in limiting government reforms and furthering distrust and dissatisfaction with the government (McGlinchey 2000, 2005; Schatz 2005). Many of the people with whom I spoke following the 2005 putsch feared instability that could lead to violence or a civil war, but they also felt resigned and distant from the political events, saying it was unlikely that political change would have any impact on their daily lives—the taxi driver still had to drive his taxi to feed his family; the worker in the market still had to set up her stall if she wanted an income.[14] And while there was a lull in economic activity immediately after events, business returned to normal quite quickly after the 2005 putsch.

Regardless of how politics impacts the uncertainties and concerns of the taxi drivers, teachers, and bazaar workers, outsiders—foreign state officials and analysts—focus on the impact of the coup and the continued instability of the Kyrgyz political system (International Crisis Group 2005a). The government killings of hundreds of civilians in the Uzbek town of Andijan on 13 May 2005 added to the image of Central Asia as a region of instability and emphasized the interrelatedness of the region (International Crisis Group 2005b; Kendzior 2007). Outsiders attributed the emboldening of the protestors of Andijan to the coup in Kyrgyzstan, despite earlier protests over taxation at the bazaars months before in nearby Kokand.[15] Fearing to lose his power, and keeping true to his earlier actions, Uzbek President Islam Karimov came down hard on the protesting population, and once again the political instability of Central Asia came to the attention of the Western media.

Earlier, Tajikistan had contributed to the impression of a politically unstable Central Asia as a result of its civil war, which lasted from 1992 to 1997. Despite lasting peace (Heathershaw 2007a, 2009), Tajikistan, Uzbekistan, and Kyrgyzstan are neighbors with a politically uncertain and unstable future. In addition to political instability, concerns about Islam add an additional facet of fear about the region. One side of the Tajik civil war purported militancy with an Islamic agenda, thereby creating a perception of a region threatened by Islamic militancy and correspondingly unfriendly to the West. This fear of Islamic militancy led to heavy courting and support of Kyrgyzstan by the United States, touted as the region's most democratic country. By contrast, when the language of democracy clearly fell apart with Uzbekistan, the United States gave its support under the umbrella of the fight against terrorism. And for more than a decade after 11 September 2001, allied forces were conducting military operations in Afghanistan with the aim of tracking down Osama bin Laden and disrupting the al-Qaeda leadership. The United States opened military bases in Kyrgyzstan and Uzbekistan as centers of support for the supposed war on terror.[16]

The fear of Islam is broad and in no way isolated or unique to Muslims in Central Asia (see Hefner 2000; Mamdani 2004; Rashid 2002; Tishkov 2004).

Though the vast majority of Muslims in Central Asia are not Islamic terrorists, there is a tendency in the public discourse and print media to overemphasize the activity of fringe Muslim groups and to talk about al-Qaeda, Hizb ut-Tahrir, and the IMU as if they are the same group. For many, these Islamic groups, and Islam in general, serve as a tool to justify measures to secure political stability.

In addition to its energy resources, political instability, and concerns about Islam, there are at least two other reasons for non-Central Asian specialists to be interested in the region (see Kleveman 2004). First, both Russia and China have interests in Central Asia, which has significant potential for transport and trade. Second, the region represents the broader dynamic of states in transition. Despite the changes undergone by their countries, the first generation of post-Soviet leaders has retained many qualities of Soviet leadership. Thus after functioning for so many years under Soviet rule, the state's leadership is developing a sense of what it means to be independent state functionaries, while the people who live in the state have to adapt to the changes of leadership, policy, and opportunities. Religion is one such change.

Religion as Life

As this book is predominately about religion, it would be understandable to emphasize the fear of religious extremism as a factor drawing people into a necessary awareness about the region. Indeed, it is an easy case to make, with the IMU having breached the borders of Kyrgyzstan; with Tajikistan still dealing with the aftermath of a civil war that pitted the government against an Islamic opposition; and with suicide bombings having occurred in Uzbekistan (Montgomery 2004). In terms of political discourse, this certainly is the context in which Central Asian States and representatives from the West most frequently discuss religion (Montgomery and Heathershaw 2016). While not discounting the fear Islamic activism evokes for many practicing and nonpracticing Muslims in Central Asia, it is critical to understand the complexities of the religious situation on the ground within the context of how religion is actually lived. After all, listening to the propaganda of any state gives only part of the story and often confuses and dangerously skews it.

Religion not only gives meaning to people's lives and motivates them to behave in certain ways; it also serves as a way of labeling and stereotyping a population. However, when discussing policy concerns for a region there can be a tendency to overemphasize religion for reasons of political expediency. The threat of Islamic extremism (an awkward term at best) has preoccupied the Muslim world of late. This preoccupation disproportionately emphasizes a section of the population that generally does not represent the whole.

As is the case elsewhere, religion is part of life but not necessarily the focus of people's lives in Central Asia. In other words, a myriad of factors compete for people's time, and everyone has obligations that extend beyond the religious ones. This is not to say that if one is not consumed with religion it becomes less significant; but there are schools to build, crops to plant, children to take care of, and lives to live, which include social relationships that often involve things that are not religious. Yes, at some level what guides people's thoughts and behaviors can be characterized as religious, or being influenced within a generally religious milieu, but religion does not necessarily become the focus of an individual's life. Or at least it would not be characterized as the focus of one's life—rather, it is always in the background, influencing moral decision making (Rasanayagam 2011).

To illustrate this point, an outside observer may interpret the fact that one Muslim prays five times a day as an indication that that individual is consumed by religious thought. It may be the case that the bulk of that Muslim's contemplative time is about living a religious life, but it is just as likely he would argue that he is also more than just that religious life, that religion is something that is being lived. And while he is Muslim, he is also a carpenter, a salesman, a taxi driver, a farmer, or a barber. Religion does not consume him beyond an ability to carry out other required functions of life. It is a part of his life, but does not prevent him from carrying out other functions that are not religious, even if the chores are carried out with religious devotion. For in Central Asia as well as in other places, everyday activities are imbued with religious gestures though not necessarily with religious meaning, be it an *omen*[17] before leaving on a trip or putting a decorative hanging with "Allah" and "Muhammad" written in Arabic on the rearview mirror.

The Idea of Everyday Religion

When discussing religion, I spend most of my time within the context of the everyday, the lived experience that is often outside the realm of theological workings. Most people with whom I had contact were armchair theologians at best. Though many were concerned with being good religious followers, being a practitioner does not require a high level of theological understanding.

There is a tendency to talk about religion through the eyes of people regarded within the community as being the most knowledgeable. On countless occasions, when interlocutors learned that I was researching religion, they would discount themselves and point to someone else within the community who was deemed the "expert" on religion. When administering my survey of religious practice, a common initial reaction was for the interviewees to say, "Oh, I am not an expert on religion. You need to speak with. . . . He knows more about religion and can be of more help." Upon explaining that I was actually interested in what they had to say about religion, they talked about what they understood and knew.

Frequently the acknowledged "experts" on religion would tell me what they thought I wanted to hear. As experts, they were less open and casual with their answers. Some spoke articulately and presented themselves as genuine in their certainty. Many of these experts were, after all, imams and other leading functionaries in the local religious communities. Their job was to

FIGURE 1.2. A driver with "Allah" and "Muhammad" ornaments hanging from his windshield as he waits for sheep to cross the road in the mountains, 2006.

present certainty, to be a source of answers to questions of religious belief and behavior.

While I do not question the experts' motivations, and while they often actively participated in my attempt to better understand the religious geography of Central Asia, they generally do not represent everyday religion as it is understood and practiced—in the full color of its interpretations and contradictions—by most people. The experts are often seen as the professionals and because of the diversity of people's obligations, few have the time to become experts, and possibly even fewer have the resources to devote themselves to religion as a profession. While I do not want to deny or discount the role these experts and professional religious leaders play in transmitting knowledge or motivating community members, they can provide only part of the picture since they represent only one of the forces influencing the realization of religion in the everyday realm.

The specialists, then, do not own everyday religion, which everyone interprets and practices with great diversity. For some, orthodox understandings guide it; for others it is a syncretism of pre-orthodox practices, traditionalism, and the contemporary religious field. The degree to which people make their own sense of this variance is, to some extent, the subject of attempts to understand contemporary religious practice.

The preceding discussion may give the impression that what the everyday contains is self-evident. The question of *whose* everyday appropriately follows, but the fact that the concept is flexible and open to interpretation does not render it useless. Most do recognize or are able to characterize, at least for themselves, what is everyday and what is somehow unique or more special than what would fall under the heading of the everyday.[18] In this sense, the everyday has parallels with religion, because religion also holds a recognizable interpretative framework even if the boundaries of its definition are not articulated.

With regard to religion, the application of the term and its contents are loosely understood. It is most clearly seen in images and activities connected to formalized religious structures—such as mosques, churches, synagogues, temples—and ceremonies and acts—such as Ramadan, hajj, Easter, Passover. But the terrain of religion and religious expression also infuses itself into the everyday in ways that are overlooked.

By suggesting that there is an everyday practice of religion, I am not suggesting that there is a laxness in one's ability to choose or to preference particular expressions of practice (see Barro and Mitchell 2004, 11–12). In one sense it is everyday, like buying vegetables is everyday, but it is also *not* the same; the same types of analysis do not apply. People do not consciously make choices about many behaviors with roots in some way connected to a religious structure. For now, however, it is enough to suggest that what is encompassed by the everyday practice of religion includes praying at home, discussions about religion on the streets, jokes about religion, common gestures, and superstitions, to name some readily observable actions. But the everyday also encompasses acts that most would acknowledge as contradictory to religion, such as a Muslim drinking vodka or a Jew eating shellfish.[19]

The goal here is not to relegate everything that one does to the sphere of religion—sometimes vodka is just drinking and sometimes talking about religion is gossip. Rather, I argue that so much of what people see as religious or as a derivative of a religious context exists in the milieu of the ordinary rather than exclusively in the realm of the sacred. Religion, and perhaps more accurately the acts and gestures construed as part of religion, pervade in ways that carry meanings of wide variance.

Defining terminology is an awkward and inexact task riddled with exceptions and caveats. The very definition of terms often creates Otherness and justifies the division between insider and outsider. One could offer a list of various definitions of religion,[20] yet for most religion is that which is recognized (by the participant) as religion, like a shade of blue that is categorized as blue in the color spectrum of blues but at some point, as the hint of blue becomes lost, loses its blueness.

I am not interested in parsing terms around the spectrum of what it means to be religious, but am comfortable enough accepting (though to some degree also challenging) the locally understood conventions of religion. The level at which I accept it is the level at which people recognize that they are practicing something they call religion. This recognition is at times consistent with considerable interpretive flexibility for one group and the imposition of that group's categories onto another group to label the practices of the second group something other than religion—perhaps even heresy (in contrast to orthodoxy) (see Henderson 1998). This is exactly the dynamic between Tolkun and Azarmat; Azarmat does not consider what Tolkun does as religion, whereas she does.

The point in which I challenge the locally constructed understanding of "religious" concerns the perception of orthodoxy; I take Tolkun's claims as seriously as Azarmat's, even if the populations in Kyrgyzstan and Uzbekistan do not as a whole. There is definitely a sense among some, as alluded to above and discussed in more detail below, that mountain Kyrgyz are religiously inferior to mosque-attending Muslims in the valley. While many mountain Kyrgyz accept being stereotyped as less orthodox or even nonreligious because of their infrequent mosque attendance, I consider their less-orthodox, or pre-orthodox, practices of ancestral veneration, mazar worship, and worship of nature to be part of religion, at least as they envision it.

Defining practice as orthodoxy creates the idea of both heterodoxy and pre-orthodoxy. But it is the case, after all, that most people do not find themselves part of a religious community wishing to be bad practitioners within that community. Both Azarmat and Tolkun are searching for meaning in what they do. And while there are certainly those who stand out as exemplary practitioners worthy of emulation, most practice a religion to the extent that they feel it is important. They do what they feel is required for them to be religious practitioners of that religion, or at least religious enough for where they are at that moment in life. They may at times wish they were more religious, but one cannot assume that they consider their actions to be in direct contradiction with local and/or external standards of practice.

Thus, there is a level at which the practitioner does what he or she needs to do to feel that it is legitimate. This may result in applying fluidity to what the practitioner calls religion. Visits to sacred sites to pray to nature and ancestors are not seen as "standard" religion because the articulation of such activities falls outside the realm of what is commonly understood as the "standard" religion, be it Islam or any other religion.

Whether this is a more liberal or conservative understanding of religion is directly associated with the issue of ambiguity and a flexible application of terms. While part of my concern is the shift from a liberal to conservative expression of religion, or vice versa, the terminology of conservative and liberal is troubling because it is inexact. Some of the more politically conservative religious groups can advocate reforms that are socially liberal, such as the Catholic Church working to improve women's rights in Latin America, or modern, such as al Qaeda's use of video and television technology to spread its message.

When trying to understand the gradations of religious belief (or affinity) and practice, terms arise that are particularly problematic. Fundamentalism, for example, is not really appropriate in a context outside of the early-twentieth-century Protestantism,[21] though one can stretch it to make it fit.[22] But insofar as Muslims root their theology in the Qur'an, all would proudly accept the label fundamentalist, because they are working from fundamentalist foundations to understand and live their faith. Yet in contemporary usage the implications of the term are almost always pejorative. When referring to Muslims who assert the literal truth of the Qur'an and the modern validity of its ritual and legal commandments, one could use the Arabic term *salafiyya*. The term does not imply that such Muslims reject change, for *salafiyya* are often at the edge pushing for change. Rather, *salafiyya* insist that change should take place within the valuated framework established in the Qur'an. *Salafiyya*, however, is also somewhat problematic, so most often I refer to its followers as re-traditionalists.

While words can create the outsider and confine a group, such terms as extremist and militant are awkward when applied discriminately and without scrutiny. Extremism is relative to some norm, which may be a local or more broadly applied norm, and there is a loose consensus regarding whom it encompasses. Militantism can imply inflexibility in ideas or a proclivity to take up arms (with or without ideas). It does imply an aggressive nature, whereas extremism implies a corresponding inflexibility but not necessarily as much aggression.

Indeed, the salient differences are not generally found in the categories of liberal and conservative, fundamental or otherwise, but rather in terms of ambiguity and the ability to deal with ambiguity. The terms of coping with the ambiguous and of coping with the Other involve elaborate and spontaneous steps of navigating the social world. And this feeds into the essence of what I am examining, which is the everyday religious world in which people are engaged and how they come to an awareness of it—through a net comprised of the social structure, corpus, and medium of knowledge.

History and the Geopolitical Context

Despite its location at the center of Asia, there has been a tendency to imagine Central Asia as closer to the edge, closer to the periphery of the world. It has languished on the precipice of the known world though it encompasses a vast area of desert, steppe, and mountains that stretches from the Caspian Sea to Mongolia and from Siberia to the Hindu Kush. It is largely associated in people's imaginations with the Silk Road—a series of trade routes between the Mediterranean Sea and Xi'an and Luoyang, China—that flourished between the second and thirteenth centuries CE. In the fourth century BCE, Alexander the Great extended his empire to present-day Khojand, Tajikistan.[23] In the early thirteenth century CE, the brutality of Genghis Khan's approach to empire expansion made its way across the region, conquering more land in 25 years than the Romans had conquered in 400 years (Weatherford 2005). In the late thirteenth century, Marco Polo traveled east along the routes of the Silk Road, where he served as both explorer and diplomat, writing of his adventures and exposing the West to the exotic world of the East as he experienced it (Polo 1958).

More recently, it was the "Great Game"—or the "Tournament of Shadows" (Turniry Tenei) as it is known in Russian—that carried with it the excitement of exploration and espionage as the expanding empires of Britain and Russia clashed in the nineteenth century.[24] While an exciting idea, the Great Game can be most easily understood in terms of two empires pursuing self-interests. In some sense, this was a precursor to the Cold War, which also had a theater in Central Asia, most notably in the 1970s and 1980s, when the United States and the Soviet Union supported opposite sides in the Afghan war.

Five Central Asian republics gained independence with the collapse of the Soviet Union in 1991: Kazakhstan, Kyrgyzstan, Tajikistan, Turkmenistan, and Uzbekistan. Prior to its independence, travel and scholarship were largely restricted in the region, which contributed to Central Asia being a dark spot on the mental maps of most Westerners. Since at least the time of the Great Game,[25] the boundaries of Central Asia have for all practical purposes been understood to be those now-independent countries bordered by Russia, China, Afghanistan, Iran, and the Caspian Sea. At times, Afghanistan, Azerbaijan, Mongolia, and Chinese province of Xinjiang are considered to be parts of Central Asia.[26] For the purpose of this book, however, I generally use Central Asia to reference the five "stans" that shared the Soviet experience.

My research focused on Kyrgyzstan though I also conducted significant field research in Uzbekistan's portion of the Ferghana Valley. As suggested earlier, there is an interconnectedness of the countries in the region and the lived and imagined boundaries do not correspond exactly to the modern state borders established in 1991. The delineation of Kyrgyzstan's boundaries with Uzbekistan and Kazakhstan was largely influenced by geography, with Kyrgyzstan having the majority of mountains and Uzbekistan and Kazakhstan finding their borders beginning just beyond the foothills, where the valley gains prominence. Prior to the arrival of the Russians and the Soviet efforts to delineate borders, there was greater fluidity, with borders loosely demarcated by trade relations and the extent of a ruler's sphere of influence. Thus, the boundaries of the nation-state are less than exact representations of the relations people have and have had historically. Uzbekistan holds claim to the bulk of land in the Ferghana Valley and the largest percentage of the valley's population is composed of ethnic Uzbeks. But as the mountains of Kyrgyzstan slope down to the beginning of the Ferghana Valley, a strip of the valley with both Uzbek and Kyrgyz residents remains within the Kyrgyz border. Despite the difficulties the border creates, there are trade interests and family relations that move back and forth and in some ways recognize the limits of a pre-Russian-delineated boundary.[27] The geographical, as well as the political, environment sets much of the tone for various options that could be pursued, and certainly some historical factors that significantly influenced the social setting of the environment are helpful for understanding the immediate situation.

Indeed, history is relevant for the contemporary analysis of today's everyday. The relations between the countries are important and the roots of today's relations are connected to the perceived reality of history, shared and otherwise. To some extent, people acting today are acting with a limited view, understanding, or recollection of history, but because the overriding explanation given for tradition is "this is how we have always done it," it is important to give the historical background with which to understand the debate. Moreover, because part of the argument is that the transmission of religious knowledge takes place in a cultural and social setting, a discussion of the history of political attempts to alter culture is relevant.

The Pre-Russian Period

History as it influences the everyday is inexact at best. The past clearly informs the present in innumerable ways—and history can be reconstructed and made useful for a variety of political purposes—but I will suggest only a few historical moments and how they continue to be viewed and utilized today.[28] This necessitates omitting some distant yet significant historical events that have little recognizable bearing on how everyday lives are being lived in the contemporary period. How much of an impact the Samanids or the Seljukids have on the individual construction of a meaningful life for an Uzbek barber in Karasuu or a Kyrgyz shepherd in Achakainda is open to interpretation, but is not the focus of this section. Of course, there are habits, customs, and ways of looking at the world that have been passed down and remain in some form a part of local culture. However, proving the origins of people's actions in antiquity is beyond the scope of this foray into history. Certainly the Mongol invasion and Turkish expansion into the region created new political environments in which people acted, as did the Russian period, but it is the broad environment that I address.

There is no question of Central Asia's historical importance. So much of what I have written above follows traditional views in legitimating Central Asia's historical place by speaking of its connection to outside actors, but it certainly has contributed to the world. The early history of Central Asia is that of nomadism, but at the same time great cities developed that fed trade along the Silk Road and advanced world knowledge (see Hansen 2012; Whitfield 1999; Wood 2002). As numerous caravans traveled with goods between China and the West on the many paths that became known as the Silk Road, the peoples of Central Asia became vital in securing the safe passage of goods. They were also active participants in the exchange of goods and culture. This is not to suggest, however, that Central Asia was a unified region that gave traders and travelers peace of mind. Largely controlled by tribal leaders and khans, at every place safe passage had to be secured and traders were aware of the importance and the danger Central Asia presented.

In the fourteenth century, Central Asia gave the world Tamerlane (Timur), who made Samarkand his home and followed in the steps of Genghis Khan, ruling as much of the world as anyone had before (see Manz 1989; Marozzi 2004). Andijan was the home of Babur, who went on to establish the Mughal

Empire of India in the fifteenth century (Babur 2002). But while the historical stories of Tamerlane and Babur had a significant impact on their world, in today's setting my interlocutors referred to both of them as sources of pride and religious inspiration. Uzbeks point to how great a world power they *were* as evidenced by the architectural masterpieces left behind by Tamerlane in Samarkand. And as will be discussed in detail below, Solomon's Mountain (*Solomon Too*) in Osh is a sacred site in part because it is believed that Babur stopped there to pray on his way to establishing an empire in India.

Islam arrived in Central Asia in the late seventh century. Prior to its dominance, there was a mixing of religious beliefs and practices, including Buddhism, Confucianism, Judaism, Manichaeism, Nestorian Christianity, Shamanism, Taoism, and Zoroastrianism (Foltz 2010). In the ninth century, the famous Sunni scholar Muhammad al-Bukhari contributed to the establishment of Bukhara as a center of Islamic learning, and his collection of *hadiths* (traditional account of sayings, actions, or habits of the prophet Muhammad) is considered to be the most authoritative. Al-Bukhari remains a central contemporary reference point for Central Asia's role in Islamic intellectualism and his hadiths can be found in almost every mosque I have visited in Central Asia and abroad. His name is among the most recognized of Islamic scholars in Kyrgyzstan,[29] and even those who do not know that he compiled the hadiths know that he was Central Asian and an important intellectual.

The Uzbeks adopted both a sedentary lifestyle and Islam before the Kyrgyz (Allworth 1990). This earlier adoption of Islam is a common local explanation to account for variations in religious practice between mountain Kyrgyz and valley Uzbeks—specifically, why Uzbeks are more orthopraxic in their Islamic expression. People will explain that the Uzbeks adopted Islam a few hundred years earlier and thus have a more developed understanding than their Kyrgyz neighbors do. This, of course, is not the case, as people learn religion within the time span of their lives, but it is an example of how historical facts are interpreted in a contemporary setting to explain differences of behavior.

A narrative descending from a lineage of historical greatness is prevalent and becomes associated with sacred sites throughout the region. In Jangi-Nookat, in Osh oblast, the eponymously named sacred site of *Sahaba* is believed to be the locus of the early arrival of Islam in the region. The Sahaba were considered to be companions of the Prophet Muhammad and locals in Jangi-Nookat point to the tombs there as evidence of the site's religious importance. Companions of the prophet came to Jangi-Nookat, this far, to share the message of Islam in its purest form.

In Naryn oblast, the sacred site of Tash Rabat is the most intact of the caravanserais along the old Silk Road.[30] It does not have the religious history of Sahaba but instead is connected to the history of the Silk Road and nomadic tradition and movement familiar to the mountain Kyrgyz. Those who visit see it as a magical place with a special closeness to nature and ancestral spirits.[31]

Figure 1.3. Two women and a child getting their picture taken in front of a photo backdrop of Sahaba, set up by a local photographer at a spring festival, 2012.

The guardian of Tash Rabat asserts that it is a sacred Islamic site because traders brought Islam to the Kyrgyz and to the mountain space.

Certainly within the contemporary imagination of Central Asians, Islam is characterized as the dominant religion, despite variations in religious practice between the mountains and valleys residents. Sahaba and Tash Rabat provide just two examples of history continuing to play a role in people's lives; as

FIGURE 1.4. Tash Rabat, a fifteenth-century caravanserai believed to have been built originally as a Nestorian monastery in the tenth century, 1999.

do the histories of Tamerlane and Babur. But equally important are the social structures of this time that have been carried down to the present.

Family and kinship relations were important then and continue to be so, because they represent survival and the functioning of society (discussed in more detail later) (see Krader 1963, 1971). It is also during this time that political structures and affiliations developed that remain relevant today. In the eighteenth century, three rival khanates—Bukhara, Khiva, and Kokand—filled the power vacuum left by the collapse of the military regime of Nadir Shah. They functioned much like city-states and no one felt allegiance to one nation, as nation is understood today. The borders remained fluid and imprecise because of constant skirmishes. And on the periphery, the nomads kept regular pressure on the khanates. During khanate rule, there was a decline in the intelligentsia, but trade remained vigorous.

The Kokand Khanate administered much of the Ferghana Valley and fostered relations and relationships that moved beyond the current nation-state borders of the Ferghana Valley: Kyrgyzstan, Tajikistan, and Uzbekistan (Levi 2007). The tendency to have fluidity across state boundaries highlights their arbitrariness, and my interlocutors often spoke—perhaps romanticizing the past—of both the importance and the utility of the state borders as well as a better time when borders did not exist and relations were better.

The Russian and Soviet Period

By the early nineteenth century, a cloud of imperialist fervor hung over Europe. Russia saw an opportunity not only to expand its empire to Central

Asia—a factious, unstable, and undeveloped region in which it already provided protection to the Kazakh hordes and had established trade relations with the Uzbek khanates—but also to secure a more natural border than the steppe. Fearing the expanding British presence in India, Russia set out to expand its empire and, as discussed earlier, the two nations became engaged in what became known as the Great Game.

The Bukharan, Khivan, and Kokand khanates maintained a trade surplus with Russia, which eventually viewed the area as space worth attaining. The Bukharan Khanate was ceded to Russia in 1868 and became a protectorate in 1873; the Khivan Khanate fell in 1873; and the Kokand Khanate lost its territory gradually: Tashkent in 1866, Khujand in 1867, and it completely fell in 1876 (Becker 1968). By the late nineteenth century, the Russians used a policy of indirect rule toward the indigenous population; they did not attempt to significantly alter the habits or lifestyles—religious or cultural—of the population as long as the locals did not create problems (see Allworth 1994; Bacon 1980; Rywkin 1988). Social and economic development came slowly, and when it did come, the Kazakhs were the first to see it because of their proximity to Russia.

The Soviets inherited the relationship with Central Asia that the Russians had established, a relationship of resentment that led to a holy war in Andijan at the end of the nineteenth century and Jadidist reforms in the early twentieth century that pushed for modernization on its own terms, independent of the Soviet agenda (Khalid 1999).

Soviet rule brought forced collectivization, construction of nationalism, and repression of opposition. But there were also benefits: increased education, improved health care and infrastructure, greater equality for women, and more support for arts (Michaels 2003; Northrop 2004). The Soviets had a greater plan of integration than the one envisioned by the Russians. They sought to change the landscape through collectivization projects, irrigation, and planned economies and they pushed the development of ethnic policies that had far-reaching influences in trying to reform boundaries and ideas of identity. While the theory of control was extensive, domination was more of a give-and-take situation than a complete takeover.

In 1924, Stalin's ethnonational-territorial delimitation program sought to undermine the existing regional power structure and weaken the ethnic cohesion that location and Islam had provided. This program created artificial boundaries that divided ethnicities in a way that fostered a sense of ethnic elitism. Stalin claimed to introduce the program as a means to unify the territory in language, economy, and culture (Haghayeghi 1996, 5, 169–70). The program's success gave credence and acceptability to newly recognized ethnicities, such as Kyrgyz and Uzbek. It was not that the Soviets created the linguistic identities of Kyrgyz and Uzbek, but rather built upon them and emphasized them as part of a national policy. This policy received support from the local people, who felt that their identity was being legitimated as they were now leaders of their own territory. To an extent, however, the new ethnicities served to destabilize the region by pitting one recognized ethnic territory against another.

To further complicate matters, under the national-territorial delimitation program in the Ferghana Valley the borders were drawn in a way that put large ethnic groups under the administrative jurisdiction of a territory in which they were minorities. For example, 2000 estimates suggested that the ethnic makeup of Osh oblast in the Kyrgyz Republic was 50 percent Kyrgyz and 46 percent Uzbek.[32] Furthermore, the area contains islands of one country engulfed by another—for example, enclaves of Uzbekistan and Tajikistan are cut off from Uzbekistan and Tajikistan within Kyrgyzstan.[33]

As a union of multiple ethnic groups, the Soviet system faced the challenge of convincing individuals, as well as ethnic groups, of the legitimacy of Soviet governance (Khazanov 1995, 105). By creating, albeit somewhat artificially and arbitrarily, republics rooted in ethnicity and surrounded with a filigree of folklore, history, and linguistics, a certain locational legitimacy was maintained; that is, the national language was not forbidden but encouraged in development alongside Russian. By making Russian the common medium of communication and the unifying language of the Federation, Moscow became the necessary mediator of conflicts.

Perhaps one of the most remarkable aspects of the policy's success was that Moscow and Soviet planners managed to convince the intellectuals of Central Asia of the historicity of their respective nationalities. These intellectuals were arguing against each other as to the rightness of their national order, rather than with Moscow about the arbitrariness of the Soviet-created nationalities.[34] The instability that partition created assured a reliance on the central Soviet administration that complicated the newly created republics' viability in independence (Roy 2000, 68, 73).

There was, of course, a difference between the ideals of the Soviet system and how well those goals were realized. The government system promoted Soviet education, women's equality, and a Soviet ideology. The system had to answer back to Moscow; at the macro level, it did. But in remote areas of Central Asia, especially places like the Ferghana Valley and the mountains of Kyrgyzstan, local officials lived in a parallel system where they also had to answer locally to elders and other community members.

The Soviet policies did attempt to control religion (Keller 2001). Control was not complete, however, and the further people were from Moscow, the more difficult it was to carry out the edicts against religion. During the Second World War, for example, Stalin was forced to ease restrictions against Islam in order to gain local support in the war effort. And even when religion was restricted, traditions were kept and many religious rituals were termed tradition.[35] Attempts to institutionalize, and thereby have an avenue for control and manipulation, can be seen in actions such as the establishment of the spiritual directorates—such as the Spiritual Administration of the Muslims of Central Asia and Kazakhstan (SADUM) (Russian: *Dukhovnoe upravlenie mu-*

sul'man Srednei Azii i Kazakhstana)—in which the Soviet state appointed official imams whose views were either more in line with communist ideology or at least more malleable. These relationships of state institutionalized religious authority continue today, and are viewed by some with the same skepticism as those of the Soviet period.

The Postindependence Period

Despite the arbitrary boundaries set up by the Soviets and the 1924 national-territorial delimitation, the roots of these borders proved entrenched enough to be accepted in the 1991 transition to nation-states. Independence was not negotiated but rather thrust upon the Central Asia republics and thus the style of governance that developed was based upon power structures that were left intact after the Soviet rule had ended. While much of the Soviet period has been understood and analyzed in ideological terms, people approached it more pragmatically, allowing the semantics of ideology to continue as part of the discourse but less as part of the lived meaning of the Soviet ideology (Yurchak 2006). In other words, as the new leaders found themselves in power, they were left trying to figure out what to do now that the Soviet system was gone. It was easiest to continue with the existing structure than to drastically reform it. But being separated from Moscow also meant being separated from the center that financed many of the social services of the communist state and also the mediation role that the Soviet framework provided.

For most people, despite the rhetoric of Soviet communism and its associated ideology, there was a pragmatic adaptation that was carried into the new system of postindependence. But it was also not the case that people saw democracy as the solution to all the problems. One can speak of the virtues of democracy, but the immediate result saw a collapse of pensions and the disappearance of the social nets people had taken for granted under the communist system.

As mentioned earlier, Kyrgyzstan was touted early on as a democratic success story. It professed a desire for change and it was the first of the Central Asian countries to adopt its own currency, begin market reforms, and enter the World Trade Organization. But soon prestigious jobs ceased being well paid and teachers and engineers turned to driving taxis rather than pursuing careers for which they had been trained. With the privatization of land and the end of collective farms, people were forced into subsistence farming and cultivating home gardens. When an electrician friend lost his job after the collapse of the Soviet Union, high unemployment made personal garden farming the only realistic way to feed his family. Now, twenty-plus years later, his garden produces enough food for his family to last throughout the year. However, with many of his neighbors also working their gardens, selling excess produce at the market yields little profit.

There has been little diversification in the workforce and people have flocked to professions that were once lucrative. This is why an increasing number of taxis can be found on the streets and taxi drivers complain that they can no longer make enough money to provide for their families because the market is flooded. The bazaar has become another place where those who control trade have become very successful, whereas the majority of traders struggle to make ends meet, with sections of the market where every stall sells the same products. The market has meant things are economically up for grabs, and many who see capitalism as somewhat of a disappointment long for the security the Soviet system used to provide.

With local economies struggling, people see nongovernmental organizations and foreign development as among the more profitable fields, although neither self-sufficient nor a system of self-generated income but rather one dependent on the generosity and agenda of outsiders. A host of countries and development organizations want to influence the future of Kyrgyzstan. And whereas the force of developmental influence before was top-down from Moscow, there is now a greater diversity of foreign interests, which does not necessarily lead to a greater sense of economic security for the larger population.

In addition to hard economic realities, there is a cultural change in how people learn about things. The Soviet system was enduring and continues to influence people's thinking and the social structures in which people function. In Kyrgyzstan, there is a greater openness and one sees religion and opportunity together. There is a continuity of traditions that stems from relatives as well as an influx of different religious understandings—primarily, though not exclusively, Muslim and Christian—from abroad. In Uzbekistan, on the other hand, the country's policies toward religion are becoming increasingly closed and restrictive. Islam is understood as the official religion, but believers know they must be careful to avoid being perceived as too religious and thus a threat to the state.

As the border between Kyrgyzstan and Uzbekistan becomes increasingly reified the different economic and social policies of the two countries become an important component of the social understanding of my interlocutors in the Osh region. Kyrgyzstan is seen as having more economic opportunities and greater freedom of religious expression.[36] And people on both sides of the border understand their current situation relative to constraints and opportunities in respect to the postindependence path of the countries with which they have affiliation and affinity.

THE ENVIRONMENT OF POTENTIALITY

My concern is with potentialities and how people's knowledge and options influence their actions, and what accounts for the differences in those actions. Of course, ethnicity and place are not innate ways of being but rather learned ways that carry certain behaviors. Kyrgyz tradition is linked to a nomadic way of life, whereas Uzbek tradition is associated with a more sedentary life. Pride is taught in these ways of being and in the rare instances where ethnic Uzbeks live in the mountains, they take pride in saying that they are Uzbek, implying that they are different, but their behavior and cultural descriptions are no different than that of the Kyrgyz who surround them. The same is true of ethnic Kyrgyz living predominately among Uzbeks in the valley (here I am not referring to communities of Kyrgyz but rather individuals); they behave much more like Uzbeks. The border regions are where things get interesting as there are a number of problems that are present precisely because of interaction at the edge of the valley and the mountains. These interactions tend to be described with ethnic and place of origin terms (for example, Kyrgyz mountain, Uzbek valley), and the ethnic divisions are understood to be associated with differences in religious behavior (for example, Uzbeks being more religious than Kyrgyz). Ultimately, however, the interactions are learned behaviors that are intimately connected to the potentials people have in acting.

In one sense, the mountain–valley border is one of heterodoxy and orthodoxy. In the mountains, there is ancestral veneration and the worship/reverence of nature alongside a self-identification with Islam. In the valley, there are the largest and best-attended mosques in the region and a belief that it is the place where the most correct form of Islam is practiced. Increasingly, it seems that religion is viewed as being most accurate when it is most restrictive, so the "bad" and "good" Muslim distinction tends to be accepted along the lines of ethnic (Kyrgyz and Uzbek) and place (mountain and valley) divisions.

There are differences between the mountain and valley with regard to how people learn about religion and culture; initially it appears that these means of learning play out differently in terms of practice. In general, learning that is centered on the mosques and madrassas tends to allow fewer options for interpretation and acceptance of difference; the more liberal forces seem to be those who learned about religion and culture in a somewhat informal milieu (this is not to suggest that these people are less religious but rather more open to accepting variations and difference).

Certainly it is more than just the location of knowledge transmission but also the potentiality of what surrounds people. The surrounding potentialities include, inter alia, the mafia, corruption, an education system where grades can be purchased, cronyism, high unemployment, and the most lucrative options for employment being either migrant labor work in Russia or Kazakhstan for men and prostitution for women. All of these—as well as a religious option—are among the potential avenues for action that people calculate in relation to their knowledge base.

In the quest for making a meaningful life and negotiating the myriad of obligations that everyday existence poses, people come to terms with their social environment, reconciling what they believe with how they behave and events that persuade them to act in a particular manner. Since before the 1999 incursion of the IMU, analyses of events in Central Asia have quite frequently centered on an Islamic threat, when in reality militant Islam is just one of the possibilities before people, at times made more appealing by the environment and the options contained therein.

This point takes us back to the case of the 2005 Kyrgyz putsch and the Andijan killings. Different things were taking place in a field of potentialities and what happened in Bishkek on 24 March and in Andijan on 13 May influenced the range of people's possibilities for action. How these events play out in the long term could be relevant to religious practice and a means of communicating knowledge in significant ways; it could, for example, mean that a foundation is being set for a more restrictive expression of religion to be transmitted. How all of this will be internalized and enacted remains to be seen, but people recognize that there is a difference they perceive as substantive.

One message from the 2005 Kyrgyz putsch was that thuggery works. While the state was not particularly strong before the coup, the power vacuum created by the ousting of President Akayev created an opportunity for power-seeking entrepreneurs to vie for authority. This led to shootouts between rival mafia gangs, assassinations of members of parliament, a second coup in 2010 that was significantly more violent than the first, and a season of ethnically labeled attacks in Osh. The feeling of many was that while life goes on as it must, there was an increased sense of lawlessness.

The Andijan killings are the bloodiest exemplification to date of the failure and draconian character of the Uzbek state, which is being met with an increasing sense of anger and despair. Uzbekistan has gone to great lengths to find individuals to blame for inciting these events and has convicted dozens in closed trials. But life is not getting better and people are becoming more desperate.

These episodes leave one searching for sources of security, authority, and morality. In both countries, the outcome of the religious character of society is up for grabs. Theorizing about this is theorizing the moving target and the shifting sand. Despite this, the means of communicating religious and cultural knowledge, as well as the pressures of coming to terms with the possibilities of action, reveal something significant about the everyday character of religious life that is, at least at first, not ideological but learned.

Returning to the stories of Tolkun and Azarmat, the cause of the differences can in part be explained by understanding how people come to know what they claim they know, and how this influences practice. Knowledge allows us to interpret. And maneuvering through life, making sense of life and coming to terms with the profound problems of existence are accomplished by working through what we have learned and claim as part of our corpus of knowledge.

The reality of action is that it is not always thought out, or at least thought is not always at the most immediate level. But by and large, behaviors are learned. And that which comes to constitute knowledge may not be recognized as such until expression brings it to the surface. It is in this sense that culture comes to constitute a body of knowledge that is utilized by all of us, with the subtleties and nuances of our own predilections or sense of boundedness.

Thus, knowledge exists not only in a formal sense of what we believe it to be, but also in the colloquial sense of everyday practice. It is knowing when to plant and harvest the crops. It is knowing how to read. It is knowing how to behave. It is knowing how to pray. It is knowing the difference between who belongs and who does not. It is not only answers to the questions of who, what, where, when, and why, but also that which allows these questions to be asked. This does not imply that knowledge is only that which causes us to act. It is both something that is derived from action and something that guides action.

Tolkun and Azarmat cannot explain most of what they do. When talking with them, the articulated justification for their actions oscillates between "because it is our culture" and/or "I know this is right (or wrong)." The references always go back to events and stories, revelations of ultimate truths and historical continuation: "our ancestors did it this way"; "Allah has given guidance"; or "when I was a young girl, I saw . . ."; "once that happened, I changed."

People come to know religion and culture in different ways, but a relationality to experience is always present to help frame the meaning of practice. Tolkun learned her Islam through practice—observation and participation with her parents. Azarmat also learned through practice—studies around a text and observation of his community. It is here—within and in relation to community—that relationships gain context. It is here that Tolkun and Azarmat fold into their respective communities and significance is created.[37] And at the heart of significance is understanding made meaningful by what an individual *knows*.

The net of knowledge is its social organization, corpus, and medium. It is the potentialities and restrictions of the state, society, and economics; it is the professional, social, educational, and religious frame of reference; and it is the manner by which what is known can be expressed—oral and textual transmission as well as experiential transmission (the doing of an act). None of this is revealed in a statistic that denotes the percentage of a population that is Muslim, but requires spending time with people. And to respect the variations of cosmology—as it impacts policy of this world and the nonnegotiable facets of an individual's otherworldly conceptions—we are more responsible in appreciating the nuances of difference.

Tolkun has intimate knowledge of nomadic living—every spring she leaves for the upper pastures with her family and their livestock—and the traditional obligations to her ancestors. Her learning was largely oral and handed down by her family and relatives. She references her actions to the conventions of her environment and those who came before her. She realizes that there are slight variations in the stories that she has learned and is more open to accepting variations of cosmological truths.

Azarmat has lived a sedentary lifestyle and privileges a religious tradition that he sees as being connected more transnationally than locally. He graduated from high school, and his religious education has been centered on a text that he occasionally reads but does not fully understand. He holds the text as

FIGURE 1.5. Women dancing at a birthday party, 2005.

being outside what can be negotiated, and thus he is not open to different interpretations. Tolkun can take him seriously, but he cannot take her seriously. Nonetheless, his community recognizes him as at least somewhat authoritative. And this restricts his behavior—in public, he will not drink the vodka he shared with me on his daughter's third birthday.

Socially and politically, we are concerned with what people do much more than with what they think. It is in doing that we come to knowing, and it is the net of knowledge that not only allows us to create meaning, but also guides the expression of ourselves. If we are to capture the meaning of a label such as the Kyrgyz population is "75 percent Muslim,"[38] we need ethnographic work to problematize our oversimplifications. Here, the caution is that in our eagerness to act as if we understand something, we risk oversimplification and the reification of misunderstandings that leave us thinking that we have it and yet we are woefully out of touch. People's stories matter. It is the human component, the lived reality of those influenced by religion that gives flavor to the structural confines in which people function. Because religion can be multivocal, because people's imagination is great, and because there is an improvisation—a social navigation—that people undertake to make sense of and to cope with the structures imposed on them, the approach of an anthropology of religious knowledge—social organization, corpus, and medium—can give a richer understanding of the context through which people come to their beliefs and develop their religious selves.

Chapter 2

"Muslim by Birth, Atheist by Belief"

The Social Organization of Knowledge

Presumably, then, the origin *we* should begin from is what is known to *us*.

Aristotle, *Nicomachean Ethics*

We are full of things which take us out of ourselves. Our instinct makes us feel that we must seek our happiness outside ourselves. Our passions impel us outside, even when no objects present themselves to excite them. External objects tempt us of themselves, and call to us, even when we are not thinking of them. And thus, philosophers have said in vain: 'Retire within yourselves, you will find your good there.' We do not believe them, and those who believe them are the most empty and the most foolish.

Pascal, *Pensées*

While it seems paradoxical in nature, many aspects of everyday life are filled with contradictions that are not perceived as contradictions by the actor. Tolkun, Azarmat, and Murat all do things that they fault others for doing— Tolkun privately discounting the efficacy of the spirits to repair certain fractures in life yet admonishing her neighbors for not having enough trust in the spirit world; Azarmat preaching against people going to mazars yet going to one when his father gets sick; and Murat speaking of the destiny of his path as being beyond his control and yet boasting about his agency in making choices that bettered him. There is a certain degree of cognitive dissonance at work here, where one holds others to higher standards of consistency than oneself. When pushed on these contradictions, Tolkun, Azarmat, and Murat give reasons for the exceptions that apply to them and not others. They understand issues but recognize the many gray areas of life over which they have little control but to which they must still respond.

It is also the case that they are familiar with the self-identifying distinction made by Muktar, a taxi driver who, in speaking about his approach to religion, said he was "Muslim by birth, atheist by belief." Around the world it is not uncommon for people to make such distinctions between the social and cultural contributions of a particular religious tradition and an actual belief in the tenets of that tradition (even if belief matters) (Pouillon 1982; Ruel 1997). But there is a tacit assumption that Muslims should have some belief and atheists should be able to free themselves of the cultural confines of a religious tradition. Thus, people looking for consistency can be quick to criticize Muktar, Azarmat, Tolkun, and Murat. The inconsistencies between what they say and what they do can lead to tensions between them as individuals and the expectations of the various communities to which they belong.

While they make exceptions for their own inconsistencies, it is the social framework of their community that holds them accountable. This aspect of social organization is what constitutes the cohesiveness of community and is the space in which the mundane world thrives and the transcendent world is given meaning. It involves imitation of others and socialization with others. And it constitutes understandings that are recognized, both latently and manifestly, as useful to belonging to a group and distinguishing an individual. The interpretative framework in which religious identity develops involves a synthesis of the restrictions and potentialities experienced as the state, the market, and the demands (and corollary expectations) of sociality.

THE ENVIRONMENT OF THE EVERYDAY

The everyday is the routine affair of sociality. What makes it so essential to our becoming who we become is its regularity and the unremarkable way it permeates existence without being noticed. Tolkun, Azarmat, Murat, and Muktar all went to school and acquired some level of formal learning, but everyday learning involves the conversations they have that lead them to affective communion with others; to laugh and cry, to relate and empathize. The environment of the everyday is one where people make sense of their experience and subsequently apply it to further making sense of situations in which they find themselves. It is making sense of the doing, of knowing how to be, of abstracting what to do, and of mimicking the conventions of what needs to be done. As such, it is a complexity of emotions that come to seem natural and almost unnoticed in their familiarity.

Experiencing Knowledge in the Everyday

In Book Ten of *The Republic*, Socrates speaks against artists, in particular poets, because he views poetry as a form of *mimesis*, an imitation (Plato 1991, 277 ff.). What troubles Socrates about the poets is that in their attempt to represent the real world in art—with its moods, behaviors, and senses—the poet does not need knowledge of what is being represented, but only the skill to present things as they appear. He therefore sees them as dangerous, because the poets pretend to be authorities on issues about which they may have limited knowledge. Plato recognizes the coercive force of an abstracted imitative representation of the world and its ability to persuade people to behave improperly. It is a thought not far removed from the idea that behaviors precede belief. For communi-

Figure 2.1. An elderly woman with prayer beads at a mazar in the mountains, 2006.

ty members discussed in the preface—who mentioned the material support of the Islamic Movement of Uzbekistan (IMU) and changes in their own religious practice—this is precisely what is at issue: elders and the youth embraced a more orthopraxic approach to Islam for different reasons: from economic to moral, from religious to fulfilling a desire for belonging. Seeing their actions in collective imitation, they grew to view their religious identity as wrapped up in a certain set of practices from which it is socially difficult to deviate.

It is through practice that we come to knowledge and it is through practice that we come to understand what religion and culture mean. And while knowledge is not knowledge in any tangible sense until it can be expressed, there is a distinction between practical knowledge and theoretical knowledge.[1] Turning from *mimetic* expression, which is a source of theoretical knowledge that has been collected largely from the experience of predecessors, to the *phronetic*, which is the practical knowledge that feeds the pool of theoretical creativity, we can see a circular relationship to knowing. Eventually more complex abstractions can be made at a theoretical level—which gives rise to rhetoric and thus an amazing capacity for inciting destruction—but it is only at the level of practice that the computations make sense.

In some ways, the theoretical is really an ideal type because it is through practice—action and articulation—that the waters are tested and the depths become known. To situate this in the context of how people learn, one can see that a farmer, for example, obtains knowledge that he views as practical in essence. There are some development projects that have aimed to formalize the setting for the transmission of knowledge about agriculture—to transform the medium of knowledge transmission—but in general people learn about farming through observation and imitation of "knowledgeable" authorities. They usually learn from male relatives and from being forced into the fields or the pastures as an extra hand, not for the purpose of tutelage. With some direction—but mostly through doing, reading the signs of nature, and trial and error—they acquire the skills to a degree that at some point the young farm hand becomes a skilled farmer.

While hands-on learning of farm operations is often not given the credit it deserves, the formalized settings of school are generally seen as the environment in which knowledge is transmitted. During Soviet times, schooling was obligatory, but since independence an increasing number of Kyrgyz children stay away from school either to work in the market or as apprentices with their parents, in an attempt to help support their families. Most children, however, do go to school and study sciences, languages, and social studies with varying degrees of attentiveness. Early on, children are tracked into class groupings where students in the "A" group are thought to be smarter than those in the "B" group.[2] Laxity in performance is often tolerated in the latter group and in almost all cases, students can purchase higher grades.[3] And like students everywhere, it is not until much later that they appreciate the importance of the foundation they are building as they study topics like math and language.

In the southern part of Kyrgyzstan, some parents who either cannot afford the cost (including the bribes) of sending their children to school or who want their children to gain a strict religious education may send their children to a madrassa. Some parents have their children study Islam at madrassa while attending public schools to study other subjects; others only require their children to attend madrassa and do not send them to public schools at all. While

FIGURE 2.2. Schoolchildren getting their pictures taken, 2012.

education plays an important role in Islam, the goals of the government-run public school and the madrassa are quite different.[4]

In Nookat and elsewhere in the region, young boys go to madrassa and spend hours reading and trying to memorize the Qur'an, either scattered around the courtyard or huddled in a room for warmth.[5] The madrassa curriculum usually does not include material outside what is necessary to read and *possibly* understand the Qur'an. Students learn the Arabic letters, the sounds they make, and thereby become able to read. They do not always develop a corresponding proficiency in understanding what they read, but some certainly do. In addition to classes on Qur'anic reading, students often take classes on the hadiths and on how to be a "good" Muslim.

A boy who only studies Arabic and the Qur'an at a madrassa at first perceives it as meaningless repetition. But as he grows older, he begins to consider himself knowledgeable about something he articulates as practical (ignoring the question of whether the knowledge *is* practical and for what reasons it is practical—political or/and soteriological), and discounts the knowledge of those in public schools who do not know Islam. He reinforces the value of his knowledge by discounting the value of what others know.

When one compares a boy studying at a madrassa and one enrolled in a public school, it is clear that these two students come away with different understandings of what is practical and important. Knowledge, as a way of viewing and organizing life, has many different facets, four of which are ac-

Figure 2.3. Madrassa students with their teacher at one of the few madrassas for girls, 2005.

tion, abstraction, phronesis, and mimesis. These components exist in relation to each other as part of what constitutes knowledge.

———

Knowledge of action is knowledge of practice. It is knowing when to plant the crops and how to carry out the ritual requirements of religion. Abstraction is a knowledge of theory, where one engages in thinking about how to make crops better or assigning/interpreting religious significance to events. Phronesis, or practical knowledge, gives a moral way of being and acting. And mimetic knowledge is of representation and re-presentation.

Returning to the two students, in a madrassa and in a public school they come to different understandings of what is practical, how to act, abstract, and re-present meaning in life. These visions are not always mutually exclusive, but they certainly can be. How these two students come to understand and interact in the world is set, in part, by the confines of how they came to know what they know, and the emphasis they place on that knowledge. This dynamic applies equally to Tolkun, Azarmat, and Murat and the distinctions that separate them.

Applying Knowledge in the Everyday

Knowledge in the everyday is not only a mixture of phronesis, mimesis, and theoretical knowledge, but it is also a relationship between what is old—mean-

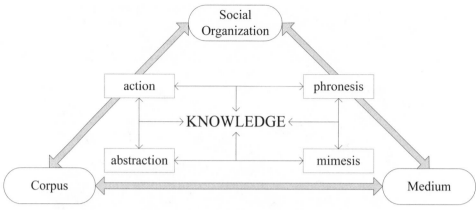

FIGURE 2.4. Facets of an anthropology of knowledge.

ing that which always was—and what is new; between the general and the specific; and between the local and the outside. There is knowledge that always was, that in people's minds came to be seen as tradition, as history, as part and parcel of the habitat in which people have always lived and where they see themselves destined to go.[6] But there is also the knowledge of seekers, trying to move beyond what they view as old, trying to embrace what they claim is new. Of course the *new* is often merely a reformulation of the *old* with select alterations or nuances that mark it as different. But both old and new knowledge exist in the present and reach toward a future under construction.

In general, the discourse between old and new moves easily. In Murat's community, a group of older men, aksakals,[7] meet everyday at the chaikhana to gossip, reminisce about their youth, and discuss community issues. Religion is always high on their agenda. When there are disputes in the community, those involved often call upon the experience and wisdom of these men to help resolve issues. In doing this, the elders generally draw their authority casuistically by precedents of tradition and rootedness in the past.

Two examples of the aksakal council show this relationship between old and new and the issue of legitimacy and change. Over the past five to ten years, a few of the aksakals in the group have gone on hajj. They are always eager to talk about their experiences, and many of those in the group who have not gone are actively trying to save money so they can also make the pilgrimage and join the ranks of hajji. Those who have gone return with an elevated religious status in the community and an attitude of greater religious authority. Their authority comes from visiting the place where the historical tradition of Islam is most deeply rooted and from joining other pilgrims in the process. When the topic of conversation can be at all related to religion—which is often—the experience of the aksakal hajjis is brought to the discussion and directives and claims are made about how the community should proceed in living a more moral life.[8]

Not surprisingly, the reason some aksakals want to go to hajj is to gain the legitimacy to be a part of this moral decision-making process. When people cannot go to hajj in Mecca, other pilgrimages are substituted—such as more local pilgrimages to Sahaba, Solomon's Mountain, or Turkestan.[9] Hajj carries with it a transformative agenda that results in a less-observant Muslim returning with an acceptable reason for transformation that absolves his past shortcomings and characterizes his present and future as more pious. While there is certainly some cynicism about some who go on hajj for possible economic or political gains, going on hajj is a way of bringing new knowledge into the discussions of the community by rooting it in the old, by referencing to a different way of Islamic behavior that, while new to local understandings, is more legitimate and more proper because its foundations are older and closer to the lived experience of Muhammad. The story of Nurbek illustrates this dynamic.

Nurbek is a young man in mid-twenties from a village near Nookat. He has a university education and now lives and works in Osh. When he visits his family, he goes to pray at the mosque and will walk over to the chaikhana while talking with—but mostly listening to—one of the aksakals, who is happy to see him back in the village. The aksakals are proud of Nurbek and see him as the future of the village. They want him to have the right wife, to raise a family, and to teach his children the traditions of their heritage. They have endless advice for him. They know that Nurbek has *new* knowledge, because he works with computers and speaks a little English. Most of his life was spent in a post-Soviet Kyrgyzstan and he understands the ideas of democracy and capitalism better than they do. Still, they are slow to embrace this *new* knowledge, arguing that greater authority rests in the *old* knowledge of their experience. Wisdom, they claim, comes from having lived experiences that affirm the importance of family and tradition.

When questioned about the legitimacy of Nurbek's views on religion or family problems in the community, the aksakals generally claim to be more authoritative and knowledgeable because their experience is broader than his. They seem themselves as having direct experience of specifics—from experiences akin to Murat's awareness after his first sexual experience to countless seasons in the life of the community—that, in the context of general understanding, give an idea of how to be in the everyday.

Nurbek, of course, has specific knowledge when it comes to computers and if any of the aksakals has reason to ask a question about computers, they seek his advice and, because he is one of theirs, acknowledge him as an expert of the highest order. But the parameters of his expertise are limited to what they do not know.

Thus, the discursive level, which includes speech and writing, is recognized as a means for knowing the surroundings, but can be questioned, overridden, or accentuated (as it can also question, override, and accentuate) the validity of knowing by nondiscursive actions. The experience of hajj or of living and watching the generations pass is one form of nondiscursive transmission of knowledge. Knowledge of something may guide the action and the action it-self may convey knowledge of what is proper or "how to be normal" or how to do "being ordinary" (Sacks 1984). But at all levels—discursive and nondis-cursive—we work on comparisons, perceiving similarities and dissimilarities, and typify. These typifications can constitute political aspects of boundaries and identities.

These boundaries and identities lead us to ideas of insiders and outsiders. For example, Tolkun is of the same ethnic group as Nurbek and the aksakals, but they do not give her much religious credence. They concede that she knows the mountains and nomadic ways better than they do, but insist that she does not know what matters. Another example is At-Bashi aksakals who go to the *jailoo* (upper pastures) in the summer and see the sedentary, valley aksakals as having a different life with a different set of experiences.

Knowledge is, of course, primarily local. It is always the case that we are local in some place and are outsiders to some people. The tendency, often a protective one, is to discount knowledge from outside. As more than one of the Nookat aksakals put it, "Nurbek knows a lot about computers, but how does that help him live here? What he needs to know are the relations here."

But the knowledge of the outsider cannot be easily dismissed as being lo-cally irrelevant, insofar as it contributes to an insider–outsider dynamic. The dynamics of insiders and outsiders are present at all levels precisely because communities are not isolated. Even the smallest village has a resident who has interacted with someone beyond the village boundaries if not someone who has visited the city. And what passes for knowledge—or is held in greatest es-teem as knowledge—in the city may be entirely useless in the village.

Before the Dolan Pass, about 40 kilometers off the main road between Kochkor and Naryn, is the isolated village of Lahol, which sits on a plateau at an altitude of over 2,500 meters. It was turned into a sovkhoz—regional collective farm—as part of the Soviet collectivization efforts.[10] Houses were built, electricity was extended out to the settlement, and products were reg-ularly transported in to support the center. When the collective farm system collapsed in the early 1990s, Lahol suffered a lot of hardship. Very little can be grown there and grain and hay shipments stopped arriving. The winters saw a decline in livestock as there was not enough food to feed both livestock and people; without other sources of income, it was better to kill the animals for meat.

Unemployment in Lahol is high, over 90 percent, and alcoholism is cor-respondingly high. And while people lament about life being better during the Soviet times and assert that it is better somewhere else, they do not have enough money to leave. Begaim, a woman in her mid-forties who looks worn and prematurely old, summarized the situation: "The problem is that we do not die." The desperation she sees in her life and in the situation of other vil-lagers comes from seeing their lives as inferior in quality when compared to outsiders who visit.[11]

The reality is that even in relative isolation, the remoteness is only relative and the isolation is not complete. Even in the most restrictive environment of the penal system, there is interaction with the outside, whether in visits from relatives or the mafia power structure that functions inside. There, knowledge of the system and ways of resisting it are intensely transmitted. The rules of the underworld are harshly transmitted and networks for surviving inside and outside are established.[12]

The local and outsider understandings of knowledge are connected not only with internal cultural distinctions, but also through the attempts of externals—real outsiders, such as foreigners working for development organizations or in education—to influence ideas and conceptions of knowledge. This includes locals who have traveled abroad for business or education and brought back ideas that are new, at least in the local context. In addition, developers and missionaries come from abroad for varying periods of time and with varying agendas.

The difference in understandings with which people enter into discourse is not just a function of culture but rather of the social organization and body of knowledge they have and can utilize to mediate their understanding of events and realities. Thus, these interactions start a borrowing of understandings and potentials for imagining, and thereby realizing, different futures.

While the aksakals offer a vision of the community that carries authority in the accumulated years of their experience, a local-born foreign-trained missionary has been influenced in ways that make him both an insider and an outsider. On one level, others accept his way of viewing the world but on another it is very much rejected. In less dramatic terms, the same can be said about Nurbek, who knows computers, and Murat, who negotiates the everyday of his world with knowledge that is at the same time old and new, general and specific, local and outsider.

SOCIAL ORGANIZATION OF KNOWLEDGE: ETHNICITY AND SOCIAL STRUCTURE

The transmission and acquisition of knowledge always exist within a socially organized frame. The organization of knowledge is socially determined and constructed. And while it seems normative and takes on a character of inevitability—this is how it always has been and has to be—social organization is in a position of potential change and modification. It is influenced by the social response to place and the outcomes of community groupings, like those of ethnicity. The logic of social organization is practical knowledge; it is mimetic knowledge; it is the expression of action and the abstracted thoughts that explain it.

The contributions of social organization to knowledge can be seen positively as potentialities or negatively as restrictions. For society to be society, there is some layer of organization that can be structured in innumerable ways and can be grouped into at least three sets of restrictions and potentialities. First, state and governance restrictions and potentialities, which are seen in the open

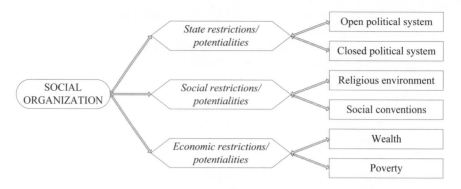

FIGURE 2.5. Social organization of knowledge.

or closed nature of the political system; second, economic, which are seen in poverty and wealth; finally, social, which include the conventions of tradition and expected behavior, as well as the constraints and opportunities of the religious environment.

Social Organization of Knowledge in Ethnicity

Tolkun, Azarmat, Murat, Nurbek, and Begaim are ethnic Kyrgyz. But Kyrgyzstan is a country comprised of multiple ethnic groups, the second largest of which are Uzbeks who live predominately in the southern part of Kyrgyzstan, in the Ferghana Valley close to the border with Uzbekistan. Ethnicity carries with it the weight of restriction and potentialities of the state, economy, and social interaction.

Ismoiljon is an Uzbek blacksmith who works in the bazaar in Osh. He is a fourth-generation knife master, an artisan of notable skill, who wanted to be a taxi driver in his youth. His father wanted him to continue the family trade, but Ismoiljon was set on joining his classmates in the quest for freedom and fast money with the chauffeur's trade. His father asked him three times if he would take over the family trade, each time telling Ismoiljon that if he did not take over, the family business and family legacy would end. After Ismoiljon refused his father's trade for the third time, his father took a hot iron rod and jabbed it into Ismoiljon's right leg. He then wished his son good luck with his trade as a driver and refused to talk to him until he returned to the shop two weeks later to become an apprentice. Now, thirty-three years later, Ismoiljon—who still limps from the injury his father inflicted—speaks of his father's wisdom, as many of his friends who became taxi drivers have asked him for loans when business became tough. That he has been able to forge a decent living is a source of pride, and he fully expects that one of his sons will take over when he retires.

Like Murat, Ismoiljon had some wayward years where he drank too much and occasionally raised his hand against his wife. He had little or no interest in religion, but as he grew older he developed a relationship with Islam that he identified as part of being Uzbek. He went to mosque for Friday prayers because everyone in the neighborhood went and he felt he had little choice in the matter. He never spoke of a conversion experience or reason for being a Muslim, other than to claim that he was Muslim because Uzbeks are Muslim.

When I returned to see him after being away a year, his excitement was evident. He wanted me to see the knives he had been working on, and told me he had gone on hajj that year. He beamed with pride about being in Mecca and repeatedly said that he was hajji now, and thus he was somebody. He had taken his wife with him and when he asked her what she thought of the trip, she told him that she married well and had the best husband in the world, for now he was hajji and a good Muslim.

Murat and Ismoiljon became aware of ethnic differences as children. They learned this because they had limited interactions: Kyrgyz children played with other Kyrgyz children and Uzbek children played with other Uzbek children. Even today, in a city like Osh where there are large populations of both Uzbeks and Kyrgyz, it is often the case that while people share the same physical place, they occupy different spaces. They, and others like them, take for granted that there is a difference between Kyrgyz and Uzbeks. Part of this differentiation is connected to traditional roles of lifestyles—Kyrgyz shepherds have different lives than Uzbek farmers. But the way in which Kyrgyz and Uzbek identities were developed during the Soviet times also provides part of the explanation.

What most likely accounts for the differences between Ismoiljon and Murat are the social structure and ways of living, though terms of ethnicity have come to imply these differences. Ethnicities have come to distinguish difference and are used for group interests. And this even extends within ethnic groupings. At local levels where different people interact, ethnic influences are used to distinguish difference. For example, between Kyrgyz there is a geographical separation of north and south, but there is also an aspect of ethnicity's influence—that is, northern Kyrgyz explain the difference in accent and slight variations in customs by saying that southern Kyrgyz have been influenced by their closeness to Uzbeks.

Before the arrival of Russians in the region, there was an emphasis on tribe, clan, and location and less concern with ethnicity in the modern sense. Ethnicities generally became more important and developed during the Soviet period. For the Soviets, this was part of a broader plan aimed at bringing people into the Union; it was not random but rather a thought-out experiment. After independence, there was a push to better understand what it meant to be from a particular nation. There have been growing pains—reified in attempts to justify difference and further legitimate the new governments—and borders and part of the identities of ethnicities had a religious component to them.

Russian and Soviet policies encouraged Central Asians to define themselves politically and ethnically. Between 1865 and 1920, the Russian empire expanded into Central Asia (Allworth 1994; Roy 2000, 25). There were hostilities among Central Asian populations in the 1860s when the Russians arrived, but despite the identity associated with homelands of groups in conflict, there was no unified political, diplomatic, or military identity (Silverstein 2002, 93). The Russian expansion, however, greatly influenced how the peoples of Central Asia came to define themselves politically and ethnically, because first the Russian conquest and later Soviet policies both physically and ideologically threatened identities based on location.

Prior to the 1924 creation of territorial boundaries by the Soviets, community ordering in Central Asia was centered on the Governorate-General of Turkestan (which included the Khanate of Kokand), the Emirate of Bukhara, and the Khanate of Khiva.[13] Each served multiethnic populations, and while ethnic terms such as Uzbek, Kyrgyz, Tajik, and Turkmen were familiar, cultures and languages were shared in ways that fostered solidarity groupings along the lines of location rather than ethnicity.[14] Thus, people would refer to themselves as Kokandians, that is, from the regions administered by the ruler of Kokand, before they would speak of an ethnic distinction of Uzbek, Kyrgyz, or Tajik. And while a Kokandian might speak Uzbek at the market and Kyrgyz at home, the base administrative grouping of Uzbek or Kyrgyz was a foreign political construction.

The administrative headquarters of the Transoxiana centers—Bukhara, Khiva, and Kokand—were not centered around direct expressions of ethnic power, but rather dynastic and religious legitimacy fitted within an accepted traditional structure (Roy 2000, 7). The traditional ruling structure, however, did not lend itself well to outsider control. Thus, the Russians and Soviets, in trying to coopt power into a system controlled from Moscow, fostered programs of nationalism that not only weakened the locational cohesion of Kokandians, Bukharans, and Khivans, but contributed to an external administrative reliance on Moscow for control over more local centers of governance.

When in 1924 the region was carved into republics and people were assigned to a republic of nominal cohesion, the Soviets tried to create a sense of nationalism that was not an ideology as much as it was intended to be a way of living. It was a form of nationalism that was forced on a people who neither viewed itself in terms of a nation nor embraced any ideology associated with ethnic nationalism (Roy 2000, viii-x). While the Soviets offered the trappings of statehood, the accompanying ideology was foreign, suggesting that the purpose of the nationalities program was not the creation of independent and viable nation-states, but rather an eventual acquiescence of the republics into the greater plan of the Soviet Union. To do this, Soviet planners sought to shift people's understanding of self from locational terms to ethnic and national terms.

Joseph Stalin set out his plan to actively transform the populations of Central Asia in his pamphlet "Marxism and the National Question" (Stalin 1913). His idea of nation involved an evolution from the clan structure to a Soviet nationality that would be of practical interest to the Soviet apparatus charged with governing a diverse multiethnic population.[15] Thus, the evolution toward nation and nationalism can be seen as passing through at least three stages.

The most basic stage of social coherence for Stalin was the clan. The clan evolved to the tribal community, a grouping that still relied heavily on kinship bonds. Nomadic populations such as the Kyrgyz were at the tribal level of community because they were not seen to have evolved to the extent of sedentary populations such as the Uzbeks (Bennigsen and Quelquejay 1961, 5).

Out of the tribal community evolves the ethnic group (*etnicheskaia gruppa*) that maintains a tribal quality but also possesses peculiarities that are ethnic or cultural in nature. The next stage is that of *narodnost'*, something which is a bit looser than the concept of nation and, though often translated as "nationality," is more a collection of people sharing a sense of belonging. The narodnost' state implies a common territory, economic bonds, and holds a cultural, spiritual, and linguistic commonality that may be diluted somewhat by the presence of numerous dialects (Bennigsen and Quelquejay 1961, 1–2). Stalin's goal, however, was the nation (*natsiia*), which he defined as "a stable and historically constituted human community founded on its community of language, territory, economic life, and spiritual make-up, the last being contained in the idea of community of national culture" (Bennigsen and Quelquejay 1961, 2–3). In short, he saw four characteristics that a nation must hold as common for its members: character (meaning mentality and culture), economy, language, and territory (Fragner 2001, 17).

Stalin's view of the nation provided a framework for manipulating social groups. Thus, it was not the tribal grouping or ethnic grouping that created the states of Central Asia, but rather the powers in Moscow that set out to transform the region.

For many in Central Asia, the characteristics of Stalin's nation were irrelevant. The largest difference between Kazakhs and Kyrgyz was dialect, but their nomadic consciousness was nonetheless complete at the tribal level. As for sedentary populations such as the Uzbeks, they would regard themselves first as Muslim and second by location of belonging, whether village or region. And directly opposed to the notion of uniform linguistic criterion as essential to community identity is the example of the Chagatai ethnic group that was comprised of both Turkic and Persian speakers but viewed its members as distinct from other Uzbeks (Bennigsen and Quelquejay 1961, 14).

Thus, identity resided either at the subnational level of clan or tribe, or at the supranational level of religious affiliation, that is, part of the Muslim community.[16] It is important to emphasize that the development of nationalities, while seemingly arbitrary, was not unplanned. Much thought and science went into fostering group identities that could be understood in linguistic terms and manifested as nationalities. Language gave status to nationality, and schools developed the identity associated with this understanding through education. The census reinforced this identity even more univocally as it required individuals to declare their ethnic affiliation. A list created by the state limited these affiliations, and the designated nationality appeared on line five of all internal passports (Roy 2000, x). Eventually, people grew to view themselves as belonging to the nationality (ethnic group) listed on their passport and locational affiliations were supplanted by ethnic affiliations.

The complete picture of identity, of course, remains more complex. For example, when "questioned as to their ethnic and tribal affiliation, people from Andijan (in the Ferghana Valley) referred to themselves as 'Uzbek' by ethnic group and 'Moghul' by tribe, in other words members of the tribe of Babur, the enemy of the Uzbeks" (Roy 2000, 16). Locational references have not been completely lost, and someone from Samarkand will continue to refer to himself as a "Samarkandi." If pressed, however, the locational reference is quickly followed by an ethnic reference such as "Uzbek," "Tajik," or "Tatar."[17] These ethnic affiliations, which have become accepted as fundamental, become particularly critical in times of struggle and conflict.

Promotion of ethnic identities in Central Asia to supplant locational identities was only one piece of the Soviet strategy. Planners also began pushing for Russian to be the dominant language in the region. In theory, this would foster a common Soviet identity. As the Soviets pushed the Russian language in public life, national languages became protected in homes and religious institutions (Marshall 1996, 20). National languages continued to be reinforced as objects of identity because they were used in spaces held with greatest reverence and served to set people apart from the Soviet people.

Although political boundaries imposed after the 1924 ethnonational-territorial delimitation program remained the same after the 1991 collapse of the Soviet Union, the newly independent states (with the exception of Kazakhstan) did not distinguish between ethnicity and political citizenship, that is, the ethnic term "Uzbek" was not delineated from "Uzbekistani," a term implying citizenship within the political confines of Uzbekistan (Roy 2000, 13). Thus, the linguistic terms of identity were maintained, but their political application was broadened beyond ethnic boundaries. This lack of a distinct separation between terms of ethnicity and political citizenship allows ethnic nationalism to serve as a potential call for unity in times of conflict. And because of this, Ismoiljon identifies more with ethnic Uzbeks on the other side of the border than he does with Murat who, like him, is a Kyrgyz citizen.

Nationalism, which was so much a part of the Soviet Union, ultimately contributed to the breakup of the totalitarian order it was intended to maintain. Citizens of the respective republics accepted the linguistic identity that the Soviet planners had implemented and resented the Russians for holding power outside the republic center. The emphasis placed on creating nationalities, however, did not in itself lay the ideological foundation for nation-building (Khazanov 1995, 73, 124). After the fall of the Soviet Union, independent Central Asian states, for which nationalism was a foreign concept, were ill equipped to transform to a nontotalitarian system of governance such as democracy. The inclination toward ethnic nationalism, which justified the move toward independence (post-facto), unified both elites and counterelites, assured the dominance of the ruling nationality, and protected the authority of those in power (Khazanov 1995, 60, 135). It was the construction of ethnic identity through language that legitimized the emergent states, and the new rulers were obliged to support the system that afforded them legitimacy.

These efforts to bolster legitimacy, combined with the success of the identity construction aspect of the national-territorial delimitation program, is evident in the fact that the states that emerged after the Soviet Union were not the Transoxiana emirates, or even a unified Turkestan, but rather the republics of Uzbekistan, Tajikistan, Kyrgyzstan, Turkmenistan, and Kazakhstan.[18] Such constructions were almost predetermined, for the construction of Otherness was not only against the central governance of Moscow, but also against the nationalities of the surrounding countries that vied for regional influence and control (Esenova 2002, 12).

All these distinctions may seem well rooted in the past; the reality is that both Murat and Ismoiljon accept them as normatively given. Even when talking with people familiar with history and the Soviet influence on ethnicity, one hears the assertion that ethnic divisions between Uzbeks and Kyrgyz were inevitable. To understand the utility of boundaries and identity to the articulation of intolerant action, we can see how events played out in the Osh ethnic conflict of 1990, creating a narrative that was capitalized on in the violence of 2010. The Uzbek-Kyrgyz nationality emphasis created boundaries and identity based on linguistic differences of dialect. This imposition of identity defined Uzbek speakers as Uzbeks and Kyrgyz speakers as Kyrgyz,[19] even though all are residents of the Ferghana Valley.

In June 1990 in Osh oblast, a group of ethnic Kyrgyz attempted to seize a portion of farmland that had been claimed by Uzbek-Kyrgyzstanis who farmed the land.[20] The group seized the land to address a housing shortage caused by a recent influx of Kyrgyz into the predominantly Uzbek area (Maynayev 1990). Tensions rose amid accusations that the government—dominated by ethnic Kyrgyz—appropriated the land for the Kyrgyz,[21] and 10,000 Uzbek-Kyrgyzstanis and 1,500 Kyrgyz crowded onto a sovkhoz (Zverev 1990). The sovkhoz director managed to keep peace until a larger group of Kyrgyz arrived. Riots broke out; over 200 people were killed over the next few days (Pannier 1999) and over 500 houses were burned down (Friedman 1990). Parliament declared a state of emergency ("State of Emergency Declared in South Kirghizia" 1990) and the only thing that stopped the riots from escalating into a full-scale war was the arrival of Soviet airborne troops dispatched along the Uzbek–Kyrgyz border (Lubin, Rubin, and Martin 1999, 10). These troops and armored personnel carriers prevented the Uzbeks of Uzbekistan from crossing the border and joining in the battle with the Uzbeks of Kirghizia against the Kyrgyz.

Rape, torture, killing, looting, banditry, and hooliganism were the trademarks of the riots (Lubin et al. 1999, 7). Ethnic Kyrgyz in Osh province were instructed to paint their doors red to escape the destruction of the rioting mob (Anderson 1997, 68). And Kyrgyz throughout the country were called to join their ethnic brothers in fighting the Uzbek-Kyrgyzstani population in Osh (Friedman 1990).

The news media carried video footage of burned houses and destruction left in the wake of the rioting mob. The media also tried to portray the instigators of the violence as extremists, bringing Uzbek-Kyrgyzstani and Kyrgyz residents together to discuss the violence and its impact on the community (Friedman 1990). The aftermath of the Osh conflict resulted in segregation and interethnic distrust.[22]

While the seizing of land was not in itself an obvious violation of ethnic identity, it was seen as a threat to the physical boundaries of what belonged to the Uzbek-Kyrgyzstanis and to the Kyrgyz. The influx of Kyrgyz into a predominantly Uzbek-Kyrgyzstani area threatened to dilute the essence of Uzbek distinctiveness. The perceived favoritism appropriated to the Kyrgyz by a government of their ethnic composition was seen as a form of action that took care of one group, thus reinforcing commitment to that group. At the same time, it encroached on the boundaries of what the Uzbek-Kyrgyzstanis claimed to be theirs. When the boundaries were threatened, violence ensued. Group boundaries were reinforced by calls for Kyrgyz to join their ethnic brothers in fighting the Uzbek-Kyrgyzstanis. Likewise, Uzbeks in Uzbekistan were prepared to join their ethnic brothers in fighting the Kyrgyz but were prevented from doing so by Soviet troops that were called in to control the border.

The national-territorial delimitation program created artificial boundaries that divided ethnicities in a way that fostered a sense of ethnic elitism. Whereas Stalin claimed to introduce the program as a means to unify the territory in language, economy, and culture, the success gave credence and acceptability to the newly recognized ethnicities. During the 2005 Kyrgyz putsch, Ismoiljon and the majority of Uzbeks in the south kept a low profile, not wanting the political demonstrations to be associated with Uzbeks and thereby possibly incite an escalation of ethnic tensions similar to the violence of 1990. To be fair, Murat was also anxious about the Kyrgyz coup, because he feared the potential of a return to fighting between the ethnic Uzbeks and the Kyrgyz. Both Ismoiljon and Murat, however, accepted that if fighting broke out, they would side with their respective ethnicities without regard to the arbitrariness of the fighting.

And in 2010, when violence did break out again, that is exactly what they did. Both expressed skepticism about the June events being really ethnic in origin, but they also saw that the ethnic distrust that drove the narrative of events was manifested in Uzbek neighborhoods being destroyed by Kyrgyz and Kyrgyz being targeted by Uzbeks (Laruelle 2012; Megoran 2012; Reeves 2010, 2011a; Wachtel 2013). Tensions came to rest on divisions viewed as ethnic difference understood to imply social difference.

Social Organization of Knowledge in Social Structure

Murat and Ismoiljon were raised differently. Part of what accounts for those differences is the ethnic preferences and prejudices they were taught. It was a sense of territory and of profession: Kyrgyz are the shepherds of the mountains and Uzbeks are the farmers of the valley; Kyrgyz are more relaxed in their work ethic and Uzbeks are industrious; Kyrgyz are lax in their religious orthodoxy and Uzbeks are orthopraxic. These are the types of stereotypes employed in the ethnicization of difference used to justify the violence of 1990 and 2010, as well as the distrust and segregation that ensued.

But ethnicity is only part of the social organization aspect of life that animates the everyday understanding for Murat and Ismoiljon. It is difficult, if not inappropriate, to use Western constructions of political and social orderings—communism or democracy—to explain many of the events that take place in Central Asia, where informal ties based on real or fictive kinship and relations of mutual indebtedness better account for behaviors centered on the interests of those close enough to be of benefit. Despite the evolving time of political transition and of flux in general, traditional social structures remain influential, with the basis of tradition serving as a means through which cultural knowledge is transmitted. Knowledge, to the extent that it elucidates roles and expectations, informs us of social statures and levels of expertise, situates patterns of action in a meaningful context, and serves as the basis for social organization (Barth 2002, 2). It becomes symbolic and plays out tacitly in the form of affiliations and discriminations.

The flag of the Kyrgyz Republic, for example, consists of a *tunduk* (the crown element of a *boz ui* [yurt][23]) situated atop a sun with forty rays to represent the forty Kyrgyz tribes. An independent new nation chose to symbolize its identity in terms of its tribal heritage, while Western countries pinned most of their excitement on Kyrgyzstan's relative openness to democratic ideas of governance. When it proved that Kyrgyzstan as an "island of democracy" was a failed moniker, many in the West were disappointed because they had placed so much hope on the idea of a democratic state emerging out of Central Asia.[24] What best accounts for this change, however, is not the ease of Soviet-inspired totalitarianism—though that plays into it—but rather the need to bolster power through kinship networks. And in a state with an ethnic orientation and a system of patronage, this not only differentiates the privileges of Murat from those of Ismoiljon, it symbolizes distinctions between Kyrgyz and Uzbek. Uzbeks, for example, are not represented as one of the forty Kyrgyz tribes.

The contextualization of traditional and contemporary social structure is difficult because what tribes and clans mean to people today is changing.[25] In general, a clan is an informal social institution that founds its cohesiveness on conceptions of kinship—through blood, marriage, or other creative arrangement—and its concomitant obligations of indebtedness (Collins 2002, 142). Among Kyrgyz and Uzbeks, clans can be regional, business, or family,

Figure 2.6. A boy leaving his family's yurt to get water from a nearby stream, in the mountains, 2006.

but they always serve as a way to shore up interests. Kyrgyz are much more likely to know their tribe and clan, especially in rural areas where there is an emphasis on lineage and ancestry. Meanwhile, many Uzbeks in Kyrgyzstan—especially the younger generation—insist that they do not have clans, while the older generations often list, and associate themselves with, historical clan names.

Putting this in the context of the interlocutors introduced thus far, all the Kyrgyz could name their tribes, though neither Azarmat nor Nurbek knew their clan affiliation (in part this was related to the difficulty of understanding what the term means). They had not been told and did not know if they should think of it as a locational, business, or historical relationship. Ismoiljon claimed that tribal affiliations were Kyrgyz and that Uzbeks did not have them. To Uzbeks, Ismoiljon claimed, tribes were unimportant, but the *mahallas* (neighborhoods) were of great importance (see Geiss 2001; Sievers 2002).

Many Kyrgyz associate the importance of their tribe with their mountain lives and nomadic pasts.[26] A true Kyrgyz, some claim, knows not only his tribe but also seven generations of his father's lineage. One reason for the importance of tribes is to be clear about whom you can count on for protection—immediate family and kin always being the answer—whereas knowledge of paternal ancestors both respects the past and minimizes inbreeding.

The implication of the nomadic life is, however, one of change and constant movement. Patrilineal relatives would, when possible, move their livestock together and share pastures. And while this may seem primitive to some, especially those with sedentary lives, in reality it was quite a sophisticated adaptation to the environment and required significant coordination to transport the household throughout the season.[27] Though materially nomads had little, they controlled trade across the mountain and the margins of the valley and the steppe (Barfield 1989).

The historically more sedentary Uzbeks organized their communities differently, generally involving relations around the mahalla, whose boundaries were known to everyone. The mahalla in its developed form is not only a neighborhood but also a local administrative system that regulates actions of the community from irrigation of fields to mediating disputes. Its sedentary orientation is a very different way of living from the nomadic ways of mountain Kyrgyz.

One interlocutor summarized the difference between Kyrgyz and Uzbeks by emphasizing the nomadic and sedentary distinctions. A shepherd, he noted, spends much of his time alone, watching his livestock to make sure the animals are safe. If a sheep gets too close to a cliff, he rushes over to move the sheep away. After this short burst of activity he returns to lying on his back looking at the clouds. This is a very different approach than that of an Uzbek farmer who must plan the steps of planting his garden relative to the seasons and each day do something different. It requires a greater level of organization, but the shepherd's approach is functionally appropriate to the task before him.

The stereotypes are that Kyrgyz are backward and lazy while Uzbeks are entrepreneurial and hardworking. A Kyrgyz may have two months to plan an event yet do most of the work in a hurried two days before the event, which often turns out to be a wonderful success. An Uzbek, on the other hand, may take the whole two months to prepare. These distinctions revolve around different conceptions of time and ways of approaching a task. Westerners frequently—and the pejorative stereotypes reflect this—bring with them their prejudices toward time and discount the utility of the Kyrgyz nomadic tradition because in many ways it does not mesh well with a world that plans.

Tolkun still closely identifies with the nomadic traditions of the Kyrgyz because she lives in the mountains and for years has spent at least part of her summers in the jailoo, migrating with relatives. Nurbek knows some of the traditions and is torn between the city and the mountains. Some of his best memories are of being in the jailoo with his brothers, and sometimes he leaves the city just to return to the peace of his village at the edge of the mountains. Azarmat does not care much for life in the mountains and prefers the medium-size village. And Ismoiljon wants to look at the mountains from a distance and insists that the place for an Uzbek is in the valley.

What happens, however, is that the specific ways of understanding time and the world become associated with ethnic labels, even though the environment in which people live and the nomadic or mahalla orientation toward social organization seem more important than ethnicity. There are very few Uzbeks who live in the mountains of Naryn oblast and those who do often act more like the Kyrgyz around them than the Uzbeks in the valley. Likewise, those Kyrgyz raised in an Uzbek environment feel more natural there than they do in the mountains. There is more leeway, of course, in those areas situated between the mountains and the valley; what tends to distinguish a Murat from an Ismoiljon or a Tolkun is the degree to which there is a connection to the nomadic or sedentary tradition, to a tribe or to a mahalla.

POTENTIALITIES AND THE EVERYDAY

Before the collapse of the Soviet Union, the son of a prominent Party official in the south was faced with a dilemma: should he give his father a proper Muslim burial or should he abide by the expectations placed on him as a member of the communist leadership and give him a nonreligious burial? After hours of deliberation and consultation with community elders, a Muslim burial was given; because of his high-profile position within the Communist Party, the official was removed from his leadership post. He lost the Party's official support but remained an important and respected figure in the community. Months later, after Kyrgyzstan declared independence, the former Party official returned to his leadership position, but this time as a democrat. Nothing had changed on his résumé. What had changed was the environment that allowed him to resume his post.

People are constantly adapting to their environment. They see potential and employ a behavior of social navigation whereby they assess the constraints of the everyday, weighing their prevailing obligations and marking them in relation to ideas about and visions of the future.[28] This is not always as smooth or linear a progression as theory would often suggest. Ismoiljon hated his father for ending his dream of being a taxi driver, but after three decades of making the most of the options before him, he praises his father's wisdom. Others may see his father crippling Ismoiljon as a selfish and hateful act, but Ismoiljon casts it in a light of purpose and destiny.

The children in the madrassas and public schools do this as well, capitalizing on what they have learned and understand to be important, and attempting to maneuver toward a meaningful life by emphasizing skills they can exploit. The level to which a madrassa student, without training in the general school curriculum, can integrate into the Kyrgyz government structure is limited and thus roles of leadership within alternative political structures such as Hizb ut-Tahrir may become more attractive. Likewise, a public school student who sees a separation between religion and the world privileges his knowledge in relation to barriers and opportunities to find utility with a religious orientation. The extent to which religion plays a role, and the role it plays, comes along lines of learning—of the perception of one's place in one's social grouping and the history of the most influential social structure.

Adaptation in the Post-Soviet State

The collapse of the Soviet state created a system that was very much in flux. There was a knowledge of one system—with its state, economic, and social re-

"MUSLIM BY BIRTH, ATHEIST BY BELIEF"

strictions and potentialities—that forced the emergence of a different system of social organization. This forced people to adapt to the new border restrictions and the collapse of state services, as well as an increased opportunity for public exploration of religion. Now, over twenty years after becoming independent, the ways people have reoriented their expectations and lives under a new system are becoming more apparent.

Pensions promised under the Soviet system are no longer enough to live on and in the city, pensioners can be found selling whatever possessions they have—old books, used household items, clothes, garden equipment. Most of the pensioners selling their goods are ethnic Russians who no longer have family to help support them or who did not have enough money to immigrate to Russia after the collapse of the Soviet Union. The Kyrgyz and Uzbek pensioners also struggle, but because of a social organization that encompasses a broader definition of family, some relative usually takes care of them.

The borders also present new regulations and adaptations. For example, independence and efforts to distinguish the state boundaries of Kyrgyzstan and Uzbekistan saw the division of the town of Karasuu into two parts with one section of the town being in Uzbekistan and another part in Kyrgyzstan; a river that runs through the town marks the border. Movement across the bridges was relatively easy until the 1999 emergence of the IMU led to a tightening of the borders and a more defensive posture on the part of Uzbekistan. The different policies of the states have resulted in the increased economic isolation of Uzbekistan and the emergence of a thriving bazaar in the Kyrgyz Karasuu.

To take advantage of cheaper prices in the Karasuu market and to meet the demand, people have found ways to skirt the border restrictions. One of the more dangerous yet creative ways is an inner tube and pulley system set up across the river that allows Uzbekistanis to enter Kyrgyzstan and bring back their goods without going through the border regime. The border guards on both sides are, of course, aware of this system but look the other way for a small fee. Another alternative is to return with goods using the bridge crossing, but this often brings more hassles and extortion. Those who do not want to take the risk of crossing via the inner tube cross back via a different border fifteen kilometers away. Those who purchase jewelry and other expensive products that they can easily carry back on their person generally prefer to return via a different border because there are fewer problems with border guards.

Corruption and patronage are ways of maintaining indebtedness that have long been part of the social system but are now being adapted to the current environment. The border guards take bribes to supplement their income and most people accept this as part of the cost of doing business. Sometimes the corruption is even calculated into the veil of legitimacy of the official transition to a free market economy. The Naryn State Property Fund, for example, initiated a closed auction to privatize a factory. The starting bid price published in the newspaper was 200,000 som, but the individual who bid 17,000 som was awarded the property.[29] Technically, the auction should have been rescheduled and a lower starting bid published. I later learned that the auction went through because the director had been personally paid 50,000 som. This type of practice was commonly known and accepted as part of the way business works, but now has become associated with the shift to democracy and a free market.

In this context, the mutual indebtedness and reification of household networks remain important parts of the social organization of knowledge and ease the adaptation process initiated by the post-Soviet states (see Werner 1998). In this period of transition, people search for ways to deal with the uncertainties of their futures. For some, religion mediates uncertainty and manages ambiguity by eliminating it. And in Karasuu, one of the communities with the most active presence of Hizb ut-Tahrir members, the religious component/contribution to the adaptation process has been responsive to political voice, social decay, and spiritual searching.

Potentiality in the Everyday

Some things seem obvious. A taxi driver spends his day in a car, hired by passengers to transport them from one location to another. A cook prepares food and a waitress brings it to a table. A blacksmith works with metals while a seamstress works with fabrics. A farmer plants and harvests while a shepherd tends animals. There are functional differences between trades, and the interactions of factory workers and teachers can be quite different. But it is possible to characterize the environment in which daily existence is typified: waking up with the presence and obligations of an extended family, going to work (or not), returning home to a dinner at a table or on the floor, and praying or carousing.

Most of the world does not experience the classical liberalism of Horatio Alger's novels where determination and pluck—the potential to self-realize dreams merely by "picking oneself up by the bootstraps"—open the doors to unbounded success (Alger 1990). On any given day, we are able to do what can be done based on the options that are realistic for us to choose. Whether or not these potentials are articulated, we are aware at some level that choices range from the magnificent to the nefarious—even if all the choices before us are undesirable and few—and we have a corresponding idea of how to categorize those potentials. The limits of action are also generally known.

The range of options available to women illustrates this point. The reforms imposed by the Soviet system created more professional options for women than had existed before, but male dominance remained a factor limiting women's access to "men's professions." Today men generally control business ventures and government in Central Asia. When women become involved, it is usually in "women's trade" or "women's issues," which include education, textiles, or social services. In Naryn, for example, most schoolteachers are women; the workers at the textile factory are women; and the vice-governor responsible for health, education, pensions, and the arts is female, while the vice-governor for business is male. This is not to suggest that women do not have prominent positions or play significant roles in the country—Roza Otunbayeva was, after all, the country's interim president between 2010 and 2011. But the reality is that most women and men see their professional options as limited by their family and family status, clan affiliation, economic constraints, and social connections.

The Soviet goals were largely fixed and now there are many more options and goals to be negotiated. As people negotiate them, they do so within the context of how they perceive their options. The following stories of Muktar and Toliq, two former classmates of Ismoiljon, illustrate this point.

Both Muktar and Toliq are ethnic Uzbeks living in Osh, who turned to taxi driving as their profession. They frequent the street corners waiting for clients. As the state facilities faltered or collapsed, more and more people have left or been forced out of careers which they still view as their rightful and proper profession, and seek to make money elsewhere. This has led to an increase of taxi drivers waiting for clients, and thus Muktar and Toliq sometimes wait for up to one or two hours for a client. Muktar is a former engineer who spends much of his time reading or performing the only seemingly requisite activity of a taxi driver: polishing his car. It is a 1976 dull-mustard-colored Soviet-made Lada that breaks down with relative frequency. It is a machine that is simple enough to repair and one that he owns. As an atheist, he sees himself as slightly ostracized from the other taxi drivers and thus even further limited in his options for economic growth. He speaks with pride about his lineage—which includes fifteen generations of his family owning a tract of land in the city-center—and despairs about his future—which begins with having to sell his family's land.

Recently taking out a loan to upgrade from a Daewoo-Uzbekistan Tico to an early 1990s model Mercedes Benz, Toliq's personality has changed. He became a taxi driver out of high school because there were no other jobs available. He presents himself as a devout Muslim and ambitious businessman who can make a respectable living out of his car. He says it is not the profession he would have chosen, but the only one that was really available to him. Since getting his Mercedes, he has become more arrogant and elitist in his interactions with his fellow taxi drivers, and he has also become more desperate because he took out a loan from the bank to buy this car but the increased profits he expected to come from a nicer car have not yet materialized. Although he prayed regularly and claimed that Allah would provide and everything would work out, he nonetheless had backup plans that included hustling more clients, losing his car to the bank, or entering the more dangerous economic territory of borrowing from a local organized crime boss.

The bazaar is filled with traders selling cheap goods that come from China. There is little that distinguishes one booth from another—stalls that sell household products sell the same household products and are grouped in the same area of the bazaar—and sellers generally work long hours seven days a week in hopes of, or in need of, making a living. Each town center has at least one bazaar, and villages that are not large enough to support a daily market will often have a weekly market. Nonetheless, for purchases of significant quantities, people will travel to the larger markets where products are often slightly cheaper. It is also from these larger markets that sellers in smaller markets purchase their goods for resale.

Baktagul is one of the sellers who works in the main Osh bazaar. She is Kyrgyz but the options for her if she were Uzbek would be only slightly different in that she could take advantage of different trade networks controlled by ethnic Uzbeks. The aspirations are the same, as are the challenges. Once a week, she or her husband go to the Karasuu bazaar, the largest market in the Ferghana Valley, which is about twenty kilometers from Osh and only one kilometer from the Uzbek border, to replenish stock. Despite the fact that her husband and son help from time to time, she is the primary tenant of the stall. It is where she trades gossip and news with fellow sellers. Although she is there every day from eight in the morning until six in the evening, she is still also responsible for cleaning the house and making meals, at least until her daughter is old enough to do it. Ten years ago, she used to be a nurse but now finds it more profitable—though "profitable" can convey an erroneous sense of the economic opportunities available—to sell soaps and toiletries.

While the bazaar provides an environment where both sexes work (though women may be more numerous), Baktagul's sister Asel is a housewife living in the village of Üser. Asel was kidnapped for marriage (*ala kachuu*) and taken to a village where she did not have any friends and where her sole responsibility is to raise her children and tend to the needs of the household (Borbieva 2012; Kleinbach, Ablezova, and Aitieva 2005; Werner 2009). She did not want to marry her husband, but her parents refused to take her back after she had been kidnapped. She has accepted her fate, though she wishes she could have finished university and lived closer to her family and the city. Although Asel was kidnapped, even if she had been forced into an arranged marriage her flexibility in making decisions about her life would have been just as curtailed. Her responsibilities to her husband and her family are the same as those of Baktagul.

Of course other means of propelling one's everyday existence and making a living exist, as do the restrictions that these forms place on people. There are politicians and prostitutes, migrant laborers and drug dealers, teachers and pensioners. In other words, a range of potentialities exist in people's lives. To say that Asel is a housewife in a village gives an image of the constraints on her life, as do the scheduled days and communication network of Muktar's and Toliq's profession as taxi drivers, a job the former took with resignation and the latter with optimism turned to anxiety. What they *do* is how they pass their time and, in turn, how they see and make their time, a schedule that in theory holds opportunity but is often articulated as laden with constraints.

Thus, the everyday is a combination of what can be based on what has already been and what can be realized as defined by the range of realistic possibilities for each person. Determined by events largely beyond one's immediate control, the potential of one's action is limited. Ismoiljon is not a taxi driver because his leg injury made pursuing that profession impractical. Muktar would rather be an engineer, but the closing of the factory where he worked, combined with having to provide for a wife and four children, forced him into becoming a taxi driver. Likewise, Baktagul does not enjoy the hours she works in the bazaar, but after four months of working at the hospital without receiving a salary, it seemed to her to be the best option to provide for the needs of her family.

To a large extent, the social organization dimension is what governs people's options in viewing the possibilities and impossibilities of their actions. And while there is always a tendency to want more, people generally adjust their desires in an attempt to reconcile their potentialities with their capacity to realize them (Bourdieu 2000, 216–17). Everything beyond that is dreaming outside of what can be expected. Toliq saw a new car as a way to get higher fares and more prestige; becoming president he said was impossible and therefore nothing he would consider. Asel wanted to be a teacher, but because she was not allowed to finish school, she has said that her happiness is more closely connected to being a mother.

SOCIAL ORGANIZATION AND POTENTIALITY

The social organization, the medium, and the corpus of knowledge can be viewed as distinct components of cultural movement, but they are not independent. Rather, they are threads of the same project interwoven to make meaning in life. The social organization, however, carries with it the restrictions and potentialities of the structures with which people build their lives.

Resources play a significant role in this. The differences between life in the mountains and in the valleys are not only about the relationship between the nomadic and the sedentary, but also include the weather—severe winters in the mountains; limited water and extremely hot summers in the valley—and diet—an abundance of produce in the valley and an abundance of meat in the mountains. It includes positive and negative aspects of the family, where the closeness of relations ensures that if one person has a decent job, the extended family would be supported. It may be the case that one person supports twenty and if something is needed, it will be provided. But the downside of this is that if one person has money, there are pressures to share it rather than invest it to make more money.

The income options can be in the formal or informal employment sector. People make ends meet through selling goods in the bazaar, bartering for items, or engaging in a shadow economy through mafia connections. High unemployment is among the social crises people face and for those who work outside the formal economy, options include participation in the drug trade, prostitution, and labor migration. Osh is considered by some to be the heroin trafficking capital of the world, with significant amounts of the drug coming through en route to Russia and Western Europe. It has a direct flight to Dubai, which is allegedly used for trafficking prostitutes from the region to the United Arab Emirates. Furthermore, large populations of men migrate to Kazakhstan and Russia for summer work. In some villages, over 70 percent of the men will leave. The community depends on this income but also functions differently in the absence of the men. The people of Osh adapt to all these factors, much as they adapt to the inconveniences of borders and the difficulties of separation.

Some of the men who leave to work abroad buy into all the vices, including gambling and spending their money on alcohol, drugs, and prostitutes. Some channel their emotions toward religion and become more pious and orthopraxic. When both groups return to the village, they influence and adapt to the familiarity of the setting and the baggage of experience they have endured. Given the options of debauchery or orthodoxy, most mothers and village elders prefer a community of order and religious devotion. These are the ways in which social navigation occur within the range of potentialities available, given the particular social organization involved.

People are aware of their obligations and options and the challenges of life are ever-present. The perception of potentiality for action and means for social navigation are aspects of people's known reality. Here, knowledge is framed within a particular social organization, be it a more totalitarian state that limits economic opportunities like that of Uzbekistan or a state that encourages a more open political and fiscal environment like Kyrgyzstan. Those who drive taxis, like Muktar and Toliq, struggle to provide food to their families, as Tolkun and Begaim do, but the potentialities and the understanding of how they struggle are very different. Likewise, attempts to locate meaningful religious lives are found in different places for Tolkun and the newly returned migrant laborers who join Azarmat and his missionary teacher in pushing an Islamic agenda to address the problems of state and society.

Chapter 3

"Our Ancestors Also Live Here"

The Corpus of Knowledge

> The traditions of belief and action arise from the fundamental necessities of human existence given the nature of the organism, the mind, and the cosmos.
>
> **Edward Shils**, *Tradition*

> What each man knows is, in an important sense, dependent upon his own individual experience: he knows what he has seen and heard, what he has read and what he has been told, and also what, from these data, he has been able to infer.
>
> **Bertrand Russell**, *Human Knowledge*

The social organization of knowledge both influences and is influenced by how people live. The totality of what people know constitutes the corpus of their knowledge and is informed within the social organization of their experience. At the heart of this corpus of knowledge lie struggles with the issues of certainty and ambiguity, as well as authority and rationality. The idea of restrictions and potentialities carries over as an integral part of this corpus, as the frames of religion, education, and profession all imply social constraints and norms of behavior. The "knowing" and "acting out" of religion is shaped not only by the experience of place—mountain and valley, rural and urban—profession, and education, but also by the relationship of history to tradition and authority to locality.

The activities in which people engage—a skilled trade (Ismoiljon), a technical field (Nurbek), or agriculture and unemployment (Begaim)—give us access to an expertise of particular frames. There are differences in schooling between the public schools and the madrassas and there are also differences that result from the level of schooling and degrees of mental adeptness. And there are, of course, differences in the environments that influence the religious frame.

Not wanting to lose sight of these relationships and the influence of social organization, many uncertainties of life are contained in and mediated by one's religious self. Tolkun and Azarmat, Murat and Ismoiljon are all Muslims

FIGURE 3.1. Men cooking *besh barmak* after sacrificing a sheep, 1999.

who have perceived and interpreted events in their lives—beyond what could be understood as objective reality (phenomenology)—and placed them within a set of otherworldly conceptions on which they draw meaning and structure their daily lives (cosmology). The following three stories add to the complexity and diversity of interpretations of the religious self and the boundaries of difference.

———

On an early spring morning that still held close the character of winter, in the mountain village of At-Bashi a prayer was offered to Allah for forgiveness of the life to be taken. In accordance with tradition, this is what is done before a sacrifice. And one should give a sacrifice in remembrance of the dead, this remembrance being of a man who had died five years earlier. Thus, with the sheep's neck positioned over a bucket, the knife moved quickly across the throat, causing steam to rise from the blood of the animal's departing life. Within five minutes the prayer was finished, the sheep was dead, and people began preparations for the meal—men methodically separating out the animal parts and women returning to the kitchen. Usually, such meals are for more than the immediate family, but in this instance the purpose was to engage the ancestors and it was better to have fewer distractions.

After consuming the meal, the family retired to another room. Under the light of candles, Mairam, the middle daughter, who made a point to dress in red, began a series of prayers and movements she learned from her mother, who sat in a corner of the room. She offered incantations and petitions to the ancestors, and at the close of the ceremony, she burned a long thin strip of un-

"OUR ANCESTORS ALSO LIVE HERE"

spun fleece. Exhausted weeping followed, which contained a sense of comfort in the weeping ability to overcome the barrier of mortality by bridging the temporal world of the family's struggles and ancestors who, at least this time, maintained a posture of reassurance that the end would be satisfactory.

———

Three hours to the north, I sat down for lunch with Aibek in Kochkor, a mountain village in Naryn oblast. While Kochkor is only two hours by car from the capital, it seems just as removed as At-Bashi to those who consider Bishkek an almost unimaginable and dreamy world that is the essence of sophistication. And just as villagers idealize the ease of city life, urbanites are often unappreciative of the harshness and vast beauty of mountain living. As the meal progressed, an interest in my questioning of religion gave way to Aibek's openness about the rumored diversity and fluctuating religious character of the village. Aibek, a self-proclaimed intellectual of the village, spoke of a neighbor who was a shaman and another who had a Zoroastrian shrine in his home, though all were Muslims skeptical of the emerging Islamic divide created by the new Turkish-built and Saudi-sponsored mosque. In his sympathy for what he sees as a more traditionally legitimate and politically indifferent religious syncretism, Aibek makes a sharp distinction between the two mosques in town. He describes the new mosque as threatening the way of life in Kochkor because it represents a more orthopraxic and more socially conservative Islam that distributes flashy propaganda in the bazaars and speaks against the tradition Aibek casually practices.

———

On the other side of the country, Friday prayers in Karasuu are a significantly less syncretic event. Uzbeks cross the border by walking across the footbridge to attend prayers at a mosque, which sits on the Kyrgyz side of the river. There, Uzbek-Kyrgyzstanis and a few ethnic Kyrgyz join them. The mosque is undergoing renovation, as are many of the more popular mosques in the south. The three levels of the mosque are filled and late worshipers have no choice but to lay their prayer rugs in the street outside the entrance. Most of the few businesses in this neighborhood close during prayers, with the life of the community finding its center at the mosque. Women are home, with the exception of a few who show up at the mosque either to sell religious paraphernalia or to beg for alms. After prayers, many worshippers covertly give local leaders of Hizb ut-Tahrir funds to support their "religious education projects" and flyers and pamphlets with religious and political positions of the organization are discreetly distributed. Regardless of whether they are members of Hizb ut-Tahrir, most of those who attend prayers are sympathetic to the struggle to be more observant Muslims and will spend their afternoons discussing the sermon, politics, and Islam in general.

These three vignettes offer three interpretations of a religious self that holds a self-identification with Islam. These characterizations contain phenomenological tensions that people often articulate with pejorative language: those in Karasuu say that Mairam is not a Muslim; she says she is and that the men in Karasuu are extremists that muddy the beauty of her traditional Islamic religion with a political agenda. What is important here is what constitutes boundaries of proper and improper religious behavior. Or, rather, the interpretation of boundaries and how people articulate the fuzzy areas are important. The degree to which otherworldly discussions of transcendence reify these boundaries, and the means by which individuals reconcile issues of ambiguity greatly influence the local understanding of religious practice. This, of course, is related to options people have for learning about religion (the social environment), but is exploited by the phenomenological encounter that contains both metaphysical and social components.

The Context of Religion in Central Asia

In any context, the range of religious expressions is diverse, and this certainly holds true for Central Asia. The fact that Tolkun and Azarmat have such difficulty accepting each other as fellow Muslims is telling of how the different interpretations of orthopraxy play out along the rightness and wrongness of accepted cosmologies, or at least accepted religious expressions. There are many contributing factors to the cosmology of Mairam, Aibek, and members of Hizb ut-Tahrir; the purpose of this study is not to give a detailed history of religion in Central Asia but rather to address history as it arises in context (see Foltz 2010). When Mairam, Aibek, Nurbek, and Ismoiljon talk about what has influenced their religious world, they seldom reference history but look to more contemporary connections with the religious, such as a teacher or relative.

The vast majority of Kyrgyz claim Islam as their most significant religious influence. But among the tensions between Tolkun and Azarmat or Aibek and Ismoiljon is the question of whether Islam can be contained or whether the practices of pre-Islamic ancestors must necessarily be seen as in contradiction with Islam. To understand these tensions, I turn to some of the various ways that the past remains part of the contemporary religious landscape. Even though the animistic and shamanistic influences found in the practices of Mairam and Tolkun have preaxial characteristics—for example, in the belief that there are spirits in trees—in a general overriding sense, these beliefs are postaxial in their soteriological conception.[1]

The distinctions of Islamic and pre-Islamic can be problematic, because some see that embracing *Islamic* as a categorical epoch lessens the validity of religious views that have roots in traditions prevalent before the arrival of Islam. However, the reality is that Islam has had such a profound influence on the character of religious understanding in Central Asia that even pre-Islamic practices are generally articulated as being part of the region's Islamic character. In this context, I use "pre-Islamic" as a neutral temporal descriptor that acknowledges the impact of Islam on people's religious imagination. Likewise, syncretism is an aspect of all religions, though acknowledging Islam's impact of structural import on the framing of religion in Central Asia implies that heterodoxy and orthodoxy are likewise intended to be used in a neutral sense.

Continuing with the problems of terminology, it should be kept in mind that there has been dynamic change throughout history. During the Soviet time, there were active attempts to emasculate religious practices, both Islamic and pre-Islamic, because of the perceived incompatibility of these practices with the communist modernization project. And while it is to some extent convention to talk about "Soviet" as a category, as it is to talk about "Muslim" as a category, "Soviet" is not one group of people acting in a uniform way but rather people interacting in many different ways. Those acting under the auspices of the Soviet Union were trying to do something very complex, and the extent to which their efforts were successful varied. Since the collapse of the Soviet Union, however, Central Asia has encountered Saudis, Pakistanis, Turks, and other missionaries in a way that the Soviet system restricted for much of the twentieth century. The revivalism of religious beliefs has both political and social aspects that animate religion and invigorate those who find answers within such frameworks.

Early Religious Traditions

Despite the emphasis given to trueness or pureness of tradition, there is probably no religion practiced today that has not been in some way influenced by another. In this sense, syncretism is an aspect of all religions. Outside ideas always have significant influence, and history plays more into determining the present than many contemporaries notice or acknowledge. Though Islam is pervasive in Central Asia, the legacy of Islam follows numerous other named religious traditions, as well as practices that may not have been recorded. The earliest religious traditions, of course, predate writing, and it is thus left to the archeologists to postulate meaning out of excavated finds from long-forgotten lives.[2]

It makes sense, however, that nature played a large role in the earliest religious traditions, especially among nomads whose lives were lived closer to the natural world than we live today. For early sedentary populations, and nomads especially, the natural world could be a frightening place where danger lurked and spirits pervaded (Berman 2000). The natural world also offered a livelihood and provided game and livestock, alongside sources of water and pastures.[3]

Early explanations of religious ideas developed over time from the idea that spirits animate life. Such spirits resided in a myriad of places including rocks, streams, sky; winds, rains, sun; trees, animals, and locations of life's departure. These explanations led to theorizing preliterate societies to be filled with spirits in an unsophisticated cosmological framework. Labels to characterize these early beliefs—"primitive," "archaic," "natural," "tribal," "folk," "native," "indigenous"—are problematic (see DeWeese 1994, 27–29) and often connote a certain pejorative character implying that greater truth rests within a more "complex" religious system of today.

The reality, however, is that people lived and practiced religions independent of clean theoretical terms to describe their practices. While capturing the exactness of descriptive terms used in preliterate times is not possible, a concept such as animism has a descriptive utility that seems to coincide with contemporary practices.[4] Thus, when using the term I do so in the most basic sense (not as a synonym for the religion of preliterate societies since it remains very much alive today): the tendency to locate spirits in tangible places in the environment with which one can have contact.

In Naryn and especially, though not exclusively, in the mountain regions animism and remnants of animistic sentiments are prevalent. There are sacred rocks, streams, sources of water, and trees laden with ribbons that all serve as testament to the contemporary continuity of a belief that the inanimate can be animated—at times functionally as a means to communicate with spirits, and at other times as a spirit itself (see Montgomery 2007a).

With spirits of varying intentions touching all aspects of the lived world, a need arose to appease the spirits—whether to restore health, secure the harvest, or protect during the hunt. Eventually a few charismatic individuals emerged who were able to control the spirits, generally through incantations, trances, or out-of-body experiences. Shamans have direct contact with the spirit world and usually receive this ability as a gift.[5] At times they claim control; at other times they claim skills of persuasion.

Mairam's mother, Dimira, considers herself a shaman and loosely connects the practices of shamanism with the understanding of Kyrgyz having migrated long ago from Siberia.[6] She has not had contact with anyone from Siberia, and when she talks about the shamanic lineage coming from Siberia, it is to the Kyrgyz ancestors or shamans that she refers. She heals and mediates with the spirit world and possesses a knowledge that is practical and mysterious in its orientation. As such, a shaman takes on a role of a specialist within a community and a central contributor to the cohesive aspect of communal being. In some communities, especially in earlier times, a shaman was at the center of the community (DeWeese 1994, 37). Neighbors and those concerned with the spirit world that the shaman mediates believe that Dimira has special powers. But when they consult her or solicit her advice on these matters, they do so secretly.

Dimira comments that of her children, Mairam was the only one who displayed the gift of spirit communication. Mairam's role during the ritual sacrifice described above was part apprentice and part ancestral mediator. While the idea of ancestral veneration is generally seen as another aspect of pre-

FIGURE 3.2. Healing rituals on Solomon's Mountain, 2005.

Islamic religious life that has been carried to the present, Mairam and Dimira point out that the ancestors are not worshiped but rather communicated with and seen as still part of a continued relationship with the family. It is, rather, an ancestral precedence that is continued, for relations are kept up: the hungry spirits appeased through periodic offerings and then consulted for advice and direction to guide the decision of the living. There is reliance on the living spirits of the ancestors and a continued relationship through which the spirit of Mairam's father maintains an active role in her family's life.

Both Dimira and Aibek see their environment as being animated by spirits that reside in places near where they live, and it is important that they visit these places. Dimira visits mazars on a regular basis, sometimes every day, whereas Aibek goes only when he needs to petition the spirits for health or success in some challenge facing him or his family. In the past two years, he has visited a mazar on three occasions—twice with his wife, who has problems with blood circulation in her legs, and once alone, to commemorate the death of his cousin. When Aibek describes his recent visits, he says that the guardian of the mazar helped with prayer, *archa*,[7] and spring water that helped heal his wife. And when he went to remember his cousin, the guardian prayed and burned wool in a mountain cove.

Aibek does not really question the efficacy of any of this. When he assumes the role of the town intellectual, he says that people go to mazars because they are superstitious and notes that he does not believe in any of it. Yet later in the same conversation, in talking about the new mosque in town, he argues for the utility of mazars and shamans because they *are* important, as are the ancestors and the need to communicate with them.

Having read a book about the history of religion in Central Asia, however, Aibek explains the hearth fire in his neighbor's house as an indication that his neighbor is a Zoroastrian.[8] Few, if any, Kyrgyz admit to worshipping Mazda,[9] and when I asked the neighbor about the fire, it was explained as a home mazar used for prayer and to help communicate with the spirits. The neighbor knew little about Zoroastrianism and claimed he was a Muslim just like Aibek.

In general, remnants of Zoroastrianism are easier to find than Buddhism, Judaism, or Nestorian Christianity—all once prevalent in the region—because fire is readily associated with Zoroastrianism. There were once Zoroastrian communities in Central Asia, and one of the former centers was Solomon's Mountain in Osh (Zadneprovskij 2000). At the side of the mountain, people come to burn cotton or wool in continuation of a practice that the mazar guardian claims was connected to the earliest communities in the area. The guardian at Osh says that fire was Zoroastrian, while what people do is Islamic and is simply borrowed from the Zoroastrian tradition. Even at Sahaba, the mazar in Jangi-Nookat where it is believed that descendents who learned directly from Muhammad are buried, there is a corner used for burning cotton.[10]

While there are tracings of earlier religious traditions, not seen as outdated but rather as continuations of the past, there is difficulty in translating the historical remnants of a religion to an individual's contemporary understanding and usage. Aibek talks about his neighbor as a Zoroastrian because his neighbor keeps fire in the house, while his neighbor claims that he burns it for his ancestors. And those who make requests or petitions at sacred sites by burning cotton or wool usually see what they do as Islamic. In all instances, they view those practices as a continuation of the past and justify them as tradition; the idea of tradition contains valence that serves as a marker of legitimacy.

The Arrival of Islam

The idea of pre-Islamic life in Central Asia does not imply sudden change or a complete disappearance of the ways before the arrival of Islam; rather pre-Islamic life refers to aspects of what Aibek and Dimira experience. The environment through which Islam came to be in Central Asia was multivocal—there were Buddhist, Jewish, Nestorian Christian, Manichean, Zoroastrian, shamanic, and animist beliefs—and Islam incorporated some characteristics of these early beliefs into its practice (see Berkey 2003; Westermarck 1933). And while very few of my interlocutors knew the details of Islam's introduction to Central Asia and its integration into and domination of their religion, they reference history as a partial explanation for variations in religious practice.

Military conquest, missionaries, and trade all played a role in introducing Islam to the region at the end of the seventh and beginning of the eighth centuries (Barthold 1992, 184 ff.). In the western part of what is today Uzbekistan, Islam had taken hold by the time of the Abbasid dynasty in 750 CE (Soucek 2000, 49–50). But it was not until the thirteenth and fourteenth centuries, and the conversion of the Mongols and the Chaghatayid khans, that Islam began to play an active role in the renaissance of native identity.[11] This was largely through Sufi orders in Central Asia that formed *khangahs*, religious complexes that often contained a mosque, the tomb of a sheikh, and lodging for travelers.[12] By the sixteenth and early seventeenth centuries, a framework had been set up that took Islam into consideration (DeWeese 1994, 135–38 ff.).

The Islamization of Central Asia, however, was a two-part process that involved the "imposition" of Islamic norms and later assimilation and "nativization" of Islamic practices and thought (DeWeese 1994, 51 ff.). Over time, Islam became a central part of communal identity, pre-Islamic practices became seen in Islamic context, and the relationship to the world was increasingly understood in postaxial terms.

People, however, have only a marginal contemporary awareness of history. And with regard to the construction of history many of my interlocutors conceived, there was little difference between the sixth, tenth, or sixteenth centuries. A few, for example, anachronistically cited Alexander the Great and Genghis Khan as important Muslim leaders in the history of Central Asia. After reflection, of course, they could see that even though Alexander the Great allegedly visited Arslanbob in the south of Kyrgyzstan, and that Arslanbob is seen as a Muslim mazar, Alexander the Great lived and died well before the time of Muhammad. Similarly, Genghis Khan was not exactly a convert. But in practice, the distant past is blurred and does not have the same borders that define the present and recent memory.

In reality, whether Islam came to Central Asia in the eighth or fourteenth centuries or more recently does not matter much. In the imagination of Uzbeks and Kyrgyz, though, it does seem to matter, at least in a relative sense. For them, the date of when Islam arrived in the region becomes an explanation for difference in practice. When I asked what accounts for the variation in religious practice between valley and mountain Muslims, most interlocutors respond in ethnic terms: the Uzbeks, who are more prevalent in the valley, are "better" or more orthopraxic because Islam took root with them sooner than it did with the Kyrgyz, who are more prevalent in the mountains.[13]

Islam has been a rooted part in both populations' lives for longer than any of the current population can recall. And religious conversion can occur in a very short period of time. (After all, it is a short period of life that leads any adherent to an understanding of his or her religious self.) The attitude people hold toward Islam and the frame in which they view themselves culturally and religiously has a lot to do with their perception of history. Some, like Mairam, view history as a continuation of ancestral religion, while others, like Rustan, trace their lineage back to the Prophet Muhammad and their Uzbek ancestry to an Islamic community of privilege, prerogative, and rightness. Rustan is a frequent drinker and socialite who has not visited a mosque in years; he is proud of his Muslim heritage even if he admits to not being a serious practitioner. In his view, there is something for him to gain from his ancestors having been serious practitioners. Mairam's connection with her ancestors (who she says are Muslim) is an integral part of her cosmology, yet the Islamic component is not what is emphasized so much as a continued honoring and respect for the spirits of her bloodline.

Tracing lineage back to history—be it Mairam and her veneration of ancestors or Rustan and his connection to Muhammad—is more an exercise of legitimacy than of accuracy. Indeed, historical concerns of most Central Asians lay primarily with claims of legitimacy.

The Soviet Influence

Soviet functionaries who implemented plans to alter the face of Central Asia impact the religious histories of both Mairam and Rustan. The Soviet policy was one of political and military control, economic extraction from the region, and the replacement of Muslim culture with communist Soviet culture (Shahrani 1994, 59). The policy was intended to culturally isolate the people of Central Asia by geographically fragmenting the region and defaming and deteriorating their adherence to Islam (Shahrani 1994, 63). The ethnonational-territorial delimitation program aimed to accomplish the former, while the government structure was intended to accomplish the latter.[14]

Under the Soviet structure, the government closely regulated and monitored religion, strictly controlling most aspects of the religious presence in public life (Haghayeghi 1996, xxi). To do this, the Soviet government had to recruit community leaders to be part of the communist apparatus. Marxism was not a popular ideology among Central Asian Muslims; therefore, in recruiting and selecting leaders for the Communist Party, the decision makers in Moscow were less discriminating than they had been elsewhere (Haghayeghi 1996, 19). The communist leaders of Central Asia carried out the mandates of Moscow, but with less vigor the more remote the community.

Communist leaders made a concerted effort to influence broad reaching reforms, such as the collectivization process that set forth the trajectory of Begaim's life in Lahol; educational reforms that resulted in public schools and the university that Nurbek attended; the economic system that meant job security to Muktar; and the certainty of a livable retirement to countless pensioners. In these reforms, leaders attempted to influence religion and the religious in all aspects of life. They used law as an instrument of change,[15] and established Muslim spiritual directorates (such as SADUM) to help control religion through institutionalization (Keller 2001; Ro'i 2000).

The Muslim spiritual directorates created an official face of Islam in Soviet Central Asia under communist control. The extent to which politicians in Moscow controlled the Islamic leaders who came to authority in the spiritual directorates or the extent to which those leaders were able to promote a religious agenda for the region can be questioned,[16] but the organizational success of these spiritual directorates can be seen today as they have been maintained and remain under the control of the titular governments.

In general, communists unevenly implemented reforms, and there were discrepancies between what they did locally and what those in Moscow understood. One cannot take the Soviet Union as a monolith with disproportionate unity in what it did—it was as disorganized and dysfunctional as any large system—but it created a hegemonic system that the population resisted. (For example, while the Jadidist and Basmachi revolts were religious in organization they were responses to social constraints [Khalid 1999] and precursors to the reified association of national identity and Islam [Khalid 2003].) Those in positions of power and who were charged with the task of implementing official policies were not only under pressures from Moscow but also under more immediate pressure from the community in which they lived. Thus, while they were expected to give an official answer to Moscow, there was a greater degree of deference given to the community at the local level than officially acknowledged to Moscow.

Many of the Soviet policies toward religion were not popular, and at certain times, required accommodations. Stalin, for example, loosened restrictions on Muslim practice when he needed troops for the Second World War.[17] But the more lasting attempts of resistance were adaptations to the environment at the local level. Such adaptations included local officials looking the other way and allowing religious practices to continue. It was Dimira continuing her regular visits to mazars—a secret that everyone in the community knew and many called on her when they were sick. And it was religious aspects of life-cycle rituals, such as burial, wherein the religious aspects of the ceremony were presented as tradition and not religion (Privratsky 2001).

The Soviet functionaries persecuted many people for their religious beliefs and closed numerous mosques or converted them to museums. But despite the restrictions placed on religion, Dimira, Tolkun, and Ismoiljon's father were among many who maintained active religious lives, sometimes in secret and other times in public. And while schools taught communist ideology, children learned traditions at home that often contained religious components: Mairam learned the sacred sites from her mother; Ismoiljon learned to pray from his father; and even Muktar, who claimed to be an atheist, believed that it was right to pray at a funeral.

Religious Worldviews in Kyrgyzstan

Many saw the collapse of the Soviet Union as marked by an opening of previously restricted expressions. It is easy to have the impression that when the Soviet restrictions were lifted, Islam surged—on 30 August 1991, people were communists and on 1 September, the day after independence, they were Muslims.[18] Such an image neglects the complex nature of religious development; it is not an either-or relationship but rather a project under development.

People throughout Kyrgyzstan have a general sense that religious expression and religious belief have been, and continue to be, on the rise since independence. Over 60 percent of my survey respondents (97 percent of whom are Muslim) claimed that religion is important to them. Only 50 percent, however, considered themselves to be practicing Muslims. Regardless, 43 percent felt that religion had a greater influence on their lives since independence (51 percent said no change) and 45 percent said it had a greater influence over the past five years (51 percent said no change).

Already a sense of the diversity of expressions of Islam in Kyrgyzstan has been conveyed, yet in order to characterize the perceived contemporary rise of religious interest I suggest three different frames of religious revival: general revival; inward-looking traditionalism; and outward-looking orthodoxy. I do not conceive of these groupings as a carryover of Sovietologists' categories that separate Islam between "official" and "unofficial" or "parallel" and "traditional" but rather as groupings of ethnographic observations.[19]

The revival of religions or the treatment of various aspects of religious life as in need of being infused with a newness presented as forward looking, capable of mediating the challenges of the present, and legitimized by a continued (though updated) connection with the past, is as much a way of politically negotiating the various levels of governance imposed on a population as it is an attempt to address the micro-level search for individual meaning in daily existence. This individual search is filled with and occurs in response to the challenges of the broken in life: death, failed relationships, and a general quest for purpose in response to personal crises. Politically, revival serves as one way to galvanize the purpose of a group toward betterment. At both levels revival generally occurs in response to a sense of misdirection, but also generally contains a sense of optimism that frees it from the fetters of despair. It is renewal and in that, it is hope.

Openness in dialogue about religion and its role in Kyrgyzstan has increased, and much of this dialogue takes place in terms of revival—that there was less religious practice and a constricted sphere of religious expression, which now allows for a rediscovery or an inquiry that can be seen broadly as a revival. This sentiment encompasses the individual as well as the collective, because both are in positions to be influenced in ways that significantly change behavior.

As suggested earlier, the religious sphere of Central Asia encompasses great diversity and complexity, despite a tendency to punctuate political discourse with the most extreme generalizations of all-or-none believers, that is, generalizations into categories that imply either radical belief or nonbelief. Everyday existence, on the other hand, involves negotiations and adaptations to the realities of existing and projected possibilities. And as we have seen, Central Asians have adapted their religious practices to the available options of beliefs—from the incorporation of nature worship into Islam as Islam became more prevalent, to the incorporation of Islam into traditional aspects of ceremonial life under the strictures of Soviet rule (Privratsky 2001). In Kyrgyzstan, a myriad of locations for a renewal of the meaningful life exist, most of which can be categorized into three loose groupings of religious sensibilities: a milieu of general interest in a religious (usually Islamic) setting; a revival of local religious traditions; and an interest in the expertise and teachings of religious practitioners from outside the region.

General Revival of Islam

With some exceptions, much of the Islamic revival in Kyrgyzstan involves attempts to discover how Islam fits into the realm of everyday meaning, to come to terms with how an increase of religious practice can make lives more meaningful and also more tolerable. Ideally this would happen in terms of a Central Asian Islam, but there is a tendency to privilege outside interpretations, such as those offered by Pakistanis, Saudis, or Turks.[20]

Thus, returning to the options of developing religious sentiments, the loosest grouping is a general revival, or the generalized idea that everything is Islamic. Conversations with most people reveal that in their religious frame they generally understand revival in Islam as what everyone else practices. Most people are not familiar with the various schools of Sunni Islam; certainly within the general frame the increased openness is general and inclusive. It is open to an Iranian bookstore that sells many Shi'ia titles, private Turkish high schools influenced by the teachings of M. Fethullah Gülen (see Balci 2003), and missionaries from Tablighi Jama'at (see Balci 2012).

Most within the grouping of general revivalism acknowledge that Islam can be beneficial for society, but they push for the middle ground. The practice of Islam, they contend, should be knowledgeable, local, and moderate. They fear the language of Islamic jihadists and find the idea of an Islamic state undesirable. For them, Islam is optional, can have individual protestant interpretations, and can be embraced without significant changes of lifestyle. Murat, Baktagul, and Rustan would place themselves within this understanding. They conceptualize Islam as always having been present in the region. Though Murat is becoming more interested in Islam and Rustan less, they both describe a desire for an Islam that is open in interpretation and in practice. And at least for Murat and Baktagul, this includes a desire to gain a greater informal awareness of formalized settings and to looking at religion in a reflective way with differing degrees of seriousness—maybe they practice religion, or maybe religion plays a less significant role in their life, but it does play a role, one that they do not question.

There are noticeable differences in practice, however, between village and city inhabitants. For example, Adilet stayed in the village, became successful and a very active and observant Muslim while his younger brother Jyrgal went to the city and became the intellectual of the family. Each brother is proud of the other and welcomes a more active role of Islam in Kyrgyzstan. But Jyrgal laments that, compared to Adilet, he is lax in his religious practice. Jyrgal says that he wants to be more like Adilet, but wrestles to find Islam's place in relation to modernity and rationality.

Within the general revival frame of religious sentiment, some struggle in their relationship between religion and modernity. Having grown up learning communist ideology in school, some are looking outside of a religious revival to make sense of their world, but are not entirely secularists in their worldview. For them, it is perhaps rather an idea of separation between cultural Islam and an uncertainty with how they might embrace religious Islam. They do not question the Islamic identity of those who appeal to a modern and Western frame that defines progress (sometimes understood as that which is modern). But sometimes they are not clear about where Islam fits within their lives. For those struggling within this more modernist frame, there is a tension between the primacy of rationality and the role of religion, which at its very foundation has aspects that go beyond the rational.

At the heart of the matter is the question of the authority to which one answers and how. Those embracing modernism generally live in the cities and look to either Russia or further West for their standard of what is modern. The post-Enlightenment project emphasizes rationality as a way of negotiating the world, and Western pedagogy has privileged an education of rationality. The Soviet system also encouraged rationality, but carried with it a stronger affinity for authority. In both instances, the answer is found in authority that lies beyond reason, for even modernist claims that authority is that which is rational look to some authority to determine what is rational.

The point here is not so much to enter a debate on rationality but rather to show that this aspect of the modernist struggle is in part one of locating authority.[21] Though enticed by what is perceived as modern, they are not quite ready to jettison the religious project altogether because it would be politically imprudent to do so publicly and/or there is a sense of uncertainty about belief—that somehow keeping open the option of belief publicly does not commit one privately to belief or disbelief.

As Islam, and an association with it, takes on greater purchase in the public sphere, it also becomes part of social projects of businessmen and politicians wanting to gain favor within their communities.[22] Thus, while funds to build many of the mosques after independence came from foreign monetary sources, it is increasingly common to see neighborhood mosques built with financial support from a successful businessman who has embraced capitalism. Some politicians place a mosque in the background of their campaign photos and calendars they distribute so people associate that politician with a symbol of moral rightness and tradition year round. Whenever a politician or businessman (who may or may not attend prayer services there) has supported a mosque, his name is made known since the public prestige of donating a mosque to the community is desirable publicity. Some politicians and businessmen have made hajj simply for the status it confers upon return. For some, then, it is a gesture that embraces a general Islamic revival, insofar as there is compatibility with their political and business goals.

FIGURE 3.3. A mosque in the mountains, 2012.

FIGURE 3.4. A mosque in the valley, 2005.

FIGURE 3.5. Men at midday prayers in the countryside near a mazar, 2006.

Religious Revival and Local Tradition

Tolkun and Dimira frequent mazars and see their relationship with Islam as a continuation of the religious tradition of their ancestors. They claim—and research supports this—that visits to mazars are on the rise.[23] They explain this by saying that Kyrgyz have a natural relationship with nature, and that the nomadic traditions make the mazars *their* mosques. Directing themselves toward Mecca, they perform namaz at the mazar when they visit, but the parallel they intend to draw in calling it their mosque is to say that their structure of Islam is more open and without boundaries.

It is true that nomadic life is not as conducive to developing the same character of knowledge as when it is transmitted in a mosque or madrassa. But in calling the mazar their mosque, Tolkun and Dimira aim to draw attention to the legitimacy and worth in their local interpretation of Islam. Religion is meaningful to them; it is living and alive in their environment. Preaxial age tendencies to see the spirits throughout nature exist, and yet they also have a sense of a transcendent world of the spirits that they embrace as Islam. They encourage a renewed respect of nature, reverence for ancestors, and devotion to Allah.

Syncretically this is the Islam that was handed down to them, which they share with their children and interested seekers. They locate their authority by tracing tradition through their ancestors, and they wish to advance an awareness and acceptance of this. Their religious legitimacy is tied to the continuation of local tradition. Seen by some as heterodox, they are not concerned so much by the wide variety of interpretations of Islam. They do, however, share

"OUR ANCESTORS ALSO LIVE HERE"

Aibek's concerns about the new mosque and missionaries who have taken it upon themselves to preach against local interpretations of Islam.

Though Tolkun and Dimira are not concerned with politics, Aibek talks favorably about supporting Tengrism, a relatively small yet (marginally) politically active movement that advocates a return to the religion of the Kyrgyz ancestors. Developed largely out of the philosophical writings of Choiun Omuraly uluu, Tengrism urges a balance with nature, a respect for the ancestors, and an awareness of tradition (Omuraly uulu 1994). The political and philosophical efforts of Dastan Sarygulov, former member of the Kyrgyz Parliament and state secretary, have advocated it as a natural religion (Sarygulov 2005).

While Tengrism is not widespread, it does show one way of conceptualizing and reviving religion in terms that are locally centered and relevant to the Kyrgyz experience in history. It also attempts to reinvent the indigenous aspects of religion by expanding connections (and an historical religious affinity) with the broader Turkic world, especially Altai, Yakutia, and Kazakhstan. The idea of Tengrism gives legitimacy to the pre-Islamic traditions of the Kyrgyz by privileging a religious relationship with the sky and nature, but most who call themselves Tengrists (and this is a small number) see it as entirely compatible with Islam. Tolkun and Dimira do not consider themselves Tengrists, but the sky plays an important role in their cosmology, and they are supportive of the idea of Kyrgyz religion being renewed within local knowledge and tradition.

Religious Revival and External Authority

A third revivalist sentiment draws on external claims of tradition in its attempt to coopt legitimacy. It does not reference back to the relations of ancestors with nature and the spirit world, but rather looks toward the early teachings of Muhammad and the time of the caliphs. People often apply pejorative labels to this grouping—such as extremist, fundamentalist, Wahabbist—but in a more neutral sense they can be seen as Salafists. Looking beyond the local, this sentiment strongly privileges a Muhammadian ideal animated by Qur'anic text and hadiths. This is the story of Iqbol, a local missionary and member of Tablighi Jama'at (Ahmad 1991; Masud 2000). Some respect him for his adherence to an idealized Islam and his devotion to his mission. But he also represents the type of revivalist who makes Aibek uneasy.

Iqbol is a young Muslim who wears a long black beard and dresses in white. He prays five times a day, teaches Qur'an at a mosque, and walks around with prayer beads moving regularly between his fingers. He comes from a small town in Kyrgyzstan; after Kyrgyzstan gained independence he went to Pakistan and India to study Islam. He has returned to his home village to teach his fellow villagers about Islam; because of his appearance and missionary work at the mosque, he is respected by some and feared by others who refer to him as an "extremist," a "Wahhabist," and a "terrorist." Ideologically he speaks of being influenced by Sayyid Qutb[24] and Bakhautdin Naqshband,[25] but when one engages him in dialogue, it is clear that he is driven by his passion to educate his fellow Muslims on the "correct" way to practice Islam. He has not been implicated in any wrongdoing or crimes against the state, though he knows that police watch his every move. He spends most of his time at home or at the mosque because he knows his appearance and devotion to Islam make others uncomfortable. He does not consider himself an "extremist" though his views are much more orthodox than those of most of his fellow villagers, who think he is an Arab.[26] And whereas those who call him a "terrorist" have bought into the state's rhetoric of fear and the stereotype of what a "terrorist" looks like (long beard and white turban) (Montgomery and Heathershaw 2016), Iqbol's work is not centered on terrorism but rather orthopraxy and his understanding of how to live a meaningful religious life, with the caliphate as his frame of reference.

Iqbol stands out in the community where he works because of his strict lifestyle. He offers an Islam-related solution to all problems, the legitimacy of which, for him is in the level of restrictiveness. During a conversation about alcohol and its prohibition in Islam, he identified alcohol as one of the causes of moral failure in Kyrgyz and Uzbek societies. I asked him about *kumys*, fermented mare's milk that is mildly alcoholic and is a popular drink, especially among the mountain Kyrgyz. He said that of course he drank kumys because of its health benefits as well as its delicious flavor. When I pointed out to him that it had some alcohol in it, his immediate response was to say that if that were the case he would have to stop drinking it. The discussion of alcohol can be problematic, especially as some within the Hanafi tradition argue that kumys is permissible, but this example seems indicative of Iqbol's type of orthodoxy, one that looks externally for authority: the more restrictive the practice, the more likely it is in line with what it means to be a "good" Muslim. For those who ascribe to it, rationality and authority are found in the restricted.

The certitude in Iqbol's discourse illustrates the attractiveness of the message that a better life is located in Islam. I was discussing with him the story of a young friend of mine who was told by a police officer that he would help her friend only if she had sex with him. The story outraged Iqbol, and he claimed that if there were better Muslims and an Islamic government, such behavior would not be tolerated. My friend, a twenty-year-old university student, said that such behavior is common among police, and while she hates it, she is resigned to it as part of the dysfunctionality of her society. She is, of course, someone's daughter, and Iqbol's message that Islam can bring a better life can be appealing to fathers wanting to protect their children from corruption and lechery (Montgomery 2015a).

The ideas of Hizb ut-Tahrir members in Karasuu contain this message.[27] While the relationship between Tablighi Jama'at and groups such as Hizb ut-Tahrir and the Islamic Movement of Uzbekistan (IMU) is not transparent, these groups are sympathetic to one another and share a common search for legitimacy. Iqbol often meets with Hizb ut-Tahrir members, and they all see themselves as brothers in the struggle to improve Kyrgyzstan's Islamic character. Despite their claim that they are remaining true to religious sensibilities and preserving the corresponding traditional ways of life of the Prophet Muhammad, they create new ideologies and organizational structures and methods in order to do so (Almond, et al. 2003, 92). While they root the legitimacy of their participation in the political process as an otherworldly mandate from Allah, much of their literature and support comes from outside Central Asia.

Iqbol illustrates perhaps one extreme of Muslims looking outside the local to differentiate legitimate religious practice from local inaccuracies, though it is not entirely fair to say that he only looks outside. He does play with history, reminding people of al-Bukhari and Naqshband as two examples of Central Asians who were leaders in the Muslim world. But he also claims that the moral example of these leaders is lost in Central Asia and is now better exemplified in Pakistan and India. Azarmat studies with Iqbol and agrees with him that "true" Islam is centered on the text and that one should be guided by tradition—though this is not the tradition of the Kyrgyz as much as the tradition of contemporaries of Muhammad. In the process, Azarmat attempts to express that certainty when he meets with friends who know less about Islam than he does.

No matter how they understand the revival, all of those who see a revival currently under way consider themselves Muslims. In all cases, however, there are differing motivations and frameworks for understanding. And the boundaries of religious difference are both imagined and articulated with a political salience. In general, they draw on different but equally relevant resources to gain their religious knowledge. Though texts are not important to Dimira's teaching of Mairam as much as is an openness to seeing the spirits, Iqbol's teaching of Azarmat centers on text for he argues that the only way to come to an openness of the spirit is through the text. As such, Dimira's vision is open to greater ambiguity and acceptance of difference while Iqbol's vision is more restrictive.

COSMOLOGY OF THE EVERYDAY

The differences between these groups are rooted in their visions of religious order and legitimacy and the extent to which those ideals are called on and taken seriously. All these things take place within the context of history as it is understood, and for many Kyrgyz the rise of Islam is seen in general terms. Some push strongly to frame Islam by drawing on local traditions of the ancestors and a relationship with nature whereas others who privilege external interpretations of religion reject this notion. These represent different ways of envisioning religion in the social world.

In reality, we do not live at an everyday level cognizant of the fact that everything—all options of action, soteriological or otherwise—is absolutely open. The world of the everyday is by and large a world primarily populated by nonelites, by people largely unaware of the issue of transcendence as a mediated construction. This, in the case of Central Asia, allows a syncretism of a preaxial shamanistic vision with a postaxial Islamic soteriology. For postaxial religious elites, this syncretism is troubling. For others, this is life.

Elites, however, are important because they are fundamental to the forming of society and thus fundamental to understanding it. They are the carriers and more important, interpreters of the charismatic.[28] But their structure and their understanding of structure is not all there is to understanding society, for the lived realities and potentialities of elites are not the lived realities and potentialities of nonelites. The categorizations of the three frames—general revival, inward-looking traditionalism, and outward-looking orthodoxy—are similar. And all three frames fit into a system that is the background of the corpus of knowledge.

The Meaning of Boundaries

Religion imposes rationalization despite a corpus of ideas that eludes understood rationality. It is the rational way of life that was originally motivated by religion and not by capitalism (Löwith 1993, 67 ff.). But the constraints of rationality are, in essence, the constraints of social action. In any ends–means relationship, it is always the ends that emerge out of action and are always reinterpreted through action. In essence, everything becomes means, because the end is never reached until one dies (see Dewey 1916). Likewise with religion: There is always a renegotiation of ultimate ends and everything becomes the means to some soteriological (or political) end.

The emergence of the transcendent and the requisite soteriological bridge results in an increased concern for boundaries and their purity. Boundaries create a distance that allows for reflexivity in viewing the self relative to the community and the community relative to that which is placed outside of the boundaries of the community. Transcendence provides a place outside of the world and allows for a positioning of reflexivity.

At a social level, a group is defined not so much by the cultural aspects of life as by the boundaries understood to define it. Events such as the 1924 national-territorial delimitation, the 1990 Osh riots, the 2010 Osh violence,[29] and the acknowledged variance of religiosity create an atmosphere of boundedness and potentiality for the political articulation of difference.

Ethnicity, for example, is an outcome of the bounded orientation of value-producing and diacritical cultural features that generate an understanding of social identity to a point that allows them to understand themselves as "playing the same game" (Barth 1969, 6). And while ethnic categories utilize cultural differences, they do so in a way that is fungible and inexact (Barth 1969, 14). The inexactness, however, is not reason enough for people to discard it as a category; its perceived exactness contains too much social utility. Once the line has been drawn and the boundary created, it becomes more difficult to transcend the perception of difference. This difference is at some levels comforting, for universal sameness is threatening; an Other there must always be.[30]

Boundaries of religious saliency create a similar level of difference, but one that carries weight beyond the temporality of what is this-worldly. Most have a desire to find religious meaning in life and to bracket out this-world's burdens with the imagined rewards of what is otherworldly. And so in a certain sense, religious understanding creates the boundaries that separate Tolkun from Azarmat. Again, religion is a part of life but not the totality of everyday life. Ismoiljon and Toliq continue their businesses and practice their religion when deemed necessary. And Jyrgal, who sees Adilet as a better Muslim but a less successful intellectual, covets the boundary of being more religious but neither acts on it nor attempts to transcend it (except for major holidays when he recites namaz and, as part of the community of believers, temporarily transcends his lax religious devotion). There are calls to be more orthopraxic, which is both Iqbol's mission and, in some sense, what Dimira wants. How they envision that orthopraxy is quite different, but they share in their concern of the importance of practice. The particular worlds they reference are, in part, what accounts for these differences.

Heterodoxy and Orthodoxy

While the boundaries of "good" and "bad" Muslims are connected in popular language with ethnicity (and the acceptance of ethnic differences between Uzbeks and Kyrgyz), the praxis of these boundaries is more connected to location and knowledge. There is a general sense that the difference between mountain and valley falls along lines of heterodoxy and orthodoxy, with the mountains being the domain of heterodoxy.[31] These terms are value-laden because they offer a sense of rightness—for the orthodox, heterodoxy is akin to heresy. Never mind that heterodox and orthodox are relative terms that limit the realm of possible discourse while capturing the sense of what the limitations are: for both ends of the spectrum of beliefs there is a doxa that appears self-evident (Bourdieu 1977).

While all contextualize and adapt religion in order to make it meaningful, the incorporation and melding of practices and beliefs from different reference points is evident, especially in the mountains among those who look to local tradition for legitimacy. There is a syncretism of practices that provides comfort through a sense of religious continuity.[32] That which is practiced locally has a relevance that can fit within a historical framework of tradition and within the context of the broader aspects of world religion—that religion is at once local with the faith of the ancestors not lost, and yet also global with a sense of legitimate membership in the *ummah* (global Islamic community). It is not merely syncretism but also a contextualized configuration of ancestral and household cult with local Muslim shrines. That which was sacred is assimilated into a framework of ritual and liturgical expression that allows what otherwise may be heretical to be viewed eventually as a preservation of the sanctity of what carries the orthodox label (Rappaport 1999, 338).

The centrality of the mosque as a locus of religious practice in the valley then stands as a marker of orthodoxy in contrast to the mazars in the mountains (though there are mazars in the valleys and mosques in the mountains). In the boundary areas—the foothills with populations that work in both the mountains and the valley—it becomes most clear that the background and framing of the corpus of knowledge influences what develops as heterodox or orthodox understanding (or a transition from one to the other).

A few examples come from one such border village, where Bakyt and Erkin live, both with houses only steps from the foothills. Bakyt was a lawyer who worked for the regional administration and retired eight years ago. He recalls, with embarrassment, that he was a heavy drinker who neglected his family and treated his wife poorly. He always had friends expressing happiness to see him and women were never far from his arm. He describes himself as someone who was important, but once he retired, he realized he had very few friends; most of those acquaintances who had been nice to him were doing so only to garner favor and now are distant and indifferent.

He is now retired and since early 2000, he has become more religious. He no longer drinks, and every Friday he goes to the nearest town to join others for *juma namaz* (Friday prayers). He is now one of the regional leaders of the town mosque who meets with the imam and aksakals for tea after prayers. He is working to build a mosque in the village where he lives and discusses the importance of such work. The youth of the village, he asserts, need good Muslim role models (which he was not for most of his life), which can best be found at the town mosque—the same one where Iqbol teaches the madrassa students. He feels that the local resources are inadequate; one must look to knowledgeable Muslims like Iqbol.

Erkin is Nurbek's older brother, who lives down the road from Bakyt. Unlike his brother, Erkin has no desire to visit the city. He graduated from high school and spent some time at a university but returned home when his father became ill. He helped raise his four siblings and does most of the heavy labor around the house. His parents were strict and his father forbade drinking. Many of Erkin's local friends drink heavily, but Erkin does not. Most days he does perform namaz, but he rarely goes to mosque. He loves the mountains because to him they are a place of tranquility where he can be part of an environment known intimately, and unchangingly, to generations of his forefathers. He is not overly interested in Bakyt's ideas for opening a mosque in the village and claims that the shortcomings of the village come not from an absence of Islam but rather from an absence of appreciating tradition.

When we speak about religion, Erkin talks about sacred places in the mountains around his house. The most sacred, he claims, is a three-day horse ride from the village, and he has only been to that mazar four times. The first time was with his father, and the last time was to pray for his father's recovery. This mazar is a stream that emerges from the base of a rock face, a place his ancestors have visited for as long as anyone can remember. The solitary aspects of being a shepherd allowed his father to teach him all the sacred sites in the region, along with the stories necessary to appreciate them. And he also does not worry much about the religious vision of Iqbol or Bakyt. Erkin wants only to be left alone and, when he has grandchildren, to teach them the way of the mountains and an appreciation of the magic it holds, a magic that is traditionally Kyrgyz and Islamic.

Not all boundary villagers are as divided as the stories of Bakyt and Erkin suggest. Rustan, for example, came from a mountain–valley border village and as a student traveled throughout the Soviet Union as a musician. He reminisces about the virtues of the communist system and has no regrets about leaving his village or about relegating his religious heritage to an artifact of the past; while he claims descent from the Sahaba, he strayed from the religious ways of his ancestors. And Farhod, Rustan's friend and former classmate, has not observed anything religiously in the last six years other than his devotion to cheap vodka. A mechanic, Farhod does not pray but explains having two wives by saying that Muhammad said it was right for a Muslim to have up to four wives. The nuances of the teaching are lost on him; he uses it to the extent that it allows him to do what he wants.

Framing the Corpus of Knowledge

The tension between variations of religious practice is over the correctness of practice. The various currents in religious revival indicate approaches to the problem of practice and how people come to legitimate what they do. In this respect, Mairam and Iqbol are two extremes. Mairam's views were developed within a sense of local tradition, of ancestral precedence. Iqbol is equally likely to claim tradition but the reference of tradition for him is one rooted in the Islamic texts and traditions of the Arabian Peninsula of the seventh century. Iqbol draws upon a legitimacy that claims universality; Mairam's legitimacy is of local specificity—the tradition of ancestral syncretism privileges personal and intimate connections learned from ancestors.

People's relationship with religious understanding is connected to the idea of precedence, which both Iqbol and Mairam can claim. And of course, tradition comes from this idea of precedence. Furthermore, precedence and tradition are realized in social memory, which in turn gives an explanation for contemporary orthodoxies and lends inertia to social structures (Connerton 1989, 102).

A complex range of factors come together to create knowledge and influence behavior. Thus, while the social organization of knowledge includes social and economic restrictions, the background of knowledge that constitutes its corpus is often set within historical, social, professional, educational, and religious frames.

Though the discussion of this chapter has largely centered around religion, the corpus of religious knowledge is far-reaching for it includes all fields of knowledge that allow us to make sense of the world and postulate the relationship of this world with the otherworldly. Ismoiljon, for example, works in a particular environment and the knowledge that constitutes his mastery is not religious but technical. Nonetheless, he discusses religion during tea breaks, and while hammering metal, he occasionally contemplates religion, his family,

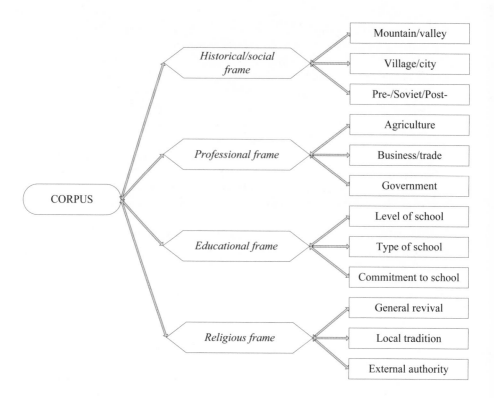

FIGURE 3.6. Corpus of knowledge.

and the "failed" state in which he lives. The solitude is similar to that of the shepherd, but the relationship with the environment is different. The environment affects one's relationship with religion and its points of orientation: the shepherd is likely to spend more time in nature while the metal worker is likely to visit mosque more frequently—out of these come different contexts of inspiration.

The historical frame is how people see themselves relative to the past and how they interpret this within the realm of their own experiences. For some, the ethnic claim of Uzbeks being better Muslims than Kyrgyz has an impact on the psychological sense of openness or obligation to religion, but so does the extent to which lives were impacted by historical events such as reforms under the Soviet Union or the religious freedoms of independence. History is, as well, individually experienced and local, similar to the importance of national and international events, and is often secondary to a neighbor's illness or an approaching winter without money for coal.

The historical frame is also part of the social frame, which includes relations with Others in the community and the pressures of change. It is gathering with friends at teahouses or squatting in conversation at the only intersec-

"OUR ANCESTORS ALSO LIVE HERE"

tion in the village. It is the pressure not to be the one in the village who does not go to mosque; or to be like Iqbol and Hizb ut-Tahrir members, offering their own interpretive way out of contemporary suffering; or to be like Mairam utilizing different traditions to combat the suffering of the world.

Moreover, profession contributes to the overall understanding of what one knows. Whether it is Muktar and Toliq talking near their taxis while waiting for clients, Baktagul gossiping with her clients and cosellers in the bazaar, Aibek working as a journalist, Erkin shepherding his sheep, or a businessman working with foreigners, the interactions with others and the information gained from this environment give a foundation for interpreting life. Educationally, the corpus of knowledge differs, whether there is advanced schooling that promotes the rational mind or religious schooling that looks for answers in the text.

In the context of the religious frame, the differences between an emphasis on the general revivalism, inward-looking traditionalism, and outward-looking orthodoxy suggest different orientations toward religion. The frames themselves do not predict what people will do or believe because human behavior is too complex and too unpredictable. But they do begin to parse out the complexity that contributes to understanding factors that lead to developing ideas that preference tradition or orthodoxy. Certain professions and forms of education, for example, imply particular settings for the sharing of knowledge specific to that setting. And it is the body of knowledge that people use to develop their cosmologies.

Mountain and Valley Muslims

Cosmological understanding and its public and private construction is an experienced phenomenon held in a corpus of knowledge. In an environment such as the mountains, which are less controlled by man, one finds a tendency to place the otherworldly in nature and the power of nature. The valley represents the city and village that are created by man, and here one finds a tendency to place otherworldly authority in the text (Qur'an) and associated institutions (mosques). Where there are differences in religious views between the mountain and valley Muslims, it is because of how religious knowledge has been experienced. This constitutes the corpus of knowledge because it is through *experience* that we know the world. The contrast between Dimira and Tolkun on the one hand, and Iqbol and Azarmat on the other, illustrates this point.

Dimira and Tolkun see magic and the spirits of their ancestors as an ever-present part of their lives, and yet the transcendent structuring of Islam is to them an entirely compatible aspect of life. They see miracles as common and superstitions may guide their behavior, but when one goes to a sacred site it is proper to perform namaz. The authority that guides them refers back to the importance and legitimacy of tradition: This is how it has always been done and must always be done.

For Iqbol and Azarmat, the ancestors are not to be venerated and true religious understanding can only be found in the revelatory text of the Qur'an and in studying the hadiths. The environment of the valley is a sedentary one with manmade structures for devotion and everywhere the mark of attempts to control the environment—from irrigation ditches to roads and fields. Their points of reference in tradition are those of a global *ulama* and a postaxial conception of transcendence. The answers to all questions can be found through study and the world of revealed knowledge stands in opposition to the "heterodoxy" of Dimira and Tolkun.

Both experiences see revival in the current context. The idea of revival and renewal carries with it (insofar as it is successful) an obligation of change, and anyone wanting to impart change must do so within a language that is legitimate. The language used to bring this about, to develop a sense of tradition and orthodoxy, is presented as a legitimate (and rational) continuation of proper behavior in relation to the obligations and potentials of the lived world and the strictures of the transcendent world. Of course this involves interpretation and claims to authenticity that reflect, not the historical understandings of tradition and orthodoxy, but rather the contemporary realities (Lee 1997, 144).

The difference between the mountain and valley Muslims relates to the environments in which they live and the understanding of tradition that they invoke. This shapes their view of one another. Because of the syncretism Tolkun employs in her religious expression, Azarmat does not accept her as a "true" Muslim. The unwavering and unaccommodating personality of Iqbol is unappealing to most of the population; likewise, Mairam's relationship with her deceased relatives is too much to accept for many.

But distinct boundaries do not exist so neatly. While heterodoxy and syncretism may be found with greater frequency in the mountains, they are also found in the valley: in markets one can usually buy talismans or beads to ward off the evil eye, or many will use archa (juniper) or *isrik* to help clean the space of bad spirits.[33] Orthodoxy is identified with the valley, but it is finding some purchase in the mountains as well. Even though Aibek complains about the new mosque, attendance at the mosque is up, and those who attend question the rightness of local tradition.

The extremes do serve the purpose of making clear the range of options available to people. Nurbek, Murat, Ismoiljon, and Jyrgal are all working within their experiences to locate themselves in a spiritual environment that makes sense. What they know of the world influences this and how they come to know the medium of knowledge gives rise to the characteristics of their understanding, and goes further in explaining why people like Dimira and Iqbol are how they are.

Chapter 4

"Listen and Watch!"

The Medium of Knowledge

The language of the first men is represented to us as the tongues of geometers, but we see that they were the tongues of poets. And so it had to be. One does not begin by reasoning, but by feeling.

> Jean-Jacques Rousseau, "Essay on the Origin of Languages Which Treats of Melody and Musical Imitation"

Telling stories is as basic to human beings as eating. More so, in fact, for while food makes us live, stories are what make our lives worth living. They are what make our conditions *human*.

> **Richard Kearney,** *On Stories*

On any given day, one can see a Kyrgyz or an Uzbek exhibiting a common gesture: with hands cupped together at chest level and open to the sky, he says *"Omen"* and in a fluid movement raises his hands to brush them over his face in a downward motion.[1] For some, the gesture is cultural; for others, it is religious. Some do it at the end of a meal, prior to departing on a trip, or when passing a cemetery or a mazar. For some it is spoken simply and casually; for others, it is preceded by a prayer or verse from the Qur'an. The fact that it is so common gives it a sense of being unremarkable. But the fact that everyone knows when to make the gesture shows the power of its social embeddedness.

The interpretation of the gesture, however, varies considerably. It is generally seen as an expression of thanks offered to Allah. For some, it is done without any sense of religious obligation; for others, it is one of many expressions of religious obligation. Aibek does it when leaving the table, regardless of whether he has finished eating or drinking vodka (and some debate whether it should be done in association with alcohol at all since alcohol is prohibited by the Qur'an). Mairam also does it when leaving the table, as well as when passing a cemetery to bless the souls of her ancestors. Toliq does it before leaving on a trip to ensure safe travel. Iqbol does it with great frequency, always preceded by a prayer. It is done before sacrificing an animal, and it is done to end all prayers. It can be done for any reason.

Those Kyrgyz and Uzbeks who have contemplated it assume that they share the gesture in common with the entire Islamic world. It is part of namaz, but Muslims in many Islamic countries do not associate it as widely with the same variety of everyday experience as those in Central Asia. What imbues the gesture with a sense of meaning and correctness for Central Asians is that it has been learned and it is known that this is what a Kyrgyz or an Uzbek is supposed to do, either as a Muslim or merely as one connected to a cultural tradition.

As a gesture, or more appropriately as a ritual, saying *omen* can mean everything, and it can mean nothing. How people learn such a seemingly simple and meaningful gesture, however, is informative, for what we know influences what we do. Asking why people do what they do when they do it often yields a reductionist answer that we know to do it because it is our culture to do it. There is some explanatory value in this argument, but in looking at knowledge we see that culture, in conjunction with a number of other aspects of information acquisition, takes us to a point of claiming knowledge. There is not only a social organization and corpus of knowledge, but also a medium. And all three components in combination hold sway over action.

As discussed in Chapter 2, social organization includes the restrictions and potentialities of the state, economics, and social relations that aid in determining the occasion and timing of action. The corpus of knowledge forms the frame—historical, social, professional, educational, religious—that imbues action with meaning. The means of acquisition and transmission—the medium—sets the field of knowing. What constitutes the medium is not only a variety of forms—oral, text, and practice—but also a wide variety of social and environmental influences that limit or impel the spectrum of action. Stories and texts, gestures and rituals, create indices that not only process experience but also bias understandings of certainty, ambiguity, and the negotiability of meaning.

Transmitting Knowledge and Understanding

Knowledge and understanding are inequitable gifts. But despite varying degrees of success, even the unlearned and seemingly unsophisticated have a mastery of awareness that allows them to negotiate their world. Mairam has more formal education than Aibek, yet Aibek provides for his family and is viewed as an "intellectual" in his village. Ismoiljon is a master of metal working but knows nothing about shepherding. Muktar can cook only *plov*,[2] and Baktagul, who can cook anything, does not know how to drive a car. Iqbol views himself as a religious authority and so does Dimira.

Expertise is, of course, relative to the act and carries the political implications of authority. But one always has mastery relative to another, and the acquisition of knowledge seemingly precedes authority, though is heavily influenced by it. At a basic level, it is influenced by the authority of the social organization in which knowledge exists. And the means by which this organization is revealed is the medium.

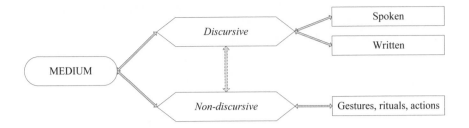

FIGURE 4.1. Medium of knowledge.

The medium of knowledge acquisition can be roughly categorized as either discursive or nondiscursive; its forms include differences of character and ultimately differences of action. The discursive medium can take either spoken or written form, whereas the nondiscursive medium includes gestures, rituals, and actions that convey meaning. The relationship between discursive and nondiscursive mediums is, of course, an intimate one. And in practice, a participant utilizes all forms available to come closer to understanding the world. Each aspect of the discursive and nondiscursive forms, however, carry nuances of difference that feed back to the medium and overall understanding of what is known and, as such, an understanding of how to act.

The spoken word holds special meaning, especially in Central Asia, which presents a cultural context keen on storytelling. Moreover, Islam emphasizes the recital of the Qur'an rather than merely reading it. But how the stories are told and understood differs according to the environments in which people live, be it mountain or valley, village or city. One group is no more honest in their telling of stories than another, for they both interpret their stories based on their understandings and needs. Their goal is to entertain and convince the listener.

Referring to a textual justification for one's stories stymies the variability of a listener's understanding. The role of the text in conveying information takes creative license away (at least somewhat) from the storyteller by moving authority from the oral storyteller to a text that can be situated as outside what is "man-made"—something that can be either authoritative because it is agreed on by "experts" or even more compellingly, something that is the direct message of transcendent authority.[3] This distinction can blur in practice, however, because people who are viewed as authorities may reference their authoritative opinion to a text, such as the Qur'an. One who hears the message may not have read the referenced text but will, in conversations with others he sees as less knowledgeable, claim to have "read the text" and thereby acquire the cover of textual authority even though he obtained it orally. This creates a problem of translation, which at some level all texts encounter, as well as the role of literacy—not only as an exponential contributor to the corpus of knowledge, but as something that influences the structure of orality.

But the medium of transmission is more than the word, whether spoken or written. One can easily observe that *omen* is prevalent, for example. The prevalence, or rather observation of prevalence, is a compelling guide for social practice that takes place at both conscious and subconscious levels. *Omen* can be either a direct observation or an indirect, passive, peripheral one, but in both senses the understanding of the action enters the body of knowledge— whether in the sense of "this is how my father prays" or, for example, in attempting to construct religious meaning out of some aspect of a wedding that may be perceived as being partly religious.

Spoken stories entertain and inform, as do texts and acts, but the negotiability of their authority is varied. The negotiability varies not only by content and the presenter, but in the positioning of authority both in what can be negotiated and in what lies outside of the negotiable realm. Texts fall outside the flexibility of the spoken, and the spoken becomes less flexible when it is written down. And while many see the discursive mediums—spoken and written—as the form of knowledge transmission in the most formal sense, the nondiscursive mediums of observation and action equally contribute to creating knowledge and guiding social practice.

A Culture of Stories

In reality, language is overwhelmingly oral. Over the course of history, thousands of languages have been spoken. But the vast majority has not been written and perhaps slightly over a hundred have developed sufficiently to generate literature (Ong 1982, 7). One should therefore distinguish the contribution of orality to the generation of knowledge, because in character it differs from its written counterpart.

Orality is, of course, a performative act of the everyday. It is dynamic, theatrical, and a means of communication that precedes writing. The spoken word can be mimicked and the meaning of intonations can be inferred, as the stories of a culture can be relayed in a mundane way or with dramatic flair. Furthermore, it takes communication beyond the gesture and adds to the richness and expediency of knowledge transmission.

At the discursive level, elders of the community, parents, neighbors, and friends all speak to each other—they gossip, tell stories, exchange views on certain situations—and inform each other about their surroundings. This certainly informs people and leads some to *know* a situation. People speak of the change in the price of onions; they speak of the behavior of their children; they speak of being discontent about their economic struggles; they speak of (and herein envision) a hopeful alternative for their children. They entertain the hopeful message and spread it to others in the community. (It is worth noting that knowledge is not the same as *objective* truth, even though those who *know* something often assign that knowledge a degree of truth.)

—⁊⁊⁊—

"LISTEN AND WATCH!"

FIGURE 4.2. As men talked in one room, elderly women gathered around a dosterkan at a wedding party to talk about the bride and groom and gossip about happenings in the village, 2005.

On a summer evening in the jailoo, something magical happens: the tradition of storytelling comes to life. Developing out of conversation with unnoticed ease and naturalness, Kubat begins to tell a story of his childhood and his family, an epic of the greatness of his ancestors, learned from his father and the community elders. A talented storyteller, he captivates everyone with his words, fluctuations in tone, and gestures. Sitting around the *dosterkan*,[4] tea (or vodka) pours freely, and when the story becomes engaging, everyone listens. Kubat is an aksakal in his mid-sixties, and in a culture that associates age with respect and wisdom, his voice is heard. The young boys sit attentively, hearing what he says, seeing how he performs it, and observing the reactions of others who are listening.[5] They are taking in information through indirect participation that will give them a sense of who they are, how they should tell stories, what stories they should tell, and what is important about the narrative of their lives.

The grandest form of the Kyrgyz oral storytelling tradition is the recitation of "Manas," an epic poem of nearly half a million lines.[6] It recounts a ninth-century battle to retain Kyrgyz independence against the Uighurs and is a particular source of pride for Kyrgyz, both for its length and its depiction of the Kyrgyz as a proud and triumphant people. Those who are particularly gifted in the telling of Manas obtain the title *manashci* and can melodically chant the story for hours without break, entering an almost trancelike state of the performative act. The manashcis do not see their telling of the story as optional, but rather as a mandate passed to them from their ancestral spirits.

Kubat is not a manaschi, though he speaks with reverence of the manaschis he has heard. For him, they are living signs of the presence of the Kyrgyz spirit, a belief that the experience of the ancestors can be channeled into the words of a storyteller.[7] And when discussions about the moral nature of the Kyrgyz arise, Kubat is quick to reference Manas as the example by which Kyrgyz should live. For example, within the story of Almambet, an ally and friend of Manas, a distinction is made between Muslims and infidels, and it is told that even before birth Almambet was destined to be Muslim.[8]

After Kyrgyzstan's independence in 1991, the new government encouraged the leadership example of Manas. In 1995, the country celebrated what was declared to be the 1,000th anniversary of Manas's birth in Talas oblast and leaders made efforts to encourage the adoption of the principles of "Manas" as part of the Kyrgyz school curriculum. Eighty percent of the Kyrgyz I surveyed felt it was important for children to learn about Manas.

Stories merge, or at least link, the past with the present and with possibilities. They create mimetic opportunities—opportunities to imitate action (Kearney 2002, 5, 12). Inherited from culture, religion, or family, stories can be narratives of place (myths of homeland), creation (explanations of existence), or narratives for solving problems (Kearney 2002, 3, 29–30). Often, oral genealogies give preference to social space (Goody 2000, 81), for they reference a connection with the past and present, of ancestors to contemporaries, with a continuity that is less concerned with temporal accuracy than spatial relativity.

Furthermore, stories can be history and they can be fiction, but they always have a purpose in their telling. They can structure the past as it *could have been*, not only as it *was* (Kearney 2002, 31). This subjunctive aspect of storytelling is also seen in rituals and can be understood to be at the heart of what religious understanding is. Whenever relevant, Kubat ties Manas to his stories, to give legitimacy and authority to what he says, aiding him in transmitting a sense of communal norms and history. Thus, not only does a character such as Manas serves as a hero who links Kyrgyz to a heroic past, but the story offers a vision of traditional behavior. And depending on its interpretation, this can further link a Muslim heroic past with Qur'anic stories of appropriate behavior.

Of course, oral storytelling is not limited to the jailoo. It is a vibrant part of life and happens as often as friends meet with time to narrate, whether at a home, a teahouse, or while hanging out on the street and waiting for either something interesting to happen or for a reason to move somewhere else. And we find community in the stories we share. To be a guest and to go as a guest is a matter of honor. And in Central Asia, guest is not only a noun but also has a verb form: people go guesting. As guests, people gather to share stories, gossip, and rumors.

While the tradition of oral storytelling remains an active part of Kyrgyz society, there is a difference in the oral communication of societies with writing and those without writing (Goody 2000, 23). As noted earlier, one important part of the Soviet planners' agenda was education reform, which aimed to give all members of the Soviet Union a similar educational background. In the early 1930s, Russian psychologist A.R. Luria conducted research in remote parts of Kyrgyzstan and Uzbekistan, looking specifically at the locals' adaptation to the influence of the Soviet Union's efforts to eliminate illiteracy, force collectivization, and infuse new socialist principles.[9] His research served as a Marxist justification for the Soviet literacy program, but also suggested that what the cognitive framing processes of Kyrgyz and Uzbek illiterate were almost entirely based on local knowledge and an inability to relate to possibilities beyond their spheres of experience. And while illiterates may have contact with literate structures, it is not until writing is personally internalized that their cognitive processes are affected (Ong 1982, 56).

In the Kyrgyzstan of today, however, the issue is not as much illiteracy but rather more the preferred mode of communication. The Soviet programs of educational reform successfully and dramatically increased literacy in Central Asia. Now, the region is no longer perceived as illiterate. Rather, the high rate of literacy served as a marker of the success of Soviet reforms. One could still contest the degree of literacy attained, but that is a different issue than the fact that the population as a whole has become more literate. Despite the dramatic increase in literacy, however, the importance of orality has not been eliminated. In fact, many aspects of orality have remained influential in how knowledge is communicated and now, with a postindependence decrease of literacy, the role of orality is on the rise.

Oral genealogies preference local social space; they are informal, immediate, and reaffirming of social relations. As protests grew following the February 2005 parliamentary elections in Kyrgyzstan, eventually leading to the March putsch, I spoke on several occasions with one organizer who mentioned the utility of rumors for organizing protests and protestors. Toliq and Muktar were always talking with their fellow taxi drivers and customers about the protests, and it was clear they feared possible instability, even though they were active in contributing to the anxiety of others who were just as uninformed. Even false stories, when presented convincingly and with enough authority, can generate verity: "what if it is true" permeates the imagination.

Going with a group of university students to Solomon's Mountain in Osh led to stories and explanations for the utility and purpose of rituals at the sacred site—does one slide down the rock three times or seven? Does sliding down the rock help with back problems, kidney stones, pregnancy . . . ? The students debated meanings, but what they eventually accepted as true came from the person whose answer had the most convincing authority. A story told with assurance leaves a lasting impression.

FIGURE 4.3. Women sliding down a rock on Solomon's Mountain to help with various health issues from spine alignment and issues with internal organs to fertility, 2005.

The Rise of Literacy

An interesting component of the 1924 partitioning into republics was that the Soviet planners, in order to create a sense of nationalism, were required to develop languages and literatures as well as national histories and folklores (Roy 2000, 61). The Soviet Union was particularly proud of the success of this Marxist project—literacy.[10] While the definition of literacy was relatively loose—in the early years, someone who could read and write his name was considered literate[11]—the Soviet system did teach a lot of people how to read and therefore enabled them to gain access to written information. While university instruction was often in Russian, students also learned the titular language of the republic, resulting in a largely bilingual population.

Despite the advances of Soviet education in literacy, independence has resulted in a decline of bilingual literacy as well as literacy in general. A push after independence tried to emphasize Kyrgyz language. In Naryn city, for example, a number of schools allowed Russian to be dropped as a subject, saying that the country's future was monolinguistic—in Kyrgyz. At the national level, the status of Kyrgyz and Russian as official languages has been a source of great debate. Those who push dropping Russian as an official language of the state also support dropping it as a requirement in school curriculums.

Russia has put pressure on the country to keep Russian as an official language, though an increasing number of young people educated after the breakup of the Soviet Union lack competency in Russian.

While nationalists do not see this as a problem, the implications for large sections of the population no longer being able to communicate with the Russian-speaking world are widespread. Much of Bishkek, for example, remains predominately Russian-speaking, and those who do not know Russian often feel lost and are linguistically unqualified for many white-collar jobs. Furthermore, due to rising unemployment, an increasing number of migrant laborers, mostly men, go to Russia to do construction and other jobs that native Russians do not want to do (see Reeves 2011b, 2012). With often inadequate language skills, they must either quickly acquire knowledge of Russian or face worse treatment because of their inability to communicate. In villages where over half the male population works in Russia during the summer months, the loss of bilingual literacy is recognized as a problem. One community response to the loss of Russian can be seen in Jangi-Nookat, where a local school began a special Russian class, and students whose parents have paid more receive instruction in all their subjects only in Russian; Uzbek is learned at home.

This Russian-language class is only one part of recognizing the important role played by a command of Russian in the success of those in the village, because it connects them to a larger world with more opportunities. Part of this dynamic is concerned with the oral, whereas another part is concerned with the continuation of knowledge transmitted through texts, with more texts available in Russian than in Kyrgyz or Uzbek.

The breaking apart of the planned socialist economy and shift to a more market-based economy in Kyrgyzstan has contributed to an increase in the country's illiteracy rate. More parents are forced to work longer hours without the social benefits of the Soviet economy. This, in combination with lax truancy enforcement, has led to a greater number of children helping their parents in the markets, metal shops, barber shops, and jailoos, rather than attending schools. This creates a whole population with limited textual knowledge and leads to the more circumscribed opportunities afforded by illiteracy.

We need to be cautious in equating or simplifying the oral mind to merely a spoken form of the written mind. The conceptions are quite different (Ong 1982, 11). Writing creates an appearance of symbolic similarity, of the ability of markings to be decoders of expression with residues of meaning. The oral story does not have the same repository aspect of writing, for the oral story exists as the potential of being told and in being told or retold, it can be altered with minor variations. It does not have to be recounted with the same exactness of the written word. Despite these differences the two modes are not in complete opposition. Oral transmission often comments on and contests the written form and as such engages and complements it (Bellér-Hann 2000, 90).

In Nookat, the juma (Friday) mosque is a few hundred meters from the primary road, situated high above a stream and with a deep sense of being surrounded by the community. Hundreds, if not thousands, attend Friday prayers, with overflow going to the new mosque along the main road. On other days, fewer people come to prayers—perhaps fifty to seventy for afternoon prayers. But on any given day twenty young boys can be seen sitting cross-legged around the courtyard, trying to memorize *suras* (chapters) from the Qur'an. Some of these boys do not attend public schools, only a madrassa.

Like most who attend mosque, the students do not know Arabic well. They can read the letters and read the Qur'an, but they cannot carry on conversations in Arabic. However, the ability to recite sections of the Qur'an in Arabic, even without knowing it well, gives people a degree of authority in oral knowledge of it. Many of my interlocutors listed knowledge of Arabic as one of the important traits of a religious leader. When people do know Arabic and can read, the Qur'an legitimates individual authority.

Zafar and Baktyor represent two cases of where authority can be seen as constructed in relation to Arabic and the Qur'an. Both men are ethnic Uzbeks who live in the southern part of Kyrgyzstan and regularly attend mosque. Zafar owns a small shop that sells household accessories in the village where he lives. For the past six years, he has been meeting with four of his friends on an almost daily basis to study the Qur'an. He has also been learning Arabic and now has a better command of the language than the imam of the local mosque, who has been there since the Soviet period. A year prior to my meeting him, Zafar had begun to challenge some of the imam's interpretations of the Qur'an. Rather than engaging Zafar in discussion, the imam countered the threat Zafar presented to his authority by saying that Zafar was too radical in his views and a member of Hizb ut-Tahrir, thus making Zafar unwelcome in the mosque.

Zafar denies that he is a member of Hizb ut-Tahrir and, at least at the time of our last conversation, I believe he had not yet joined the organization. Being ostracized from the mosque he had attended for years, however, has made Zafar consider joining Hizb ut-Tahrir. He is angered that his attempt to become a more learned Muslim has put him in conflict with the religious establishment in the community and believes they are more concerned with controlling dissent than with supporting Islam. He is increasingly skeptical of the state, especially as the police routinely hassle him because they have taken the word of the imam as an indication of Zafar's membership in Hizb ut-Tahrir. Zafar no longer attends the main mosque but meets with friends in his home and has plans to build a mosque in his neighborhood, which would teach (according to him) a "more knowledgeable" version of Islam. By "more knowledgeable," he means an Islam guided by a more literal interpretation of the Qur'an and hadiths than what is taught at the mosque.

Baktyor on the other hand, is a member of Hizb ut-Tahrir. Most everyone knows he is one of the leaders of the movement in his community and at juma namaz he can be found opposite the mosque entrance standing with several other members of Hizb ut-Tahrir. They are part of the mosque community, and those who support their activities embrace Baktyor with greetings, and discreetly give him money as they part. The other Hizb ut-Tahrir members record who pays dues and distribute literature if there is any update that needs to be passed along.

Engaging Baktyor in conversation, however, is more like arguing with a bully who finds himself cornered and whose only recourse is to raise his voice and insist that the other person is not knowledgeable. Baktyor's discussion tactics are limited to quoting excerpts from the Qur'an—excerpts that come from the official Hizb ut-Tahrir literature he has memorized. He has a rudimentary understanding of Islam and does not know Arabic besides the phrases he has memorized. He claims his legitimacy based on the façade of familiarity with Arabic. Though he does not have the same command of theology, for example, as Iqbol, he is an effective organizer and distributor of the polemical message of Hizb ut-Tahrir.

Zafar and Baktyor differ in what they know, though both couch their authority in a written text that allows them to exclude those unfamiliar with it from the argument. Throughout Central Asia and other non-Arabic-speaking countries, the Qur'an is learned and read in Arabic. Most who recite the Qur'an and pray in Arabic often do not know Arabic but rather have learned the meaning of the utterance or text. Most can neither understand the text in its written form nor translate it; their learning is the skill of verbatim memorization (Goody 2000, 34). Learning to repeat the Arabic text—or any text, be it Russian, Kyrgyz, or Uzbek—can create a setting where the issue is less about engaging in ideas and more about protecting (and projecting) dogma.[12] When turning to the textual, the difference is in the locus of authority: that which is textual, or referenced as textual, takes authority outside of negotiation. The oral has a tendency to allow greater interpretive flexibility. In other words, ideas are expressed in writing; the spoken word relays feeling. Writing formalizes language, creating a perception of language being crystallized, but it is also forced by a set of conventions (Rousseau 1966, 21–22).

Writing restructures consciousness and print encourages a sense of closure, of acceptance that what has been written is of greater significance than what has merely been spoken (Ong 1982, 78, 132). As such, Iqbol, Zafar, and Baktyor all reference, and find authority in, the written word. It was quite common to encounter someone who references a particular writing and claims familiarity with it, even without having read it. Murat does this with his less knowledgeable friends, and to a certain extent, Baktyor and the imam from Zafar's old mosque do the same thing. Murat, for example, assesses what he knows relative to what the person with whom he is talking knows and then passes off something heard on a cassette, in a mosque, or on the street as connected to an authoritative text. He would say, for example, that it is a particular teaching in the Qur'an with the implication that he has actually read it himself.

To a great extent, the interpretation of what is written is influenced by the prevailing winds of culture (Street 1999, 225). That does not explain everything, though, for it takes a certain amount of time for cultural norms to be developed. And at times religious texts can be seen to support a view counter to what is culturally accepted.[13] This countering of accepted norms occurs in a way that privileges the written text as the authoritative foundation that provides an unchanging description of truth and moral behavior. Because it is written, it is privileged more than the "telephone-game" quality of orality.

While all traditions, as living traditions, are malleable, their malleability takes on a different and more enduring quality when they are placed in the medium of the written word. Written traditions can be carried to different settings of place and time with the idea that they are cumulative and quasi-permanent (Goody 2000, 11). And religious texts in particular have a conservative quality, the text serving as legitimator of dogma and doxa (Goody 2000, 15; Myles 2004). At all levels, though, literacy creates a problem of translation—of translating text to accessible language and translating a message into culture and action—but the resulting negotiation of meaning is a melding of oral, textual, and active experience.

Practice as Social Learning

Knowledge is precious. It is acquired though smiles and tears, through celebrations and sorrows. And in a culture that has a strong oral component, the elders are specialists charged with the responsibility to preserve the learning of the ancestors through stories. As repeaters of the past, they are more highly regarded than when knowledge is stored in writing, outside of the mind (Ong 1982, 41). The written form dislocates authority from the oral-wisdom stories of the elders by placing it in text. But what makes sense of the oral and written is the experiential, the realm of practice and action.

Language is an abstraction of what is experienced or emoted. Oral memory functions as a reworking of experience, and written history can be obtuse without a frame of experience. One only needs to think of the relationship between stories told and written about love—from novice to more adept encounters or shortcomings in speaking for the heart—to realize the intensely personal nature of participation as social learning. As an analogy, it may seem out of place or at least awkward and uncomfortable in a discussion about knowledge and religion, but like any craft, the reality of experience is informative. It is knowledge that is secretive and made more real through the experience.[14] For as with all forms of knowledge, experience is a generative process that is personal, unique, yet shared.

Experiential mediums of knowledge encourage a cultural and social interpretation that guides action. But experience can be either direct (participation) or indirect (observation), and active or passive. A father teaching his son to pray is one example of active direct experience, whereas the son mimicking his father can be a form of passive participation. In both instances, the act of how to pray is under development, but the father plays a more active role in knowledge transmission in the first example. The son can be equally engaged in the process of mimicking prayer, possibly in mosque for the first time, but

"LISTEN AND WATCH!"

FIGURE 4.4. Experiential mediums of knowledge.

draws upon his own observations more than on what he has been taught. As with participation, observation plays an important role in experience and the difference between active and passive indirect experience comes from the intensity with which one observes. Active observation would involve a son watching his father pray with intent to pray and passive would simply be noticing that his father prays. There is a level of social and cultural interpretation that leads to action and a way of conceiving oneself within the community.

This implies only that around us are a variety of experiences that we take in at different levels. It could be a father in Naryn who does not fast but encourages his son to fast or a child's passive awareness that in other parts of the country—though maybe not his own—people are fasting. It could be the difference between sitting down before one of the Islamic programs on Osh television or doing some other task and realizing that one had caught a few bits of the program when people talk about it the next day over tea. It can also be the peer pressure that leads everyone in the neighborhood to go to mosque for prayer.

Looking at the mimetic and phronetic aspects of mediums of knowledge, then, we begin to see different characteristics that develop (though all these characteristics are interrelated). The oral referencing of tradition allows for the ambiguity of a changing narrative. Dimira and Tolkun are much more open to variation in what they do, and consequently the differences between the ways they address their ancestors or heal the sick can be discussed and tolerated as interpretations of the oral tradition. Oral referencing to a heard text, as Muktar and Baktyor practice in arguing religion with people less familiar with the text, leads to uncertainty and ambiguity (Muktar) or inflexibility around discussions of the meaning of the text (Baktyor). Iqbol has studied Arabic and the Qur'an and has a higher level of competency than most. For him, the text is inflexible and the meanings nonnegotiable.

The experiential, however, helps process knowledge by giving meaning to the oral and textual modes as well as to the experience itself. Mairam is able

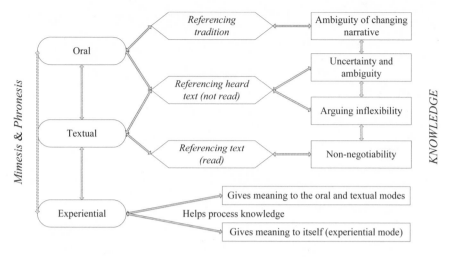

FIGURE 4.5. Oral, textual, and experiential mediums of knowledge.

to make sense of what her mother, Dimira, has told her through the accumulation of direct and indirect experience; by growing up in an environment of visiting mazars and praying to ancestors; and by being put in a position where she is called upon to lead a ceremony honoring her father's death. Baktyor understands the relationship between his authority and text in part because he is able to observe people's reactions to him. And while Zafar is emboldened to challenge the imam because he commands a deeper understanding of the text, his experience of being pushed out from the community also emboldens him in the certainty of his actions.

What people know theologically and practically about religion can be quite different things. The process of knowledge is referential and in the end, what comes to be taken as most authoritative in life is experience, though in theology it is often the text. The authority of a sacred text—and often text in general—mediates the vertigo of ambiguity and lies outside what can be negotiated. That is why Iqbol feels so certain about what he does; all answers to his questions, he claims, can be found in the Qur'an. But Tolkun is also certain about what she does, though for different reasons. She claims that she has experienced the effectiveness of visiting mazars and that the oral tradition of her ancestors is a precedent of authority. All the same, she can more easily accommodate variation in religious practice than can Iqbol.

THE INFLUENCE OF ACQUISITION

Culture constitutes knowledge, but as argued earlier, knowledge includes more than what is contained in culture. The social organization, corpus, and medium of knowledge matter because the message and means of messaging carry both legitimacy and authority. Thought is tied with reasoned conclusions and the legitimacy of those conclusions. Legitimacy is vested with a certain authority, however, and as noted in Chapter 3, authority trumps reason (even—to the extent it remains authoritative—when it seems unreasonable). What persuades authority is rationalized through what people experience and how it is interpreted through language (a translation at best). Force can be one aspect of persuasion, but it is an authority of suspect legitimacy—as Talleyrand allegedly remarked to Napoleon, "You can do anything with a bayonet, Sire, except sit on it"—though the mode of knowledge transmission cedes a particular aspect of legitimacy's viability and malleability.

Kubat's experience of storytelling (orality) draws upon different frames of reference than those of Iqbol, though this is not to suggest that Iqbol ignores the role of storytelling or that Kubat minimizes the text. On the contrary, Iqbol tells short stories to his students to illustrate the relevance of Islam in their lives and Kubat incorporates what he reads—newspapers, religious texts, novels—into his stories to add depth and relevance to his narrative. Thus, as long as literacy remains a variable, the tension between oral and textual forms is not usually so demarcated as to exclude the other. Experience makes sense of them both.

What matters is authority of the message and interpretation. And the tension then becomes situated in what constitutes learned and revered opinions. Being part of multiple affiliations that shape individual identity, we assess the medium of knowledge in relation to whether it comes from inside or outside our community and how it allows us to foster our desired relationship between tradition and modernity. This is not always straightforward and sometimes is an exercise of indirect, passive awareness. But all of it fits into the creation of the knowing self.

Missionaries

As categories, outsider and insider are, like most identifying terms, fluid in their interpretation and application. They represent new ideas as well as the maintenance of old ideas and can be in tension with each other because their juncture is the place where people's experience and understanding of the right life collide.

Though Begaim's life in Lahol is isolated by all accounts, even there, the influence of the outside is an ever-present part of the imagination of what a better life entails and what is local that is worth keeping. Nurbek maintains his connection with his village but lives in the city, and this makes him more cosmopolitan than a classmate who has never left the village. What is more, Nurbek is computer savvy and is connected to an outside world through the Internet in ways that his father cannot comprehend. Toliq listens to the world news on his car radio as he waits for passengers. Baktyor lives in Karasuu, Kyrgyzstan, but his work in Hizb ut-Tahrir, despite being illegal, extends his local connections to networks in Uzbekistan, the headquarters in England, and in a similar way, he is connected to India and Pakistan through his acquaintance with Iqbol.

The outside—identified here as ideas and thoughts that are external to the local—influences a number of aspects of Kyrgyz society in a variety of ways. Television programs such as the Brazilian telenovella *O Clone* (The Clone), set in both Brazil and Morocco, captivated people throughout Kyrgyzstan in 2004-5.[15] It led to young girls wearing headscarves as fashion—the "Clone-look"; women talking in the market about how *O Clone* taught them about how a Muslim woman should act; and men discussing on street corners what it means to be a wealthy Muslim with two wives. It was infrequent that any of the discussions were critical in engaging people on a theological level, and in fact most imams with whom I spoke saw *O Clone* as an indication that Islam was important in world culture.

While *O Clone* had a large fan base of people interested in the Islamic culture it depicted, Asel and Baktagul found themselves trying to come to an understanding of how they, influenced by the characters of *O Clone*, could make an Islamic life happier and more meaningful. For Asel, it made the headscarf a more fashionable accessory, while Baktagul felt she was more knowledgeable of her religion because of the serial.

In addition to *O Clone*, there are religious programs on television aimed at people like Azarmat and Murat who want to learn more about religion. These programs often present religious teachers deemed knowledgeable because they have either studied abroad or are themselves foreign. Toliq sometimes listens to recordings of sermons in his taxi, which his passengers overhear at times. And Iqbol has a number of video compact discs of religious themes that he shares with interested Muslims who have the technology to play them. What is interesting about the various media—television, videos, compact discs, cassette tapes—is that they give little time to educating about, or supporting, Islam as understood by Aibek, Tolkun, and Dimira. The media presents its message more orally than textually, though it gathers its authority by claiming reference to the text.

Missionaries searching for converts and others wanting to improve their religious knowledge use a variety of sources to increase their competence. There are some who come as religious authorities, such as Iqbol, who studied abroad. And there are others who, through their oratory skills and demonstrated knowledge, reformulate themselves from former everyday practitioners to Islamic authorities, such as Zafar and Baktyor. In presenting themselves as authorities, however, the relationship between insiders' and outsiders' experience and knowledge plays a role.

Iqbol, for example, is both an insider and an outsider. He was raised locally, went to study abroad, and returned to the town where his parents live. Now, however, he thinks differently, discounting local knowledge of Islam and emphasizing what he learned during his studies in India and Pakistan. He dresses differently than others in his town, and this causes some in his town to pointedly say he is a terrorist and to avoid him. The level of his activity within banned Islamic groups is unclear, but he does have a vision of the

FIGURE 4.6. Men in front of a mosque after Eid prayers, 2000.

reestablishment of the caliphate as a better way to remediate the social ills of the country.

In Naryn, the former *kazi* (Islamic legal scholar and judge) at the juma mosque was an outsider in the same sense as Iqbol. Trained in Saudi Arabia, he was originally from a valley town along the Uzbek border. He tried to present himself as a local, but many did not see him as a true insider because he was from a different region of the country and not from the mountains. Though people took him seriously as a religious leader because he had studied abroad and was from a part of the country stereotyped as more orthopraxic, he was still talked about as an outsider in the same way as the two Turkish imams who helped staff the mosque were foreign. The Turkish imams and the Saudi-trained kazi had different frames of understanding Islam and modes of initiating reform, but the nuances of their differences and points of conflict between them were lost to most people, who merely saw them as outsiders knowledgeable about *proper* Islam.

Certainly, though, the kazi and the imams are more welcome in Naryn than many of the Christian missionaries, who have a mixed legacy as outsiders. Kanibek, a Kyrgyz teacher in his early fifties, believes (like Tolkun and Dimira) that ancestors remain a valuable part of his life; that it is effective to tie a piece of cloth on a tree and make a wish; and that burning archa clears the room of unwanted spirits. He attends mosque only on Orozo Ait (Eid al-Fitr) and Kurban Ait (Eid al-Adha) and considers himself both a Muslim and a communist. I joined him for lunch one afternoon on Orozo Ait; we met later in the day because he said it was important to visit seven houses to celebrate the holiday. By the time I arrived, he had already consumed a substantial amount of alcohol, and in his drunkenness he expressed his approval for the work being done at the mosque to make community members more knowledgeable and observant Muslims.

As the conversation continued, he spoke about tolerance and an openness to outsiders, with one caveat: "We love everyone, except the Baptists. We hate the Baptists." His reason for this animosity toward Baptists, while expressing love for Catholics, Methodists, Jews, Buddhists, and Hindus, had little to do with knowledge of religion. Rather, Kanibek knew about a family whose son had become a Baptist and no longer talked with his family because they were not "believers." Kanibek could think of nothing worse than a religion that would lead an adherent to leave his family and reorient himself toward a family of "fellow believers" rather than blood kin.

The details of the story were probably more complex, but it was enough for him to oppose the Baptists (he did not know they were Christians) and support the work of the Turkish imams and Saudi-trained kazi.[16] Nargiza, an Uzbek woman in her late forties, wears a headscarf against the wishes of her husband and lives in the south. She is more conciliatory toward Christians when she talks with people from the West, but overhearing her conversations with locals indicates that her feelings are more negative. She is a theologically conservative Muslim who is supportive of the efforts of Iqbol and Baktyor, but claims to be unwilling to take money from them to open an Islamic educational center. In reality, what she wants is an Islamic school that teaches regular school subjects as part of a strict Islamic education. She complains that the madrassas do not teach education beyond Islam and students need a more rounded education so that they can go on to be qualified for a variety of jobs and remain rooted in Islam.

She is soliciting money to develop her Islamic educational center and has applied to a handful of Western development organizations for support, selling the idea of the Islamic educational center as a place to foster religious pluralism and understanding. She says that the Christian missionaries have been successful in her town because they teach about a God of love rather than a God of fear and this message is appealing to many people who do not completely understand what it means to submit to God. This, she claims, is a trait that would be good for Muslims to emulate—to emphasize that love is one of the names of God. But with her friends, she is much less open to conversations about pluralism and sees the Christians as a threat to the community.

Politics

To Nargiza, Christian missionaries are the ultimate outsiders because their ideology threatens the Islamic community she wants to strengthen. One of her arguments is that they are not local. Interestingly, however, to support her efforts, she is writing grants to Western embassies and development organizations, which are clearly not insiders but outsiders with their own agendas of influencing the social environment. The influence of other countries can be seen in educational exchange programs to the United States, religious programs in Saudi Arabia, or Turkish high schools in Kyrgyzstan.

Religious and educational programs, however, are not the only areas where outside ideas have an impact on the local. There are a number of civil society development projects aimed at teaching new ways of thinking about the community, the state, and the role of an individual's public voice. These include trainings in pedagogy, business plans for a market economy, and how to improve production quality. They also include civic education projects that encourage free media, an openness of government, and accountability of and through community organizations. And like O Clone, most television programming comes from abroad and gives a picture of life elsewhere.

Though Begaim has not left Lahol in years, she knows life is better in Russia because on the days that the television works she can watch programs that depict a more comfortable life. Baktagul assesses where life is better based on the country of origin and quality of products that she sells. She claims that Kyrgyzstan is too poor to produce anything—though she believes it is a poverty of leadership because the country has everything it needs to be self-sufficient—and the products she sells are from China, Turkey, Iran, and Russia. The Chinese products are the cheapest and least reliable. While she considers the Russian and Iranian products to be of good quality, she favors the Turkish products for their price and quality. She adds that life must be pretty good in Turkey; certainly better than here.

The marketplace is an area where local entrepreneurs utilize insider and outsider networks to create opportunities and alliances. Aidar has exploited his local networks to develop relations with international businesses. He was one of the first businessmen to take advantage of the new openness of the borders after independence, and his success in controlling the borders has increased his international economic connections. As a successful local businessman, he entered politics. Connected to the power elites through his success, he moves beyond his local relations by restructuring clan relations along economic lines. He welcomes the opportunity to be seen as a patron of a general Islamic revival, but toes the line on extremist discourse because it is threatening to his economic well-being and because there is political utility in labeling his opponents Islamists.

Baktyor, being unconcerned with the state, is the type of person who is most threatening to Aidar (Montgomery 2015a). He discounts politics—though he is political—and sees religion as the only solution. Many in Karasuu view him as a bit extreme. He is an insider, but also an outsider because his views on Hizb ut-Tahrir are more radical than most and because he draws on political legitimacy from abroad, grounded in a text.

The relevance of stories about Nargiza and Baktyor, Kanibek and Aidar, ties in to the issue of politics and religion, as well as to the problem of legitimacy and authority. Both politics and religion seek legitimacy and claim authority. When missionaries come to an area, they maintain that the message they bring has greater authority and will yield a more meaningful life. A number of outside entities try to influence politics, ranging from the West's project of encouraging democracy and supporting programs that develop civil society, to the legacy of the Soviet Union and a Russian approach to market economy.

The insider attempts to adapt to outside influences that appear compelling or at least useful for their own purposes. Within Islam, politics and religion are inseparable and authority is otherworldly—from Allah. Politics sometimes argues a separation, that authority is this-worldly. Negotiability, however, is relative to the reference point of authority. Many of the mediums through which people learn to distinguish between the insider and outsider are passive and indirect. Asel and Baktagul watch *O Clone* and by doing so it becomes part of how they understand Islam. Toliq and Zafar listen to sermons on cassettes. Nargiza rejects the foreign ideas of Christianity but is willing to use the resources aimed at developing civil society to educate people on the importance of living a more orthodox Islamic life.

Others, however, experience the outside as active and direct. Aidar sees the negotiability and fungibility in his business and political endeavors. Kanibek makes sense of his religious life by keeping it formally occasional and connecting it to the tradition of his surroundings, resisting the Christian missionaries who challenge that. Kubat is happiest with a good story.

The reference point for Aidar, Kanibek, and Kubat resembles an oral form of negotiable authority. Aidar makes business deals all the time and knows they last until another deal supersedes the previous one. Kanibek is committed to no particular place of authority and listens to the imam as attentively as he listens to Tolkun, whom he visits more frequently than the mosque. And while the stories Kubat tells may sound familiar, there are always minor variations that he accounts for by remarking that the idea is true and some details are ornamentation. For Toliq, Zafar, and Nargiza, their inflexibility is reified by their assertion that the written word—and their interpretation of it—is true and holds little negotiability for variation. Asel's and Baktagul's vision of Islam is more uncertain, though watching *O Clone* has given them the confidence of a better understanding of Islam. There is flexibility, however, when they are in contact with Toliq, Zafar, and Nargiza, whom they see as more knowledgeable because they are closer to understanding a text. And for them, there is more authority in the text, and therefore less negotiability.

DEVELOPING A WORLDVIEW

How people understand their reality is based on the events and objects they experience. But the means by which people come to knowledge are more than just the stories they read or hear. It involves a constant interaction with challenges of everyday life that can be influenced greatly by local and national politics. Both Aibek and Bakyt, for example, may have contact with a missionary, but how they hear the message of the missionary, and the likelihood of them hearing it, can differ significantly because of the local needs and understandings of the individual and the community in which he lives. Thus, the difference between the populations is seen, in part, in terms of their means of sustenance and the political environment in which they live, because these experiences are significant in providing an understanding of the religious self and accounting for nuanced difference.

The narrative medium—oral, textual, experiential—conveys meaning to phenomena and events as they are experienced and replicated, discursively and nondiscursively; the medium guides the individual in what is seen as moral, legitimate, and authoritative ways to act. Missionaries like Iqbol, the kazi and Turkish imams in Naryn, and even Nargiza draw heavily not only on outside legitimacy, but also on a textual framing that is either nonnegotiable or at least inflexible. Politicians like Aidar refer back to a textual frame of the constitution, or the Qur'an when it is politically expedient, but also are open to the negotiability of an oral frame that recognizes the utility of fungibility. And for aksakals like Kubat, decisions are made casuistically in the context of inherited tradition.

The agendas of a religious-ordered and a political-ordered world are intertwined, but they are also different in their authoritative frames of reference. The everyday never lives up to the ideal. And because of that, all states are failed states that can never adequately meet the desires of the population, though they may meet the minimal needs. Periods of cosmological disintegration are periods that are open to the charismatic.[17] History has yet to make an assessment of whether Kyrgyzstan is in such a period, but among some—especially Iqbol, Baktyor, and Zafar—there is the very real sense that the morality of the world order is fundamentally threatened.

The nature of the threat is a local one, though invariably it is given a more sweeping presentation: the world is collapsing and what is done locally can right the wrongs of the world. There is the ability for local action to be felt or presumed to have impact in more distant places, as if through cosmological transference. And thus, times of great disillusionment, which can include successful propaganda that has local relevance, yield opportunities for the charismatic message to find a ripe audience anxious for an authoritative message to guide it. If the soteriological vision is this-worldly, then politics are important, for this is the world where one does what needs to be done to gain salvation. And this is where politics are interpreted as being related to the soteriological project; where, for Baktyor, what the state and what the religious community do becomes politically important as an obligation to right the lived world.

Ritual

We imbue life with meaning in endless ways. As children, we mimic and are taught to interpret; as adults we also mimic and are taught to interpret, while at the same time we try to create experiences for children that instruct and protect them. Imbuing life with meaning is complex, intricate, and intimate, and not only as a process of learning and acquiring knowledge—though this is really just an extension of the process of knowledge acquisition—but also as a process concerned with the most significant events of life: birth, entering into adulthood, marriage, death. Knowledge exists in the possibility of expression because if it cannot be articulated or acted, it cannot be shared. Rituals constitute a portion of religious understanding that is also a social understanding of difference and behavioral correctness. And it is here that we often see a combination of oral, textual, and experiential mediums of knowledge.

As is traditional for many Kyrgyz, Asel marked the first year of her daughter Cholpon's life by having a *tushoo kesuu toi*—a ritual celebration that prepares the way for the infant's growth into a successful life and also reaffirms social obligations within the community.[18] The more people invited and the more extravagant the ceremony, the more prestige accrues to the family. When asked about its importance, people express a belief that it is essential if the parents want their child to grow up to be rich and prosperous.

As with all rituals, the details vary, but the basic events are as follows. The paternal grandmother, who is considered the most important figure of the family, takes two tufts of fleece, one white and one black. With the white representing good and the black symbolizing evil, there is almost a Manichean dichotomy inherent in the process. She twists the white wool toward herself—bringing the goodness in—until it becomes a strand; she twists the black wool away from herself—sending the evil away from the body and setting the precedent for good to come and evil to depart. Taking the strand, and sometimes with the paternal grandfather, she ties it around Cholpon's legs. A prayer is recited that begins with the *Basmala*: "*Bismillah ir-Rahman ir-Rahim . . .*"[19] While some consider this phrase to encompass the meaning of

FIGURE 4.7. Two elderly women preparing a young boy for a *tushoo kesuu toi* by tying a rope around his legs, 2006.

the Qur'an, there is in general no reading from the Qur'an at a tushoo kesuu. The paternal grandfather holds a knife as family members support the infant, who is surrounded by family members, neighbors, and fellow villagers.

The strand is to be cut to encourage the forces of the future to aid Cholpon in walking rightly in life. But unlike so much of the established order of Kyrgyz society, neither age nor kin relations designate who cuts it. Rather, the person is chosen through competing in running races. The first of three races is between the young boys present. From a short distance away from Cholpon, the boys run toward her, and the first to reach her is given the honor of cutting the strand. The winner then takes Cholpon's hand and helps her walk a short distance. The fastest boy is also given a gift that may be as valuable as a sheep or even a horse, depending on the wealth of the family hosting the tushoo kesuu (Asel's family gave a sheep). The event is repeated after retying the strand; this time the young girls race to the infant. Again, the fastest cuts the strand, helps Cholpon walk, and is rewarded with a prize similar to that given the boy who won the first race. A third time, the process of strand tying, racing, and strand cutting is repeated. This time, the older, more respected members of the community race to guide Cholpon in her first steps. At the conclusion, everyone joins in wishing Cholpon a safe path for the future—*ak-jol*—and a blessing is given publicly before the gathering turns into a party.[20]

The ritual is filled with symbolism and an array of roles and purposes for all involved. The requirements are negotiated—who is present and how many, who substitutes for key figures unable to attend, and what minimum components have to be done for it to be successful. The meanings are also negotiated: is it a religious ritual, a traditional ritual, or a hybrid? There is consensus that the ritual is an obligation of the Kyrgyz for the future of their children, and even many of those who discount it as superstition believe that the rite should be undertaken if for no other reason than to serve as an extension and continuation of the past.

Meanings, however, are an entirely different matter. For some, the ritual marks the infant's transition to childhood, explained by saying that during nomadic times, when the death rate was high, a baby was not considered a "real" child, but rather a guest of the family, until it was one year old. At the moment of cutting the strand, the baby becomes a real person. For others, there is no explanation and none is needed. It is just how it is.

—⁂—

The ability to make something symbolic and meaningful is critical to the essence of being human. As discussed earlier, discursive language functions as an important way to encode the world with meaning. The words we use to remember help shape memory itself. But there is more to the development of memory, meaning, and knowledge than words. The very essence of engagement in the lived world involves movement that is characterized by conscious and subconscious action. This key aspect of knowledge acquisition and transmission must be recognized: what we do informs us about our world both in the very act of doing and in the act of interpreting. Action informs or guides meaning, and that meaning in turn informs or guides action. In other words, knowledge is acquired and transmitted through the act of doing and interpreting *and* the doing and the interpreting inform each other. Thus, ritual becomes a form of knowledge and a form of action. Any ritual is more than just action. It may, and often does, employ words. But it is always more than just words and is generally connected to something beyond the event itself. As with knowledge, ritual fits within a social organization (Asel refers to tushoo kesuu as a Kyrgyz obligation), a corpus (it is for the future of Cholpon), and a medium of transmission (it is part oral, part direct participation, and part indirect observation).

Ritual, of course, is not the only form of action that informs us about the world since every form of action has that capacity. Nonritualized mediums of action are a constant characteristic of the everyday. But having set out in earlier chapters an approach to seeing knowledge as constituting a social organization, a corpus, and a medium, it is important here to draw attention to the intersection of ritual, praxis, and learning.

The relationship between knowledge and action is intimate, and perhaps the soul of understanding resides there. In tushoo kesuu, people gather around a child and engage in a series of actions that connect the present to the past and create a future that is manageable. The act of doing it once creates an awareness of what must be done in subsequent enactments and provides an explanation for how to manage meaning. Ritual, and praxis in general, is knowledge as action, not merely as theory. Even when someone does not understand a conversation or interaction, the sensibility with which it is presented can suggest that a meaning is made out of it, even without the language to follow or internalize the meaning conveyed.

Focusing on the relationship of action to knowledge, my concern is broad in application, looking not only at ritual and ritualized mediums but also at nonritualized mediums of knowledge acquisition. I begin, however, by looking at ritual, which has been an often-overlooked, or at least discounted, medium for its contributions to people's ability to navigate the world. Though exceptional and extraordinary rituals do certainly exist, the majority of our ritualized acts are more mundane, though no less significant in a social organizational sense. Further, my concern with ritual is not so much as a series of events that give meaning, but more broadly as a component of a life filled with meaning, and as an aspect of life that helps that meaning to be lived with all the challenges of indifference, ambivalence, and ambiguity of meaning. I am less interested in what ritual means but more broadly interested in what it does and how it goes about contributing a space of knowing and understanding in the world—how ritual is an active medium within a particular social setting.[21]

Focusing on what ritual does means examining it as a generator both of a form of knowledge and of action. It includes a concern with the significant and infrequently performed life rituals such as tushoo kesuu; with ritual-related tensions, for example, over variations in weddings and funerals; and with everyday rituals that convey a sense of connection within the community and provide a deep understanding of the roles and responsibilities of one living within a particular community. These everyday rituals include the drawn-out obligations of daily greetings as well as gestures of respect that are directed toward people and places, such as the *omen* brushing of two hands over the face when one finishes dinner or passes a cemetery. Of course, there is a difference between a formal ritual—civic or religious—and that which is merely ritualized, though here I do not make much of the distinction other than to note that while the ritualized is at times thought to be somehow less imbued with meaning, it is a medium for the transmission of knowledge, along with formal ritual.

One aspect of ritual (which also applies to the ritualized to a large extent) that is foundational to the creation of knowledge is its ordering aspect. Accepted ordering communicates a statement of authoritativeness and, as discussed earlier, authority plays a crucial role in legitimacy. In the case of tushoo kesuu, which has a clear ordering, the paternal grandparents play the most respected and perhaps most significant role in determining Cholpon's future. They play this role in an environment in which they are surrounded by the community and which engages the youth as active participants in Cholpon's life. There is also an ordering aspect of the ritual itself that is presented with a regularity and inflexibility that conveys a sense of the order of ritual that should be continued in subsequent generations. Such ordering aspects exist in acts ranging from *wudu*[22] and the reconciliatory preparations before hajj, to prolonged greetings and the pouring of tea as signs of respect.

The relationship between ritual and acceptance is interesting and precarious. When necessary, people can interpret what is being done. For example, Bakyt could provide a rational explanation for the tushoo kesuu; he explained that it as an extension of tradition from a time characterized by the fragility of infant life when people viewed life as beginning at the age of one and chose to mark that milestone by a community ritual. There is not a consensus in this rationale, however, as some are quick to dismiss Bakyt's rational explanation. People often perform rituals assuming consensus, but conflicts may arise at the point of discussing meanings. If they must explain their actions, people know how to interpret what is being done or at least offer two rationalizations: one that they present as plausible and the other that they categorically present as given—"this is just how it is"—to end the discussion. In a sense then, ritual both creates consensus in the collective process of performing and also gives a false sense of consensus. When Iqbol and Kubat perform namaz, it can seem that they share a consensus about meaning, but in discussing it with them, it becomes clear that the situation is very different.

What is interesting, however, is not so much the divisive aspect of discussing meaning, but rather the speed and ease with which ritual order and ordering become assumed and supported. On one level, the world's ordering is arbitrary. But very early on, stories of creation produce narrative frameworks for ordering society. And rituals reinforce this order. It takes only minimal observation of tushoo kesuu by an outsider, for example, to not only join others in accepting the proper progression of events, but to recognize when there are certain deviations from that progression. The ritual creates and reflects the assumption that a particular order is normative, that it is as it should be, and that while deviations may be possible, they are less effective to the future of the child (Cholpon), the success of a prayer (Toliq), or the calling of ancestors (Mairam). And that is an argument of meaning. So the medium of ritual as action becomes intimately embedded in a relationship of social organization and corpus of knowledge. People *know* what to do, and this exists in relation to how they see the world—their social structure and order.

Observing everything that people do enters into a corpus and social organization of knowledge at varying levels of consciousness. Observation and participation present meaning, action, and the ritualized as a medium of knowledge transmission that can be seen in almost every aspect of religion, civility, and social existence in general. On the streets of Osh, for example, Toliq and Muktar greet each other and fellow taxi drivers with a handshake, hand to the chest, and a series of questions inquiring about the well-being of the other; Ismoiljon is seen closing up his shop and going to the mosque for juma namaz; and Tolkun, with her prayer beads, herbs, and borsok, can be seen preparing to visit a mazar. These acts can be private or public, observed at home or noted by onlookers on the streets. They are unsensational, ever-present, and yet quite informative.

Repetition and Variance

Ritual not only allows a way to accommodate the ambivalence and brokenness of the world (Seligman et al. 2008, viii), but it is also, at a very fundamental level, a way of knowing. While rituals exist in all aspects of life—including civility, religion, politics, and nation—people's approach to and understanding of ritual, influences behavior. Moreover, how people view ritual is a way of getting to how people understand the common world. As a medium of knowledge transmission, ritual also is part of a social organization and corpus that creates and transcends boundaries, normalizes social behavior, and transmits a sense of collectivity over time and space. Much of life, but of course not all of it, is ritualized. It is worth drawing attention to the richness of the ritual experience because it sheds light on the breadth of the learning project that constitutes so much of the everyday. And as with so much of active life, ritual is not isolated—discovery and habitual learning spread from one realm to another with creative richness.

Some of the best potters in Central Asia live and work in the Ferghana Valley. To become a master potter and painter involves years of apprenticeship. As artists, they express creativity and imagination in the work they produce, and often this is a combination of continued tradition nuanced by a contemporary interpretation. But to learn the craft involves hours of repetition and basic acts that are the components of art and skill, though as isolated acts they are seemingly mundane and uninspired.[23] For the potter, it involves countless hours throwing clay until molding a plate or cup becomes second nature. For the apprentice pottery painter, it is years of copying established patterns under the supervision of a master painter.

Befriending some of these pottery painters, I observed hours of mimicry and repetitive action designed to teach proper technique. Young students who wanted to become master painters, or whose parents wanted them to learn and thus sent them to the studio of the master painter, practiced the same brushstrokes over and over. Young music students do the same, as do children in the madrassas. Some of the students, of course, become more artistically skilled than others and gradually, after learning the fundamental techniques of the craft, they develop individual styles and expressions.

The basic pattern of painting is of geometrical designs; one master painter said it took him ten years of constant repetition before he reached the level of master and possessed the expertise to reproduce the geometrical designs in a style he made his own. Even within the accepted norm of geometrical designs, an artist develops his own style. Life is very similar to learning pottery. Much of it is mimetic, with creative interpretations that result in the development of a particular style and sense of self (see Auerbach 2003).

FIGURE 4.8. A master pottery painter and teacher at his workshop, 2005.

Interestingly, a few of the young students in this particular studio began to bring Arabic script and words from the Qur'an into their art. The master said that it was a new trend and that he himself could not read Arabic. Of course, he said, he could copy the letters and reproduce the ornate script with a mastery greater than that of the students, but it was not his style and, as a self-declared nonpracticing Muslim, it had no meaning to him. He, as well as the students themselves, explained it by saying that the introduction of Allah, the basmala, and short suras into the student's paintings was influenced by the student's rote memorization in the madrassa (similar to the rote learning of their craft), where they sat before a text they did not necessarily understand but the recognition of the letters and associated sounds found their way into the student's work. The creative is an attempt to extend and express the self and for the students, the mimetic learning of one field found an outlet in art, as it often finds an outlet in life (see Hirsch 2002; Wuthnow 2001).

That the students felt proud and progressive in differentiating themselves from their fellow students and their master teacher is but one example of how the learning from one part of life melds into another that, for practical purposes, could be unrelated. The pervasiveness of all action, however, has extensive implications for the continued transmission of knowledge; while there is creativity in some levels of the artistic expression, the basics gained through the mimetic learning is foundational and difficult to unlearn.

FIGURE 4.9. Women working together to finish a shyrdok, 2001.

Mountains and Valleys

The students who have started to incorporate Arabic script into their paintings do so for ornament purposes, but also because of their study of the text. (Contrast this with *shyrdok* [felt carpet] artisans in the mountains whose symbolism is always connected to nature; they do not generally welcome the idea of incorporating text.) In this case, it is a sacred text that carries with it, especially to those who cannot read it, an aura of otherworldly and almost magical authority. It may seem to be a pedestrian example, but the master painter will not tell the students to avoid Arabic script (though he does suggest to students that the traditional style of geometric designs rarely includes religious reference) because the implications for doing so could reach back to the students' religious teachers. And the religious teachers argue that the authority of everything Qur'anic lies outside worldly endeavors. For the master painter, it is just something that he allows, focusing more on the technical aspects of art and, once that is developed, encouraging the students to find their artistic voice.

The relevance of the text to the discussion of ritual and learning brings us back to earlier discussions of locating authority and allowing variance and ambiguity. In places where there is an emphasis on the oral, there is not the same focus on the storage of knowledge in the text as there is among those who privilege the written word. An emphasis on orality allows, and requires, less exactness in the storage of information and the continued reproduction of rituals (see Goody 2000; Ong 1982). Though we generally focus on memory, it is also the case that forgetfulness and the limitations of memory can characterize the variation of ritual and what is taken from it. The process of writing tends to reduce variation (Goody 2000, 54), and without the ability to refer back to the text, the generative aspect of language becomes more focused around the performative of rituals and storytelling.

The written word tries to manage and control variance. In Kyrgyzstan we see an influx of books from Turkey, Tatarstan, Iran, Pakistan, and Saudi Arabia teaching people how to pray and understand Islam. All the books push a normative interpretation that is not seen as an interpretation but rather as truth with authority resting in the written word. Writing helps to not only foster orthodoxy but to standardize the very notion of orthodoxy as it relates to truth and identity (Goody 2000, 55–61). Thus, we see that one aspect of variation that can be found between the mountains and valleys is around the text and different ways of acquiring knowledge, the variance in ritualized and nonritualized learning.

The push of groups like Hizb ut-Tahrir and Tablighi Jama'at is heavily centered on the purification of society where all answers can be found in a text. It is mimesis and study that aims to standardize behavior and bring change. And when the books are brought into the mountains by missionaries claiming that the mountain understanding of Islam is incorrect, those who reorient themselves to truth-claims in text bring a different understanding to tradition. This is the essence of Aibek's complaints about the new mosque in town, and this is Iqbol's job.

In the end, however, we do not escape rituals. They do what text and literacy cannot. Tushoo kesuu and other rituals convey the panoply of what it means to be part of a community. Likewise, basmala, salat and even the protocols of salutations contribute to the development of knowledge and the self. Knowledge as held in its social organization, corpus, and medium makes us aware of our potential to act and our limits to act. And always aware of this, we navigate ourselves socially, addressing the basics of existence and searching for meaning (this-worldly and otherworldly) in an ever-changing world.

Chapter 5

Framing Politics, Morality, and a Practice of Understanding

Demand for the solution of a perplexity is the steadying and guiding factor in the entire process of reflection.

John Dewey, *How We Think*

Moral neutrality, here as always, is no guarantee of political innocence.

Talal Asad, "The Idea of an Anthropology of Islam"

For all of my interlocutors, meaning is created in a lived space that leads them to make distinctions about *knowing* the world, of having a worldview that guides them in interacting with the world. But despite the widespread use of the idea, "knowledge" is not a straightforward concept of study; it is an abstract, fluid, and real concept that is used to many ends, not the least of which is negotiating a relationship with the communal and the everyday. Examining the social organization, corpus, and medium of knowledge allows us to get some purchase on a concept so integral to our existence, and to begin making sense of how we socially navigate the world.

The significance of this is real and highlights one of the most relevant contributions anthropological engagement can make: observing the nuances of life construction is not merely an academic exercise but rather part of the project of social engagement in which all should see themselves as part. What we think about the Other influences our actions, so it is not a passive, purely intellectual relationship in which we find ourselves engaged.

While thus far the focus has been on an anthropology of knowledge as a tool to understand life in Kyrgyzstan and its surroundings, it would be wrong to suggest that the process of understanding stops there. Understanding public and private is a political and moral project influenced by, for example, how Islam is "known" and experienced—contextualized both morally and politically—in discussions of the role Islam should play locally, nationally, and transnationally. But even if passive, we are not neutral observers; how politics and morality get framed influences the anthropology of knowledge of all of my interlocutors. Thus, it is imperative to also recognize the agendas that the observer brings to the observed. We may assume all are well intentioned, but one who studies Islam with a policy agenda may understand what is observed differently from the ethnographer, while the ethnographer often fails to appreciate the real constraints in knowing a community under which the policy frame often is restricted. Both of these external frames of understanding influence the way religion is socially navigated.[1]

—⁘—

At 5:52 on a cold morning in January, *azan* (call to prayer) can be heard crackling from a single speaker wired to a deteriorating concrete electric post in southern Kyrgyzstan. Kadirbek has prepared himself for *fajr* (morning prayer); Nurdeen is milking the family cow before marking the anniversary of his brother's death with a pilgrimage to a nearby shrine; and Kuban does not have to be at work until 8:30 and is still asleep. All three men are Kyrgyz. All three are Muslim. And all three consider themselves ordinary. They also represent ideal types that shape policy, confuse public (national and international) discourse, and make real the problem wherein descriptive labels hold captive assumed threats.

Acknowledging Central Asians as Muslim is so much a practice of common parlance that noun comfortably becomes adjective: *Muslim* Central Asia.[2] But as already argued, this is not as informative as some unfamiliar with the region are inclined to believe. In moving from describing the region to categorizing the people, the interchange of noun and adjective—Central Asian *Muslim*—carries a range of assumptive meanings and potentialities. The disagreements begin with what it means to be Muslim and to whom; or to borrow the language of the playground, what it means to be "a *real* Muslim." The moral dichotomy of *good* Muslim—*bad* Muslim, while certainly imprecise, becomes the way most categorize the differences and argue their particular position on any number of disagreements.[3] Such dichotomization of *otherness* is not unique to Kyrgyzstan, Central Asia, or even Islam, but can be found in any community. Saudi Muslims; Israeli Jews; American Evangelical Christians: all are labels where characteristic is ascribed, and thus described, by place. And in these instances—where religion is noun and place is adjective—there is a stereotyping that melds the imagined with the political (see Anderson 1991). What is more, this imagined familiarity leads us to act *as if* we have a certain predicative capacity to capture, in a few words, the essential nature of a population.[4] And much of this is political. Unfortunately, the essentialized nature of a population is largely conformed by the needs of political efficiency and only partially informed by ethnographic engagement.

In fairness, ethnographers attempt the same thing, but with more words over more time. Far too infrequently, there is little attention given to the strictures of the policy frame, assuming those who view Islam with the agenda of policy to be unconcerned with the conditions of local life as it is being lived. Of interest here, however, are the implications of the different frames through which a population is viewed. The policy frame and the ethnographic frame present two very different visions of the population. While ethnographic engagement is also filled with its own subjectivities—the observer is never completely objective (see Rabinow 2007)—more time with a population reveals more complexities, and complexity does not breed efficient policy. In the case of Muslim Central Asia the narrative of the policy frame is a story of threat and danger; the narrative of the ethnographic frame is of diversity and disunity temporally navigated. Both are correct from their own view, yet in failing to engage each other in recognizing the impacts they have on each other, both overlook the roughness of the ground upon which they walk.[5]

A series of "recent" events have contributed to the sense of urgency about religion, though in most situations, discussions of "recent" events do not age well because the contemporary is filled with unfolding uncertainties that are interpreted and reinterpreted in response to what information becomes available. These "recent" events stretch back as far as one wants to look—indeed, history is always interpreted in relation to the transformative wake of "recent" events—but the factors noted to have influenced the Kyrgyz landscape in the past twenty-plus years include: easing of Soviet regulations, independence, the 1999 incursions by the Islamic Movement of Uzbekistan (IMU), the Aksy riots, the 2005 putsch, and the 2010 putsch and subsequent ethnic violence (see Lewis 2008). The local experience of these events has shifted from freedom and optimism, to fear, dissatisfaction, anger, and helplessness; all in response to new forms of corruption, uncertainties, poverty, unfulfilled aspirations, and insecure futures that are part of the everyday challenges people experience.

The common presentation of Islam in the West is one of threat and danger.[6] Steps may be taken to distance violence from the "essence of Islam," which presents an explanatory out but is often not taken to heart: we know not all Muslims embrace violence, just the ones that are talked about, but the seemingly public absence of Muslims voicing opposition comes to imply that Muslims actually embrace violence or counterhegemonic acts. Of course this is not true (see Kurzman 2011; Martin and Barzegar 2010), but the message still dominates the imagination of the Western press and policy world, which connects (conflates) various events in the region—the perception of increasing piety with the end of the Soviet Union; the 1992–1997 civil war in Tajikistan; the IMU's armed incursions in 1999 and 2000; the Taliban and al-Qaeda's activities in Afghanistan and the military campaign against those groups after 11 September; the crackdown on Islam and the 2005 Andijan killings in Uzbekistan; and the overthrow of two governments in Kyrgyzstan (2005 and 2010)—as interrelated indicators of the threat Islam poses to political stability. The events that attract media attention, however, generally lie outside of—though do impact—the everyday religious world in which the majority of Muslims in Central Asia reside.

The nature of events leads to the prediction of stereotypes, and depending on the situation—more so with Islam, for example, than with health care—the outliers of society receive disproportionate attention. The policy frame is more concerned with the few Muslims labeled as "threats" than it is by the majority of the population because the extremes make better stories and are the concerns that policies seek to change. By policy frame, I do not mean just that of policymakers working for governments, but rather a particular orientation that includes journalists, policy makers, development workers, and others whose constraints are those of time and action; that is, they have to act and, in order to do so, generalize from the constraints of their own biases and the demands under which they work. The constraints of needing to act can lead to fetishization of the extremes, catchier news stories, and an added sense of urgency to what we, as policy makers or ethnographers, do, but it misses the everyday life of the majority of the population (de Certeau 1984). The middle ground of a population—the average, seemingly unremarkable populace concerned more with the daily obligations and burdens of their own lives than with devoted political engagement—is commonly underrepresented.[7] This is not to suggest that Muktar and Toliq do not talk about these things with their clients in their taxis, or that Baktagul and Ismoiljon do not talk about it with their clients in the bazaar, for they do. But they contextualize it differently than outsiders who in focusing on the outliers—the subjects of news stories and policy fears—direct policies that affect everyone in disproportionate ways.

Frames are perspectives, and when we understand the policy frame as a perspective concerned with action—where the person engaged has a particular end goal related to some implementation of reform or change—we can make a distinction between the need to generalize in order to act and the importance of the particularities that emerge from the ethnographic frame. The ethnographic frame is a way of viewing concerned with characterizing both how people think and how they understand the cultural distinctiveness of experience in a local context. These frames represent not merely different ways of presentation, but also both methodological and epistemological preferences that are more biased than neutral. People switch perspectives, of course, between "policy" and "ethnographic" ways of looking at problems in relation to their need to act and their ability to listen and reflect, but each perspective can be limiting if the conditions under which such decisions are made are not taken into consideration.[8]

In certain instances we use labels as shorthand for when we know less than we acknowledge or we encounter the limits of language or time to describe. Labels lead us to believe we have predictive capacity to capture the mood and movement of people. "Muslim," "radical," "extremist" all send the hearer of those terms on a trajectory of assumptions that are often more political than accurate. The capital of such terms is greatest vis-à-vis the needs of the state, where an inverse bias toward the group in question holds hostage the freedom of the majority middle.

Sketching Islam within a policy frame and an ethnographic frame creates images of contrast, and in the case of Kyrgyzstan, it is different enough to make one believe we are talking about two different places. We are, at least, talking about two very different ways of seeing and, subsequently, of acting.

The underlying assumption in both is that the relationship between labels is descriptive enough to guide action. They are, of course, sufficient for action but not necessarily sufficient in capturing the nebulous category of truth or reality. Curiously, both labels and theories tend to fall short precisely in relation to the assumed stability of populations and their actions. In merging perspectives of the policy frame—a pragmatic, sometimes occluded, view of the world set on securing collective self-interests (national, collectivist in macro engagement)—and the ethnographic frame—a locally engaged, oftentimes affective, view of the world set on preserving relations perceived as intimate and everyday (friendships, individualist in micro engagement)—we gain a messier yet more informed understanding of people and how they see themselves (and we see ourselves) in the world.

The understanding of religion in Kyrgyzstan, as well as anywhere else, is richer (though descriptively more cumbersome) if approached through a theory that acknowledges the friction that animates sociality, the terrain where people act and are acted upon, where, as Marx recognized, people make their own histories but not independently.[9] The policy frame has an agenda that affects the ethnographic frame, reifying certain categories founded upon sometimes fallacious understandings,[10] yet in certain instances the assumptions of the policy frame get reified through their public insistence. The "terrorist threat" that "extremist" and "radical" imply within the policy frame is grounded in the understanding of outsider objectives, not insider or local realities that may view the extremist/radical not as pariah but as humanitarian.[11] Capturing the insider, or "local," realities is often the stated concern of the ethnographic frame. Yet despite its noble sense of purpose, in its analysis the ethnographic frame all too often fails to synthesize the influence of the policy frame.[12] Both frames present a picture of community that holds utility in the generalized sense of their concern, but the impact of the frames on the community is seldom connected.

How we see them and how they see us are not two separate pictures but rather reliefs of a picture analyzed differently. The hues of the policy frame differ from those of the ethnographic frame because the light in which it is viewed differs, and therein what meaning is ascribed to the picture comes to differ. Merging these frames, a task filled with friction and roughness, casts new light on the subject of understanding the local, on our own engagement with and *knowing* of the subject. Recognizing that the biases in the policy and ethnographic frames—which constitute part of our own biography, our own anthropology of knowledge—influence our understanding of the situation, pushes us toward greater epistemological humility, and better explores the middle ground, the area where most people live and where people are impacted by how they frame their lives and have their lives framed by others.

Though it is through experience that we make sense of the world,[13] we too often assume the stability of the categories and groupings we make, and the theories we use to describe them. Neither categories nor groupings—or more pointedly, neither knowledge nor identity—are unchanging, despite being presented within a particular frame as being set (see Bourdieu 2000; Jackson 2007, 174–91). There is both subjectivity and intersubjectivity in described experience—the policy and ethnographic frames—as well as in lived experience—the socially navigated modus vivendi that contextualizes the everyday. As Jackson notes, "we are so used to construing understanding as a meeting of two minds, an intellectual empathy or compatibility between separate selves, that we often overlook the extent to which human affinities reflect forms of mutual recognition that are difficult to put into words or pin down" (Jackson 2007, 184). Similar shortsightedness obscures the view of groups, who articulate understanding in relationship to the compatibility of goals and agendas. The convergence of the policy and ethnographic frames is an overlapping of understandings, a reciprocity of agendas, and a step toward making sense of the socially navigated context of the everyday. This is not only a move toward understanding the lived dynamics of the local, but it is also a move toward theorizing the dynamics of influence and change.

The Policy Frame

Actions ascribed in response to characterizations of prejudices and interests, and messy boundaries are made less messy by delimiting the parameters of concern. Conceptually, the policy frame is not limited to state or group actors for individuals make use of it in dealing with those seen as Other and it serves as a way of reifying the connectedness of individuals to a larger collective to which they identify. In the case of policy vis-à-vis Muslim Central Asia, emphasizing the fear associated with particular characterizations of the population—the "increasingly Muslim" part of Central Asia—pushes policies along a reactionary path (Montgomery and Heathershaw 2016; Heathershaw and Montgomery 2014.)

Religious labels are filled with countless assumptions, many—if not most—of which oversimplify the complex realities of how religion is experienced and managed. This is not to say that religion is necessarily experienced as complicated or burdensome, for it is not, but rather that we are quick to assign generalizable meaning to a label in order to manage the time we must spend reacting to it. This is, of course, the importance of categorization, for it allows us to assume similarities and apply casuistic reasoning to actions. But the similarities *we* assume are not always the same terms of analysis *they* assume (*we* and *they* being ever-fluid groupings), especially in discussing danger.[14] What is dangerous to one for whom religion is a lived category is dissimilar for another who views religion differently.[15]

Religion is, of course, complex and multivocal, experienced and understood by individuals vis-à-vis the communities in which they live. This refers back to the stereotypes mentioned earlier—Saudi Muslims, Israeli Jews, American Evangelical Christians—and depends largely on how the setting is framed. All these terms set in motion a particular trajectory of understanding (such as Kanibek prejudicing the Baptists) that in turn influences the perceived potentialities of the population. In the crudest sense, the policy frame imagines Kyrgyzstan as a place of dramatic natural beauty yet in desperate need of political and social reform and a generally unpleasant place to live. There are Kyrgyz like Begaim who agree—in part because she imagines life being better elsewhere—but such descriptions only get to how some people imagine their lives. For all who live there, it is, of course, not a remote place, or a place on the periphery, but rather the center of the world. Some are unconcerned with reform, being indifferent or resigned that nothing meaningful will significantly change, but the correlation between wealth and happiness is always specious. By many standards, it is poor, but there is happiness in neighborhoods and family gatherings and people are not everywhere despondent (Montgomery 2013b). (It is important to note this, as it is something one sees in the ethnographic frame that is all too often left out of the policy frame: this is also a place where people can be happy.)

Media representations of the country, however, rarely depict the happiness people find in their lives but rather focus on despondency, urgency, unsettledness, harshness, and injustice (as viewed from the outside.) Connections to Islam are made in sensational ways—emphasizing the threat of Islam or categorical indifference to religion—not the complex, evolving, socially navigated reality of religion that responds to events, environment, and relationships of influence. The policy frame sees three general ways of categorizing Islam—threat, tradition, or modern—and reacts according to these conceptions.

Muslim as Threat

Kadirbek begins his day with prayer, and for many this rouses suspicion. The image he personifies leads those engaged in shaping the policy frame to expend a great deal of energy and resources; Kadirbek is understood as a threat not simply because he prays regularly, but because he is outspoken about the role Islam should play in governance, wants change, *and* prays regularly. To Western policy makers and even the titular governments of Central Asia, those like Kadirbek represent a threat to the maintenance of hegemonic order. One can say very little about Kadirbek, his family, friends, beliefs, or desires, but knowing more is not part of the policy frame; one needs to categorize and step away in order to act. Knowing more about him at this point emasculates the image he is assumed to represent. It is enough to note that he was arrested once for possessing "Islamist" literature and associating with an Islamist group banned by the Kyrgyz government. Kadirbek (along with Baktyor) is a member of Hizb ut-Tahrir, a characterization that is enough to satisfy the policy frame disposition for it is contextualized in terms of what is generalized about Hizb ut-Tahrir as an organization and the threat it represents is inserted within the assumptions about the region.

The assumptions are constituted by an array of quasi-facts that support an image of threat. The precedent of history emerges in discussion of the Great

Game that since the eighteenth century located Central Asia within the greater colonial power conflicts and fixed the region in Western imagination as a place of mystery and notable danger (Hopkirk 1992; Levi and Sela 2010; Meyer and Brysac 1999; Yapp 2001). The proximity to Afghanistan, essential to the Great Game narrative and the "war on terror," heightens the anxiety created by Kadirbek's involvement in Hizb ut-Tahrir, as the organization gets collapsed into jihadist movements like the Taliban or the IMU. Organizations like the IMU (which is of questionable strength and uncertain numbers[16]) that advocates Islamic governance as alternative to current corruptions of governance have a message that resonates with the concerns Kadirbek articulates, with one significant exception: Kadirbek eschews violence. The IMU's 1999 and 2000 forays into the region and the use of force to instigate change created a policy of fearing their return, as well as expansion of their activities to similarly disaffected ideological groups. Thus, despite Hizb ut-Tahrir's insistence on pursuing nonviolent means to the restoration of a caliphate, Kadirbek gets collapsed as analytically identical to jihadist movements from more distant lands. Furthermore, the dissatisfaction with governance that resulted in the 2005 and 2010 overthrows in Kyrgyzstan unsettles officials who hear Kadirbek, along with Iqbol, offering Islam as a model for addressing issues of bad governance. Thus, unlinked and uncontextualized pieces of information—from the historical conflict between tsarist Russia and colonial Britain to the rise of the Taliban and jihadist movements in the region—suggest threats from one place as impending threats to a different locale.

Threats, especially when speculative, are analogized to make them impending and relevant. The assemblage of information comes from a variety of sources that are neither standardized nor objectively reported; while there are some very good reporters in the region willing to challenge perceived injustices,[17] many are aware of who pays them and the stories their editors presume the public wants to read. In the field, there were many instances when I talked with reporters for major Western newspapers and human rights reporting organizations and found the agendas of their publisher forcing a story that distorted reality. This is not to claim that bad things do not happen in Central Asia, that there are not egregious abuses of human rights, or that Muslim groups are unwilling to resort to violence against the state. There are countless draconian abuses of rights and the freedom of religious practice and expression is increasingly regulated by state functionaries, but many reporters have confessed to searching for angles to stories they knew were misleading but were more likely to get their articles picked up and read.[18]

An ongoing reading of news sources presents a very similar image.[19] Often, however, the media sources find legitimacy in citing other news outlets and print takes on meaning more distant from truth than it purports to report. With enough frequency, the report takes on, in image, a "truth" of its own that fits hegemonic agendas, guides assumptive categorization of groups, and forms policy initiatives. This makes Kadirbek—husband, father of three, and active Muslim—representative of a potential threat to the state. Kadirbek believes that the state should institutionalize a Muslim moral framework precedented by Muhammad and the Rightly Guided Caliphs. The state sees such calls to integrate religious order—at least on terms other than their own—as counterhegemonic and threatening. Kadirbek renounces violence and complains at length that those who take up arms against the state are wrong, at least in his understanding of Islam and moral advancement. The state and media disbelieve the nuanced understanding of social change Kadirbek aspires to and while through serious reflection—and time spent with Kadirbek and his friends—we know the image is a pale reflection of reality *in situ*, the stereotype of "terrorist threat" is advanced as a plausible description of something that drives the machine. The image of Muslim as threat, militant, and terrorist becomes representative for all that can be seen as challenging, and makes Kadirbek "known" without being *known*, setting aside the point that the degree of Kadirbek's involvement with Hizb ut-Tahrir is unknown to most.

Kadirbek's association with a transnational Islamic movement, which is a representatively small portion of the population, disproportionately influences policy concerns. In a sense, he is seen as being at one extreme of the spectrum where orthopraxic devotion assumptively leads to orthodox inflexibility and public exposition of moral correctness. Characterized by some as a "good" Muslim, by others he is seen as practicing an imported version of Islam that in its expansion undermines local traditions of Islamic practice. Terms like "good" and "bad" are value labels that frame the debate in moral terms, against which threat is assumed. But what is threatening to Kadirbek differs from what is threatening to the state.

Muslim as Tradition

History's experience suggests that tradition includes variance in what it means to practice Islam. Religious traditions have great local variance expressed morally in orthodox and heterodox labeling—the contrast of Tolkun and Azarmat attest to that. In the Kyrgyz setting, orthodox Islam is mosque- and text-centered and has dominance in determining the other extreme of heterodoxy; heterodoxy is rarely a label of self-description. Another edge of Islamic practice is displayed by Nurdeen, Kadirebek's neighbor. Nurdeen identifies as Muslim but, like Tolkun, Dimira, and Aibek, roots his sense of belonging deep within Kyrgyz tradition. He does not question his Muslimness but views the obligations of a religious life differently from Kadirbek, viewing reverence for ancestors and sacred places not merely as tradition but within a cosmological frame that makes the past relevant without historical discontinuity.

It has been the case that Muslims like Nurdeen have not been politically involved, or at least not through an institutional form of Islam that challenges state leadership. Nurdeen's vision of Islam is not taken seriously by Muslims like Kadirbek, who see its syncretic aspects as heretical and view tradition to be separate from religion when it veers from the interpretation of a "universal" Islam. Whatever we call the merging of tradition, ancestral precedence, and Islamic understanding—"folk Islam," "Islamic Shamanism," "pre-Islamic Islam"—the labels are usually pejorative from a religious view yet, to the extent they remain private, are encouraged in state policy. Islamic reformers—from Indian missionary groups like Tablighi Jama'at and Turkish followers of Fethullah Gülen to transnational organizations like Hizb ut-Tahrir and returning nationals who have studied Islam abroad in places like Egypt and Saudi Arabia—want to (re)educate Central Asians on what Islam is, and thus should be (Balci 2003; Masud 2000).

The knowledge of Islam in Central Asia is considered to be weak, in large part because of the Soviet Union's success in regulating Islamic learning (Khalid 2007). But the role of Islam in the public has been growing since Kyrgyzstan became independent in 1991 and people feel more open to practicing and expressing their Muslimness. Yet discussions of Muslimness connecting back to reclaiming tradition has led some to consider what it means to be a Central Asian Muslim in general and a Kyrgyz Muslim in particular, to recognize that the drivers of what Islam should be do not have to come from outside (abroad) but rather from revitalizing the ways of the past. To an extent, this fits within postindependence language policies that mandated more extensive teaching of the Kyrgyz language (over Russian) in public schools and even as a political requirement for presidential office.[20] But it also became part of sculpting a new post-Soviet Kyrgyz identity.

There have been a few instances where this Kyrgyz identity has turned toward tradition to give historical continuity to the distinctness of being Kyrgyz as part of a moral and legitimate nation. As mentioned earlier, during the late-middle years of the Akayev presidency, alongside the renewed emphasis of teaching Kyrgyz, children were taught the Seven Principles of Manas to create sentiments of morality shared in a common heroic tradition.[21] As well, Tengrism emerged as a revitalization of Kyrgyz religious tradition as intimately rooted to the territory of Kyrgyzstan and the ancestors who inhabited it. Having origins in pre-Islamic Kyrgyz cosmology of venerating the sky god, Tengri, it was reformulated by Omuraly uulu and Saraykulov.[22] While few label themselves as Tengrists, and some see it as heretically pagan and un-Islamic, those who identify with it, like Aibek, generally find it completely compatible with Islam, seeing it as the Islam practiced by their ancestors before the arrival of Islam. It thus becomes a more legitimate local expression of religion. And while Nurdeen does not call himself a Tengrist—he is unfamiliar with the movement though familiar with the implications of the word Tengri—the practices of Tengrists are ones he practices.[23]

Reformist movements like Tablighi Jama'at and Hizb ut-Tahrir find the practices of visiting mazars and venerating ancestors problematic. The increased attention to sacred sites creates tension with these groups who take on the eradication of these practices as part of their reeducation purpose. The local understanding of Central Asian Islam, while generally labeled as

FIGURE 5.1. A man praying near a mazar, 2006.

"weak"—a reference to mosque-centered orthopraxy—has a locally rooted cosmological heritage that has a continuity of truth that tradition offers. And in its emphasis on local and personal religious duties—harmony with nature and respect for ancestors, living and dead—it poses less of a threat to state hegemony. As such, it is of little concern to the policy frame and either ignored or supported under programs of cultural heritage.[24]

Muslim as Modern

As far as the state is concerned, Kuban represents the vision of an idealized modern. Enough Muslim to consider it part of his national identity, he does not know how to pray, is unconcerned with practice, and sees the presence of Muslim missionaries like Iqbol as a social nuisance. He is concerned not with the transnational connections of Islam so much as the economic opportunities of the market, the market imagined globally though primarily experienced locally. He desires a better life, which he sees as within the realm of his own making, and his entrepreneurial spirit trades on both sides of what is legal. The driving discourse for Kuban is of an interconnected modern, shaped by the emergent market economy, the dissolution of the social welfare system, and technological individualism that is part classical liberalism, part patronage network.

Kuban has managed to take advantage of the existing political system and makes a profit in his business endeavors. For him, Islam is something to be kept at a distance, for if Islam became too active in public life it could threaten his way of business. He wants the government to crack down on the activities of people like Kadirbek (he views Nurdeen as innocuous) and supports state regulation of religion. For him, and others in the policy frame, the main concern of the state is maintaining a sense of order that allows governance, or at least those in power, to continue in power. In breaking from the Soviet Union, the legitimacy of the state has been less connected to provision of social services and emphasized more a model of the neoliberal market with the privatization of services and economies being turned over to public responsibility. This means, in general, that people take care of themselves to find livelihoods outside of government dependence and assistance. The state presents not as an ally in providing services, but as an inconvenience best avoided when it comes to making a living. Independent of declining literacy, an inadequate health system, and decaying infrastructure (International Crisis Group 2011), Kuban is concerned with business and increasingly unconcerned with the failings of his community, though he does complain about the general poor conditions of public services. He still acknowledges the state as a legitimate authority, but Islam is not much of a concern for him. This seeming lack of interest in religion, from a policy perspective that assumes religious activity as threatening, makes Kuban a manageable religious, more likely to support how the state views Islam than how Kadirbek or Nurdeen view it.[25]

FIGURE 5.2. A village market in the south, 2005.

THE ETHNOGRAPHIC FRAME

Caricatures of Islam and authority, of security and value, guide much of the stereotyping of religion. Who is speaking for a particular group, who is motivating groups to action, how engaged is Islam in ameliorating social woes, and what groups are in conflict with the state are all interest-driving questions of the policy frame because they attempt to locate power and motivators in struggle. Labels, while necessary, obfuscate the details beyond what is experienced, and as such can create categories that take on a life of their own.

The literature on Islam in Central Asia generally, and Kyrgyzstan more specifically, is growing. This is both a response to the greater ease with which Western scholars have been able to access the region and a growing interest in the region as a place relatively unexplored by Western scholars and of increased geopolitical interest. While some of this literature is very insightful,[26] the bulk of what is written from the policy frame approaches the region with a fear of religious change. There is a penchant for writing about Islamic extremism, of essentializing an increased religiosity with threat and danger (from the view of the state and as corollary, international order), and while a good deal of this makes the news seem apocalyptic, it also elides how the dynamics of the everyday impact the local interaction with religion.[27] This interpretation and reinterpretation is influenced by labels often reified by what is published rather than informed by long-term ethnography.[28] Ethnography, at its best, gives depth and feeling to the understanding of its subjects' lives, struggles, hopes, and aspirations, making people *real*, not merely objects of manipulation.

The reality of religious practice anywhere is that it is complex, that individual attitudes often differ—though not always significantly—from the group to which they align (identify) themselves. The challenge to the social scientist, and particularly to the ethnographer who embeds him/herself in the everyday, is to recognize categories that allow the group to be identifiable from other groups yet at the same time acknowledge that individual agency creates a number of moving parts that can be independent of the category or be moving in multiple categories at the same time and, even if the categories seem mutually exclusive, that this is not always an untenable contradiction. Most people function with a degree of cognitive dissonance that allows for seemingly contradictory religious views to be made manageable, at least for them though perhaps not for the analyst who longs for set (rigid) categories. Together, the various interlocutors met throughout describe a very fluid and dynamic environment where boundaries are not always walls—though to be sure, walls are at times put up and, in certain situations, brought down—but more like semipermeable membranes where movement of some interactions are allowed whereas others are restricted, at least publicly.

Fluidity between Center and Periphery

Ethnographies are not always concerned with the majority within a population. Often minorities, or those living within different margins of society, become the focus of extended study; how these peripheries interact with the center is a long-standing concern in social analysis (Giustozzi and Orsini 2009; Shils 1975). In most instances, however, there is fluidity between the center and periphery, so the stories of Kadirbek, Nurdeen, Kuban, and others are all part of the description of Islam in Kyrgyzstan; caricatures of an intimate, and to varying degrees, public, relationship 5.5 million Kyrgyz have with Islam. And to an extent, the stories Kadirbek, Nurdeen, and Kuban represent are moral narratives of self and ways of religious engagement.[29] As stories, they represent everyone and also represent no one. Kadirbek is of greatest interest to policy circles; he is most threatening to the interests of those within policy circles. Nurdeen appeals to tradition and those looking for exotics—though Nurdeen does not see what he does as falling under "exotics"—of an Islamic vision infused with Kyrgyz ancestors and the sacrality of pre-Islamic landmarks. Kuban represents a modern more concerned with capital and self than the everyday vestiges of a religious life. And while they all are threatening to each other in terms of religious correctness, there are other areas in which they are not, or at least the threat does not keep their children from playing together.

The ethnographic is messier than stories. It is the public sentiments, the collective orientations, the range of beliefs felt to be common. It is that which is repeated most often, and thus not necessarily the stories that make news but the local understanding gained from being a local. It is how being Kyrgyz is understood in the most general of terms. It is taking quantitative descriptions that seem unifying—such as 97 percent of those surveyed self-identify as Muslim[30]—and complicating it by adding the qualitative. For example, while 97 percent may self-identify as Muslim, further breaking it down along lines of practice, 50 percent consider themselves to be observant or practicing Muslims; 34 percent sometimes observant or practicing; and only 14 percent describe themselves as unobservant or nonpracticing. Adding the qualitative, we better appreciate the differences at stake when both Tolkun and Azarmat consider themselves practicing Muslims despite their understandings of observance not being the same.

Percentages independent of narratives afford categories a stronger sense of coherence than everyday life reflects. It is helpful, however, for seeing populations as averages of characteristics. Saying that "over 80 percent of the population characterize themselves as at least somewhat practicing of their religion" makes clear that religion plays an active role in the life of those in Kyrgyzstan. The meaning of "active role" is different to Kadirbek, Nurdeen, and Kuban, but in an average outside of individual narratives, a quarter of those surveyed do not pray whereas 30 percent pray five times a day and over 40 percent pray with more variable frequency. A higher percentage of people visit sacred sites (around 66 percent) than visit places of worship (around 52 percent), though this is by no means a mutually exclusive category because some who visit sacred sites also visit places of worship. Only 15 percent of the surveyed population does not talk about religion with friends; for 35 percent of those surveyed, discussions of religion come up on at least a weekly basis (see Appendix B).

Over 90 percent claim religion is at least somewhat important to their lives, only slightly (though not significantly) more than those who feel tradition is important. And as with Nurdeen, tradition and religion are not mutually exclusive categories but rather ways of understanding the same phenomena. For the majority of the population, religion has a significant influence on behavior, yet its compatibility with the modern world is split between those who view it as compatible, those who do not, and those who are uncertain. The implications for all of this is that religion cannot be discounted—despite some who claim that the Kyrgyz, in comparison for example with Uzbeks, are not religious—for people see it as playing a role, albeit to varying degrees and expressed in varying ways.

In short, we see that most of the population consider Islam to be important and practice it to varying degrees. How the quantitative data overlays with the qualitative stories of Kadirbek, Nurdeen, and Kuban is in the richness of neighborhoods and interactions with differing degrees of connectivity, both imagined and real. How this translates to the policy and ethnographic frames is largely around needs and agendas. If one is concerned about the edges, the middle can be either a reassuring, stabilizing vision or representative of a population under threat of becoming subsumed by what is threatening. It is, of course, both of these things, and more, but the frames with which we view it often sacrifice neutrality for the sake of neatness.

Neighbors near the Speaker

Kadirbek, Nurdeen, and Kuban live within earshot of the loudspeaker that projects azan, and thus share many of the same public sounds, though respond to them differently.[31] They all have low wages, experience corruption, and are impacted by increasing food and fuel prices. Their children go to the same school, their wives shop in the same markets, and, having grown up in the same neighborhood, they know—and shared in—each other's history. They are neighbors in their community, but they are no longer close; in their twenties, their lives diverged and they developed different interests, different friends, and different ideas of what was important in life. When in the privacy of their homes, or the companionship of their own friends, they may share their opinions on what is missing, or wrong, in the lives of Kadirbek, Nurdeen, and Kuban, and this "what is missing" is inevitably a reflection of what one believes to be important and how one imagines one's own religious and moral life. Kadirbek believes Nurdeen and Kuban should heed the call to prayer with greater frequency; Nurdeen believes that Kadirbek and Kuban are neglecting tradition; and Kuban believes that Kadirbek and Nurdeen are holding on to ideologies of the past and should focus their energies on embracing the modern world.

But all of this is tidier than it is in reality. There is an interconnectedness in their histories and, knowing many of the same stories, they take part in mutual stereotyping. They greet one another when they meet on the streets and are friendly, but they do not guest at each other's houses or share leisure. From gossip between neighbors and rumors of the streets they know a bit about each other's activities—presume to know more than they do, and certainly know enough to make judgments—and when appropriate may convey important information. At one wedding party where the three were present, for example, Kuban warned Kadirbek that the police were likely to show up at one of the prayer meetings he attends, and suggested that Kadirbek ensure there was no literature lying around that might cause him to be detained.

Though their ideas and practices of Islam differ, as do their notions of what the state should be, there is a complexity of interrelations that stems not from what is shared but what was (once) believed to be shared—friendship during school days, common acquaintances, and distant and not so distant relatives. Very little in their relations is entirely straightforward, for even as each is representative of stereotyped personalities, they are themselves less those stereotypes than is assumed. Kuban is nonpracticing though he does claim he is Muslim; he does not pray or visit mosques or sacred sites though he talks with friends about religion quite frequently—about once a fortnight. He claims that neither religion nor tradition is important but believes religion influences his behavior and may be compatible with the modern world. He and Kadirbek share this sense of uncertainty about the compatibility of religion and the modern world, though they share little more. Kadirbek is observant, prays five times a day unless he is traveling, does not visit sacred sites anymore, talks with his friends weekly about religion, and claims that Islam is the meaning of his life. Nurdeen characterizes himself as somewhat observant, has conversations about religion about as often as Kuban does, believes both religion and tradition are very important, is uncertain about the compatibility of religion with the world of today but acknowledge it influences (or, he clarifies, he at least wants it to influence) his behavior a great deal.

The ethnographic frame is not a place where three ideal types of individuals live three neatly distinct lives, but rather where all three still interact in ways that are at times inconsistent with their beliefs. Much is happening around and between those who hear the call to prayer from the neighborhood loudspeaker. There is a sense of boundaries as "separating," yet also "connecting," among Kadirbek, Nurdeen, and Kuban. In addition to their shared past as schoolboys and their children knowing each other, they go to many of the same cafés, shop at the same market, read many of the same newspapers, watch many of the same television channels, and go to the same neighborhood barber. While they can be presented along a spectrum of religious difference, their lives are intertwined precisely through historical and contemporary experiences that distinguish and join them in their communities. There is a significant corpus of knowledge that is shared, though navigated differently.

THE SOCIALLY NAVIGATED ASPECT OF KYRGYZ RELIGIOUSNESS

Characterizations of Islam that seem to guide reporting and policy also drive scholarship and public opinion—a key to getting research funding is to play off the concerns of policy interests, to suggest that Islam is a threat and one's research can help better inform the policy frame in mitigating the threat. The ideal is that the ethnographic frame influences the policy frame and that the two work harmoniously together. But when the terms of "threat," as understood by the agendas of policy, are accepted by the ethnographic frame, the analysis can become one that reifies state agendas and this may be different from the ideals of the population being studied. And with regard to religion, this may mean suggesting that the aspirations of someone like Kadirbek, who is happier with and more confident in the rule of his religion than that of the state, needs to be dampened by policies that favor the tradition of Nurdeen or the modernism of Kuban.

Some of these issues are not new. Early sociocultural works on the study of Islam, such as Geertz's *Islam Observed* (1968) and Gellner's *Muslim Society* (1981), emphasized the distinction between scripturalist and saint-worshiping

Islam, creating a dichotomy of structural and political significance, where the two sides fit neatly into ethnographic systems intelligible to the policy frame. (Kadirbek is the scripturalist and Nurdeen the saint-worshiper, though the caveat "to an extent" must be included here. What is more, the policy frame supports the image of Nurdeen over that of Kadirbek precisely because the boundaries between the two are assumed to be real and the scripturalists are imagined to be more uncompromising in relegating their faith to the private sphere.) Asad criticized this dichotomization, arguing that "Islam is neither a distinctive social structure nor a heterogeneous collection of beliefs, artifacts, customs, and morals. It is a tradition" (Asad 1986, 14).[32] The issue becomes the way in which people refer back to traditions, something that Kadirbek and Nurdeen do differently in finding different loci of tradition: Kadirbek the universal focused on Mecca and Nurdeen the universal on local shrines familiar to his ancestors. Going further, Eickelman notes that the most productive area for understanding the religious traditions practiced by Kadirbek and Nurdeen is to explore the "middle ground" they inhabit (Eickelman 1984, 11).

As suggested earlier, however, while the middle ground is a descriptively muddled terrain, it is richly instrumental to understanding the normative sentiments of a society. What is more, there is a particularistic aspect to discussions of difference among Kadirbek, Nurdeen, and Kuban, and a push within ethnography to accept their self-definition of Muslim as legitimate because of how it has been framed and experienced by each of them. But all this takes place in an exceptionally complex and fluid environment that is socially navigated.

There is an analytical disjuncture between the policy frame and the ethnographic frame in part because the aims are different. The policy frame is more concerned with the outliers that pose a threat to existing structures. It can acknowledge that the population is not threatening but it emphasizes the nature of that which may constitute a threat in hopes of staving off that threat. The policies become directed toward encouraging a view of Islam as part of an individual's private world and therefore unthreatening to secular society. In some settings, this model may be successful, but it is not always ethnographically informed. It is rather a model of how to make *them* more like *us*. The ethnographic frame, for example, makes clear that a number of those seen as a threat by some have well-founded reasons to view their struggle as moral and just.[33] They want a meaningful life and are unconcerned about the issues of outside funding organizations. The ethnographic, however, gives a reading of where the community is (ideally) from the perspective of those for whom religion exists in the everyday, how "locals" see it and how they make use of labels that are applied to them. Making a distinction between policy and ethnographic approaches draws attention to the differences in who is framing the question. Islam, as made sense of locally, engages with both the policy and the ethnographic frames, but not in independent ways: Kadirbek, Nurdeen, and Kuban respond to both frames in relation to their own surroundings and

FIGURE 5.3. The arrival of a granddaughter leads to discussions about the future world in which she will grow up, 2005.

without recognizing differences of agendas implicit in the policy and ethnographic approach.

Revolutions and monumental life events are exciting times for uncertain futures. But to capture the descriptive friction of everyday life, we must realize that the policy and ethnographic frames collide "in the field" where people's lives are constricted by seen and unseen realities, relationships of varying closeness, and potentialities inherent to their ability and environment, and manifested in what they come to *know*. What policies assume of Kadirbek, Nurdeen, and Kuban has an impact on how they live and understand local and world order, even if the policies are independent of any grounded knowledge of the categories and assumptions of religiousness that people hold. A state where there is little to no recourse for the wrongdoing of its functionaries can always be bettered by an ideology of transcendent retribution. And, of course, international policies based on specious understanding—for example, that Kadirbek is somehow inherently more dangerous than Nurdeen or Kubat—do not remain neutral in the environments in which they are engaged. Furthermore, the ethnographic frame can romanticize the local as traditional and unique without fully appreciating the policies that frame all of our worlds, including those of our ethnographic subject. Kadirbek, Nurdeen, and Kubat all see themselves as actively engaged in a world beyond their neighborhood, which places them at a number of intersections where change and influence are likely to alter their ideas and ideals.

What influences religious belief in Kyrgyzstan (or anywhere else for that matter) is found where neighbors interact and are forced to socially navigate a multitude of demands placed on them by their engagement with the policy and ethnographic frames (sometimes their biases as well as ours). And where all of this converges, the ground is rough, but real. Theorizing rough ground is looking at the multitude of agendas put forth as analysis and seeing them not as directing linear outcomes but as influencing shifting trajectories of life, religious and otherwise. Kadirbek's understanding of Islam is influenced by his membership in Hizb ut-Tahrir and policies toward Hizb ut-Tahrir influence the status of the organization, his religious identity relative to others, and his understanding of the world outside of his local sphere. Likewise, Nurdeen's or Kubat's understandings of Islam get ethnographically characterized as traditional or modern, though that is neither static nor consistent. How they all come to be religious is influenced by the experiences they make sense of, and the ethnographer can be as influential in this as the policy maker. The tendency in theory is to smooth out the edges. And here is the utility of an anthropology of knowledge and a theory of rough ground, for it allows Kadirbek, Nurdeen, and Kubat to be Muslim in their (as opposed to our) conception of religion—and allows them to contest the Muslimness of the other—precisely due to the experiences they navigate.[34]

A theory of the rough ground keeps forms of analysis more in check. Policy and ethnographic frames do not live independently of each other despite the tendency of those who have them to downplay one at the expense of the other. In respect to Kadirbek's membership in Hizb ut-Tahrir, the rough ground recognizes the role corruption plays in bolstering the agenda of the state and increasing membership in counterhegemonic organizations. It also makes clearer that the agendas of such organizations are not necessarily antistatist but viewed as morally purifying. Misguided policy can push people to a form of engagement contrary to policy intentions and synthesizing the policy and ethnographic frames sheds light on the rough ground in ways that do not essentialize a population but guide programs around what local people envision as their needs. Furthermore, such an approach reminds ethnographers that the policy frame influences how they view the context of sociality and thus cannot be ignored as a factor contributing to local imagination and potentiality. Thus, by bringing together two groups that have largely ignored each other—or at least not taken seriously the contributions that policy and ethnographic frames make to community—such an approach better explains experience and its subsequent articulation. Recognizing the rough ground, then, is the application of an anthropology of knowledge.

Conclusion

Social Navigation as Knowing Enacted/in Action

When some event takes place, men express their opinions and desires in regard to the event, and as the event proceeds from the combined action of many men, some one of the opinions or desires expressed is certain to be at least approximately fulfilled. When one of the opinions expressed is fulfilled, that opinion is connected with the event as the command preceding it.

Leo Tolstoy, *War and Peace*

Explanation is where the mind rests.

David Hume

The process by which Islam emerges as a category for analyzing the world is a socially navigated endeavor framed locally, vis-à-vis the social organization, corpus, and medium of knowledge transmission, and interpreted politically and morally as the elucidation of a meaningful—or at least manageable—life. Yet in trying to understand human behavior there is a tendency to simplify cause by assuming rationality. This linear approach to theory is often inadequate to capture the complexity and fungibility of everyday decision making; negotiations are made individually and with others that are economic, political, social, and religious. And people do not always act rationally. Perhaps one of the more illustrative examples of this can be found in John Dewey's discussion of a man lost in the woods, which metaphorically gets at the trajectory of social navigation.

> Taking this case as typical of any reflective situation in so far as it involves perplexity—a problem to be solved. The problem is to find a correct idea of the way home—a practical idea or plan of action which will lead to success, or the realization of the purpose to get home. . . .
>
> Just what is the environment of which an idea is to be formed: i.e., what is the intellectual content or objective detail to be assigned to the term "environment"? It can hardly mean the actual visible environment—the trees, rocks, etc., which a man is actually looking at. These things are there and it seems superfluous to form an idea of them; moreover, the wayfaring man, though

lost, would have to be an unusually perverse fool if under such circumstances he were unable to form an idea (supposing he chose to engage in this luxury) in agreement with these facts. The environment must be a larger environment than the visible facts; it must include things not within the direct ken of the lost man; it must, for instance, extend from where he is now to his home, or to the point from which he started. It must include unperceived elements in their contrast with the perceived. Otherwise the man would not be lost. Now we are at once struck with the facts that the lost man has no alternative except either to wander aimlessly or else to *conceive* this inclusive environment; and that this conception is just what is meant by idea. It is not some little psychical entity or piece of consciousness-stuff, but is *the interpretation of the locally present environment in reference to its absent portion*, that part to which it is referred as another part so as to give a view of a whole. Just how such an idea would differ from one's plan of action in finding one's way, I do not know. For one's plan (if it be really a plan, a method) is a conception of what is given in its hypothetical relations to what is not given, employed as a guide to that act which results in the absent being also given. It is a map constructed with one's self lost and one's self found, whether at starting or at home again, as its two limits. If this map in its specific character is not also the only guide to the way home, one's only plan of action, then I hope I may never be lost. It is the *practical* facts of being lost and desiring to be found which constitute the limits and the content of the "environment."

. . . Now suppose one uses the idea—that is to say, the present facts projected into a whole in the light of absent facts—as a guide of action. Suppose, by means of its specifications, one works one's way along until one comes upon familiar ground—finds one's self. *Now*, one may say, my idea was right, it was in accord with facts; it agrees with reality. That is, acted upon sincerely, it has led to the desired conclusion; it has, *through action*, worked out the state of things which it contemplated or intended. The agreement, correspondence, is between purpose, plan, and its own execution, fulfillment; between a map of a course constructed for the sake of guiding behavior and the result attained in acting upon the indications of the map. (Dewey 1916, 237–40)

Life is filled with varying degrees of elasticity. Not everything social is fluid, for the social is constrained within an organizational frame that includes peer pressure, political limitations, and moral restrictions. But that does not imply that people are statically bound by their environment. Certain aspects of behavior may be privileged by the knowledge and potential one has to act in a particular way, but some form of navigating social relations and lived experience is always taking place. Social change is always around us, though with an intensity that varies across individuals in both time and place. Social navigation then is movement within movement, a way of maneuvering within networks and in response to events (Vigh 2006, 12–15); it is an evaluation of knowledge and the fine-tuning of praxis; it is in being lost in the woods and figuring out how to get back (or somewhere) that life is filled with as much meaning and comfort as possible.

One does not navigate the challenges of life alone, but within a community. The definition of who is inside and outside of that community varies, but the community is a significant factor in change and the degree of change. There are correctives everywhere, some minor and others major. The collapse of the Soviet system, for example, required a new approach to learning how to make a living. Aidar was more successful in this respect than Begaim. For Begaim, when the collective-farm system fell apart Lahol became an even less desirable place to live. The resulting unemployment forced her and her family to live a more isolated and independently sustainable life, living off their one cow, five sheep, and twelve chickens. A former accountant, she redirected the focus of her life in order to take care of her family. She became less optimistic about life and more resigned to a life that "could never be as good as it used to be."

Aidar was able to benefit from the collapse of the Soviet system and he redirected his life by navigating opportunities and chance. His economic success led to political success and his vision of change and social order is markedly more optimistic than Begaim's. Part of his maneuvering through change was by relations with business partners from abroad, especially China, Kazakhstan, Russia, and Turkey.

Likewise, Azarmat's studies and Murat's search for religious meaning were in response to a desire to better understand the contribution religion could make to their lives—a corrective aimed at informing religious practice and knowledge. And as Dimira corrects Mairam when she performs a ritual out of order or says a prayer improperly, Azarmat and Murat refine their religious practice based on their relationships with a source of knowledge they believe to be more knowledgeable. Within the system of correctives is the issue of legitimacy and authority—of whose voice counts most. For Azarmat, Iqbol is influential as a missionary trained outside. For Dimira, the tradition handed down from her ancestors is the foundation of authority. For Zafar, the Qur'an and his reading of it are authoritative; he challenges the local imam, whose word is usually the authority for Islamic understanding in the village.

The idea of correctives and social navigation does not necessarily imply agency, for there are limits to everyone's experience and ability to respond in different ways. One's potentiality (ability to act in a certain way) is constrained by a number of variables and it is in response to this, and in relation to this, that social navigation takes place. One's potential to act is limited by, among other things, desire, physical ability, mental capacity, economic resources, and political opportunities. One may be handsome, strong, intelligent, and wealthy, and have very different recourses for action than a neighbor who is homely, handicapped, lacking intellectual savvy, and poor. Aidar's ability to pursue options is markedly different than Begaim's because of the economic realities they face, and Zafar is able to command greater individual authority in his reading of the Qur'an than Azarmat (who relies on the authority of

FIGURE C.1. Eid prayers in a public square, underneath Lenin's outstretched arm, 2004.

Iqbol's interpretation of the Qur'an) in part because Zafar was more adept in learning Arabic.

Neither Kanibek nor Bakyt can afford hajj, but because of his work in the mosque, it is quite likely that Bakyt will be able to go within the next few years (or so he believes). Kanibek does not envision an opportunity to travel to Mecca but he believes that visiting Solomon's Mountain three times is equivalent to hajj in Mecca. He explains this by saying that Solomon's Mountain is a trip he could do and is also a sacred place—though not as sacred as Mecca, he admits—because the spirits of his ancestors certainly visit there. Bakyt also once thought that visiting Solomon's Mountain constituted a mini-hajj—and he continues to regard it as a very sacred place—but with the idea of hajj to Mecca within reach, he expresses conviction that all "true" Muslims visit Mecca. Kanibek could get involved at a mosque, studying with the Saudi-trained kazi or the Turkish imams, but he feels more bound by tradition and states a greater affinity for Tolkun's vision of Islam than that of Baktyor's.

Because he lives in Kyrgyzstan, Baktyor is able to be a more openly active member of Hizb ut-Tahrir. If he lived in Uzbekistan, his religious activity would be more closely scrutinized and constrained. The authoritarian government of Uzbekistan is notorious for human rights abuses and torturing (practicing) Muslims perceived to be a threat to the state and labeled as "Islamic militants." Kyrgyzstan's more liberal political environment allows Baktyor greater freedom of expression. This is in contrast to a wedding I attended in

FIGURE C.2. On top of Solomon's Mountain, one can purchase religious books, prayer beads, and refreshments, as well as have a photo taken, 2006.

Sokh, where vodka was produced minutes after the arrival of the Uzbek police in order to avoid scrutiny for having an Islamic wedding. The family could have exercised free will and opted not to serve alcohol, but as they assessed the consequences of what it would mean for them socially and politically, they settled for acting in a way other than how they wanted.

Not everything, of course, is religious or political. Or more accurately, there is a negotiation of responses and emphasis relative to the task or challenge before the individual. Ismoiljon considers himself a good Muslim and is proud to talk about having gone on hajj with his wife. And though he claims to live a religiously informed life, religion is only one part of his life. Most of the day he spends forming and polishing metal. He is a husband, a knife maker, and a Muslim.

His trade, the nature of those with whom he interacts, and events in his life, however, are what made him want to be a practicing Muslim. Being crippled by his father; going to mosque because all his colleagues did; seeing that he was more financially secure than his high school friends who became taxi drivers—all this led him to understand his life and to eventually develop his religious self. The everyday speaks to much, creating a reservoir of experiences waiting for the right time to be understood and incorporated into meaning.

UNDERSTANDING VARIATION

The majority of people in Kyrgyzstan consider themselves Muslims. But what this means to Rustam and Nargiza, Aibek and Murat, brothers Adilet and Jyrgal, or neighbors Kadirbek, Nurdeen, and Kuban is that Islam as a term carries with it a meaning with great internal variation. When the meaning of life is different for different people, it becomes difficult for some to accept the generalization, for example, that all are Muslims. A perfect example of this is the case of Tolkun and Azarmat: Azarmat does not accept Tolkun and Tolkun sees him as missing the beauty in variation that Islam can offer.

There is great variation in religious understanding and practice. And what accounts for this variation is most richly understood when examined in the context of knowledge, of how people come to know religion and culture, and how this influences their practice. This involves an awareness of praxis as well as acknowledging that actions feed back into ideas and understanding. We know more than what our actions reveal yet we can do only that which is within the limits of our potentiality. There is a constant process of social navigation where the challenges of change are responded to within the confines of what is known and what can be acted on. For all they entail, the social organization, corpus, and medium give parameters of tendencies. Events can alter the projection of the tendency—as the collapse of the Soviet Union did for Begaim and Aidar, or a crisis of religious identity such as that felt by Murat and Bakyt—but as sense is made out of the events, we come closer to Dewey's lost man finding his way out of the woods. Understanding the frame of knowledge better explains the nonlinear progression of everyday life and any theory that tries to explain it.

The influence of social organization as a component of knowledge can be seen in potentialities or restrictions imposed by the state (open or closed political system), economics (poverty or wealth), social conventions, and the religious environment. Phronesis and mimesis are components of the knowledge structure and the approach to what is learned by children in the madrassas is different than what is learned in the public schools. What sets up these differences can be seen in the organizational structures inherited from the Islamic educational system (madrassas) and the Soviet reforms of teaching sciences and liberal arts (public schools).

The policies of the Soviet Union had an impact on social structure. For example, it increased the framing of identity in ethnic terms. As such, Ismoiljon remarked once that he was going to mosque because that is what Uzbeks do. Shepherds tend to go to mosque less frequently and the idea of place and space is structured differently among nomads than among those with a sedentary lifestyle. This plays no small role in influencing people's ideas and how these ideas are transformed into action and/or abstracted to the level of cosmologies. Kubat has lived a very different life than Ismoiljon. Kubat accepts the shorthand of ethnicity as a way of describing his life in the mountains and says this is what it means to be Kyrgyz.

Associated with this, however, is a different lifestyle entailed by living in the mountains and living in the valley, by having a nomadic social organization or a sedentary social organization. We see this, for example, in one of the border communities where Bakyt and Erkin live. Both are Kyrgyz, but Erkin sees a closer relation of religion to nature because he is more greatly influenced by a nomadic social organization than Bakyt, who has come to know Islam at a mosque.

The corpus of knowledge contains a number of frames that carry settings of information unique to the experience of history, society, profession, education, and religion. Living in the mountains, the environment is confronted in different ways than in the valley. Likewise, the understanding of history's impact in the mountains and the valley has been realized differently. Dimira and Aibek live closer to the rawness of unmanipulated space, of land less altered by man, and their understanding of sacredness is connected to the mazars they visit. In a similar way, Ismoiljon and Toliq view the mosque as religion's center for where they live. It is the center not because it is required of Islam but because it is through the gatherings at the mosque that Islam makes its way into their understanding of society.

Tolkun and Azarmat have different ideas of how religion was revealed to them and the role of history in their experiences. Tolkun sees Islam as revealed through tradition and a generative connection to the land; Azarmat sees it as coming directly from the Arabian Peninsula. What they know to constitute their cosmological understanding of the world reinforces and is reinforced by their approach to promoting a religious frame that advocates either local tradition or a revival guided by external religious authorities. There is a syncretism and negotiation at all levels, the terms of boundaries and who or what lies inside and outside of the rightly guided religious community is essential and essentialized.

The medium of knowledge transmission is complex. It is discursive as orality and textuality, and it is nondiscursive as gestures, rituals, and action, all of which is experienced directly through participation and indirectly through observation. The way the message is delivered, however, can matter. People learn by watching and doing, but what matters in the message and the messenger (the performative), is the question of legitimacy, authoritativeness, and flexibility. The stories Kubat tells in the jailoo, or even at home with guests over tea, are entertaining and authoritative because the presentation is convincing and his age garners respect. He speaks of the value of tradition, the legends of the ancestors, and the spirits of the surroundings, but there is a degree of ambiguity and variability that is allowed in his slightly changing narrations.

Zafar and Baktyor ascribe greater certainty to the Qur'an (even though it is not the only written text they use), which they claim as infallible and without change. Their presentation is also convincing, referencing the text to the history of Islam and its ornamentation. But in general, they remove the authority from the individual and locate it in a text that (while an interpretation for some) is nonnegotiable.

Kubat, Zafar, and Baktyor process their knowledge through the lens of experience. They try to make relevant to others the stories they tell in the same way they try to make experiences relevant and meaningful for themselves.

Sometimes, however, the answer is not to clarify an issue but to find an ambiguity with which one can live.

Ritual is one example of managing this ambiguity, whether a ritual like tushoo kesuu intended to secure a prosperous future for Cholpon and her family or daily salat that structures Iqbol's day and reaffirms his feeling of divinely inspired purpose. But ritual is also an example of the dynamics inherent to knowledge, where ideas are translated into action and action is translated into ideas. In its character as subjunctive, ritual brings people together *as if* there is connectivity that spans both time and space. Through ritual, Mairam feels she can transcend the boundaries of mortality and communicate with her deceased father. Differences of meaning can be quite tenuous when discussed openly, but in performing namaz, Iqbol and Kanibek are part of the global community of Muslims, despite their different understandings of namaz. Furthermore, rituals of civility, like the protocol of greetings adhered to by Muktar and Toliq or respect given to elders, are essential for maintaining social harmony and are most noticeable in their absence.

The required actions of ritual are both always familiar (known) and learned. They are a social organization, a corpus, and a medium. What then accounts for the difference between Tolkun and Zafar or Bakyt and Erkin can be discussed in shorthand as a difference between place (mountains and valleys) or ethnicity (Kyrgyz and Uzbek). But the reason these distinctions have utility is because they imply a certain knowledge. Uzbeks who grow up in Naryn are more like Kyrgyz who grow up in mountains than Uzbeks who grow up in Osh. Likewise, Kyrgyz in the valley identify more closely with Uzbeks in the valley than the Kyrgyz in the mountains. And like the understanding of ethnicity, beliefs do not begin with ideology, but are developed.

Tolkun and Dimira accept more variation in religious practice and their interpretation of Islam than do Iqbol or Ismoiljon. Aibek and Kanibek are willing to accept other interpretations of Islam insofar as those interpretations are not perceived to threaten their existing way of life. Most people resist change. But significant events, of course, can bring about change. Bakyt, for example, has opted to preference his orientation to the text later in life. It does not necessarily have to mean that he reads the Qur'an, for example, but rather that he sees something static in the text that is nonnegotiable. Dimira also speaks of following tradition as being nonnegotiable, but as Kubat knows, a story passed down orally carries with it alterations in the retelling that do not dilute the truth of the story even if what the characters do changes a little. This is certainly not intended to imply that there is no change in text, for despite some claims, interpretations are ever present. It is an issue of interpretation that differentiates Zafar from the imam and it is their social background that accounts for the difference: the imam was appointed to the mosque during the Soviet Union's last years of existence because he was able to be both religious and, to a certain extent, a functionary within the system; Zafar had the opportunity and the mental capacity to approach the text in a very serious way by learning a language.

The picture that begins to develop, within the loose parameters of tendencies, is one where there is greater openness to variation when learning is referenced to authority that is negotiable and resides within an experience of openness. A feedback relationship between action, abstraction, phronesis, and mimesis bring individuals to an understanding of the social organization, corpus, and medium of what constitutes knowledge for them and because experiences differ, so too does what people know. Tolkun is more open to accepting Azarmat as a Muslim than he is to accepting her as a Muslim, and this has to do with her oral referencing of tradition, her locating sacredness in surroundings, where mazars and rituals serve different purposes for different needs. Baktyor's embrace of Islam and activism in Hizb ut-Tahrir, however, is connected with political struggle and tied to an uncompromising vision of absoluteness. Having done poorly in school, the breadth of his knowledge is curtailed and he has managed by speaking loudly and with certainty about topics on which others are even less familiar.

There are always constraints in addressing the issue of agency in change. There is social navigation but there is also potentiality that limits agency. But viewing life in terms of knowledge—social organization, corpus, and medium—comes closer to understanding the challenges of agency, the problem of authority, and the trajectory of change.

A lot of political discourse is concerned with fears of liberal Muslims becoming militant Muslims. And this is an issue framed by both a policy and ethnographic interests. Attempts to address such concerns generally focus on either isolating that segment of the population as beyond the pale of reason or labeling them as desperate in dealing with deficiencies in material wealth. Not everything, of course, is about religion. But religion is influenced by a myriad of sources and it is largely part of people's everyday existence, an existence where meaning is found in family, friends, and gathering places—not just mosques, but also schools, neighbors' houses, and markets. Understanding the ways people come to know their religious selves provides both a more complete understanding of the complexities of religion and the role education, in a broadly defined sense, can play in addressing concerns about religious practice and the challenges of the Other. Likewise, understanding the policy and ethnographic projections of external observers afford critical reflection on the biases that influence actually understanding the Other.

CONTEXTUALIZING SOCIAL NAVIGATION

To some extent, everything we do, short of experiencing something itself, is an oversimplification. But three points are to be made: religion is a fundamental aspect of life for many and is a dynamic part of the social navigation of the everyday; understanding the mechanisms of this can be most fruitfully explained by an anthropology of knowledge that notes the social organization, corpus, and medium of/relation to thought and action; and the ethnographic experience of such communities adds to the phenomenological understanding of religious life in Kyrgyzstan and beyond. The relevance of these points can be seen anywhere where people struggle with the challenges of life and its brokenness in death.

Religion is complex. What is more, individuals' personal relationship with religion is complex and at times contradictory. And yet when we talk about religion, there is a tendency to look at dogma and emphasize textual prescriptions that hold together the body of a religious belief system. Very few people, however, are sophisticated enough, or have enough time, to analyze and assess the veracity of dogma and thus rely on the guidance of those dogmatically versed to authoritatively present a belief system that is manageable and meaningful. For most, religion is a lived experience that complements the everyday. Though religion exists at two levels—that of dogma and that of everyday lived experience—there is fluidity in recognizing the expertise of one relative to another, and there is a continuous process of evaluation, reevaluation, and negotiation that attempts to reconcile the shortcomings of uncertainty in the relationship between mortality and its absence (immortality or nothing).

In history and in policy, however, dogma is assumed. It is the formality of fundamentalisms and the tenet that generalizes "believers" as a unified cohort of people agreeing to play by the same rules, or at least on the same playground. A profession for some, dogma carries with it the obligation of creating its own legitimacy—as both form and a feature of authority—and the threat of illegitimacy. Religious functionaries are the elites who carry the mantle of dogma, but generally it is only a fraction of the richness of ideology that is shared beyond the elites.

The everyday is filled with contingencies and jury-rigged regularity. Much of it is mundane and lacking the stories that animate and excite us. Significant events are often recorded and retold as part of everyday conversations and exchanges; but so are seemingly insignificant events that are taken for granted and only noticed in their absence. Religion as part of the everyday is often one aspect of what people do and not necessarily the essence of what they do. Certain events can give a spike in the religious activity—when people are threatened, desperate, or thankful—but the intensity of religious expression oscillates between different levels for different people at different times.

Religion is serious. It matters and it should not be discounted as an active part of the lives of many, by those who are not religious or project their apathy or disdain onto the religious. Arguments of enlightenment and rationality may have philosophical traction for ardent secularists, but those who actively integrate religion into their worldview have good reasons to fight over certain issues and be slow to waver about that which is perceived as threatening the foundation of their religious identity. Transcendent truths are nonnegotiable and soteriological concerns are enough to make rational people do irrational things (as the emotions of love and desperation do also). But we live with ambiguities that religion helps to mediate and make sense of, and certainly this should not be pushed aside as superstition, backwardness, or intellectual inadequacy.

To understand the relation of religion in the everyday—filled with statements and acts that contradict those statements, as well as acts and statements that contradict those acts—it is important to realize that people are always socially navigating themselves; this is an acknowledgment of dynamics under change and an attempt to theorize them loosely, noting the contingency in action. Behaviors can be persuaded but not unilaterally forced. And the limits of theoretical predictability need to take into account that people socially navigate because there is change and they are required to respond to events in order to live their lives.

Inherent to an individual's understanding of an event, and his or her activity relative to that event, is an associated embodiment of knowledge. Calling what people do "knowledge" privileges the actor's vision of the world and respects a channel of anticipated behavior. There can be a frequented path that most follow, but what accounts for deviations from those paths cannot always be predicted, though generally can be explained in relation to an individual's experience. Calling what people do knowledge legitimates what they do and acknowledges the fact that people know more than what is culture. And here, I do not wish to get rid of culture but rather to cast a wider net that includes individual explanations for their actions, that includes references both to culture and to knowing.

An anthropology of knowledge pursues the question of existence and meaning making by investigating the social organization, corpus, and medium of knowledge. The division of knowledge into three components is, of course, more of an analytical tool than an attempt to suggest that knowledge is portioned so neatly in the lived world. Rather, social organization, corpus, and medium cannot sit independent or separate of each other; their relationship to knowledge is akin to parts of the body necessary for survival. But looking at how the three aspects intersect and are influenced by the outside is important to understanding action (and the constraints on action) in the world.

The social organization component includes the restrictions/potentialities of the state—an open or closed political system; the limits/opportunities of economics—the difference between wealth and poverty; and a social environment that includes the conventions of religion. The corpus varies in depth between individuals but can be understood within a handful of frames: historical, locational, and social; professional, educational, and religious. In other words, how history is experienced in the mountains and valleys, cities and villages, and among those in different social groups, with different levels of education, different professions, and different attitudes toward understanding religion. The medium of knowledge transmission and acquisition is oral, textual, and experiential; discursive and nondiscursive in form; and derived from being both participant and observer. All of this comes together in the rituals of religion and of civility. The rituals of civility are essential to the proper functioning of society. With the rituals of religion, the isolation and broken-ness of the *as is* world is transcended by the collectivity and imagined whole-ness of the *as if* (subjunctive) world; the uncontrollable is controlled; and the everyday can be made more meaningful as well as be temporarily replaced by the exceptional.

Intimate to the social organization, corpus, and medium of knowledge is the contributing relationship between action, abstraction, phronesis, and mimesis. In action, we abstract ideas and in praxis, a related process going the opposite direction, we draw upon what it is we claim to know. The practicality of experience and the repetition of doing equally influence both what it is we claim to know and what it is that we do. Yet key to the awareness of knowledge and guided action is the relationship with authority, certainty, ambiguity, and negotiability.

Life is filled with ambiguities and uncertainties that must be negotiated to get beyond inaction and to address the demands of living. Central to this is that which is authoritative and constitutes authority. The value of this approach to knowledge is that it comes closer to capturing the complexity of the religious experience by noting the relationship to authority that is part and parcel of any social organization, corpus, or medium of knowledge transmission and acquisition.

The ethnographic picture I draw of the phenomenology of religion in Kyrgyzstan reveals the complexity of the project. Different ways of learning (oral, textual, experiential); different ways of living (location, profession, historical experience); and different ways of ordering (political, social, economic) contribute to what is taken to be authoritative and in turn to what is understood as proper action and legitimate (religious) belief. In theorizing the generalities of the everyday—of describing the channel, the most common path of social navigation—it is argued that, at least in Kyrgyzstan, a Muslim living in the mountains who remains influenced by a nomadic heritage and an oral connection to the precedents of ancestral relations can accommodate greater variation than a Muslim living in the valley who is tied to a sedentary history and a textual referencing to a nonnegotiable religious worldview. It is not that the medium or location alone account for variations, but there are tendencies in the experiences that can be observed.

Generalizing Kyrgyz life is often done in terms of culture—that it is the peculiarities and particularities of their culture that makes them Kyrgyz—and to a great extent this reveals a lot about the population. What someone knows may have aspects of culture, and certainly culture is part of knowledge, but not every aspect of knowledge is reducible to culture. Simplifying everything to the level of culture is more a sound bite of policy than of ethnography, and parallels the "clash of civilizations" arguments that inadequately capture variation within cultures. The utility of an anthropology of knowledge helps in explaining individual variations based on what people know. Thus, in trying to understand why some Kyrgyz turn to embrace a foreign-based Islamic organization like Hizb ut-Tahrir or become Christians when the culture is generally contextualized as Islamic, the details of looking at knowledge tell us something important about what people do that seems to require an explanation outside of culture.

An anthropology of knowledge explains the impact of the Soviet educational system and the Islamic madrassas, which is a frame within which Kyrgyz have learned about the world. It also explains adaptations to a nomadic or a sedentary life, which is often articulated locally as culture. But distinctions between mountains and valleys are not enough, just as ethnic distinctions are insufficient, in and of themselves, to account for differences in religious practice. Events and the experiences resulting from those events give people what they know and lead them to action. And it is in putting the pieces of knowledge together that a more complete picture develops.

Life in the mountains implies a different way of relating to the environment than life in the valley. The movement of pastoralists, as well as the referencing to a nomadic heritage, associates time to place and as such change as part of the environment, relating it to location and the time at a particular location. Sedentary life is situated in a place that is altered by the seasons (time), but the association with place is cohabitation with change. Just as the ecological environment (social organization) responds to inputs of association, so does the medium and corpus. The oral narrative allows for greater variation in the retelling than does the written text, which is in a sense codified to posit a "truth" and limit variation. Thus, the privileging of variation in stories and place can lead to a tolerance for greater ambiguity in life. And all of this is done relative to the sum of knowledge, the corpus.

The connection to location and narrative form can be discussed as culture, but there are variations within locations, ethnicities, and economies that are part of people's life stories and are best understood in terms of knowledge. While one may be raised in a mountain environment with a close relationship to a nomadic culture, various life events could bring about one's study at a madrassa that reorients and recontextualizes one's knowledge base. Likewise, dissatisfaction with the textual certainty of the valley, or the disjuncture between textual guidance and action that becomes labeled hypocrisy, can lead one to be skeptical in putting any stock in the prevailing religious environment.

In other words, living in the mountains does not mean that someone is locked to a particular way of behaving. The conditions of employment, level of education, experience of history, and religious frame further enrich the picture of individual potentiality and collective restrictions. And though it may suggest a particular behavior is preferenced, there is a fascinating mix of possibilities that come together to make the emic particularities of Kyrgyz social structure; the everyday lived experience brings together individual choices while also producing what becomes understood as a Kyrgyz worldview and a corresponding cosmology. Islamic orthodoxy and orthopraxy among Kyrgyz is most frequently seen in sedentary environments where textual orientation prevails, and where legitimacy is drawn from the referencing of external religious authority (foreign missionaries who advocate restrictiveness of behavior and the example of Islam under the caliphs). Conversely, heterodoxy among the Kyrgyz is seen more in a nomadic setting where orality predominates as a medium and legitimacy is drawn from the referencing tradition and the precedents set by the ancestors as authoritative. Thus, looking at the social organization, corpus, and medium of knowledge tells more about not only the trends of how one would expect the religious environment to be in different regions of Kyrgyzstan, but it also provides a phenomenological explanation for differences within those regions.

While my argument is largely about the Central Asian case of Kyrgyzstan, the theoretical implications of the approach are much broader. To understand change, the everyday, and the religious environment anywhere—including parts of the world as diverse and seemingly unrelated as, for example, the Balkans, East Africa, Southern Africa, or elsewhere—an anthropology of knowledge is useful and theoretically rewarding. In Albania, the context of living under the restrictions of a closed communist politic formed a basis of knowledge that made the pyramid schemes of the mid-1990s plausible, and unrest and dissatisfaction tenable; as villagers flock to the city in search of gainful employment, the understanding and experience of religion is influenced by Christian and Muslim missionaries with differing agendas and differing claims to authority. In Bosnia, the context of war transformed one of the world's most liberal Islamic countries to an experience of decreased openness, where mosques are rebuilt and staffed by supporters of a nonlocal school of Islam less accommodating of religious pluralism; where religious dialogue is complicated by memories of injustice and tensions of distrust; and where the religious is discussed more as political than phenomenological. And in Uganda and Zambia, differences in Christianity, influenced in the context of colonialism and the relationship of tribal leaders to territorial cults of possession and mediumship vis-à-vis interpretations of Christianity, affected various ways of accounting for and accommodating to the hardships of everyday life. Each location holds similar stories of local understandings.

The cohesive connection of events and the everyday is in the nexus of social organization, corpus, and medium. In all cases, people are negotiating the temporal world in relation to a vision of a cosmological world that they can make fit. Recognizing and respecting this casts policy (public and foreign) and intellectual discourse in a more realistic light. Turning to issues of conflict, tolerance, and peace building, the religious frames must be understood for what they contain and not a simplification of what they should contain, independent of the factors that contribute to knowledge and attempts to live a meaningful life. Religion is often essentialized and simplified as a cause of conflict. There is a fungible utility in the essentialization, but religion can also be a source of resolution, when issues (and limits) of authority, certainty, ambiguity, and negotiability are recognized. An anthropology of knowledge helps us to that end.

In the end, the process of adapting to one's environment is a necessarily ongoing endeavor and social navigation is, writ large, the way of responding to one's surroundings that combines the past and present situation to make a future. For much of the world, religion deeply influences one's worldview, for it gives a framework for negotiating the challenges of everyday life. And as with all skills needed in life, one must practice to gain any mastery. It is the practice—the doing—that leads to the knowing, and as such, all of my interlocutors see themselves as Muslims (of some sort), *practicing* Islam.

Appendix A

Overview of Interlocutors

Every community contains people of varying degrees of closeness, whose stories impact each other in one way or another. Many of the interlocutors below know each other; those who do not know each other personally have heard stories about one another (or the ideal types the Other represents). This list serves as a reference to the interlocutors central to the story of *Practicing Islam*. It is a reminder that all accounts of practice and interaction are populated by a large number of people whom we may know intimately and whose details we sometimes forget.

BIOGRAPHIES OF NAMED INTERLOCUTORS

Adilet (Jyrgal's brother) (Chapter 3, Conclusion) stayed in the village and became successful. He is a very active and observant Muslim.

Aibek (Chapters 3, 4, 5, Conclusion) is a self-proclaimed intellectual of the mountain village in which he lives. He supports a more traditional understanding of religion, which he perceives as respecting the ancestors, and speaks against those at the new mosque whom he describes as threatening in their orthopraxy and social conservativism.

Aidar (Chapter 4, Conclusion) is a businessman who exploited his local networks to develop relations with international businesses. He was one of the first businessmen to take advantage of the new openness of the borders after Kyrgyzstan declared independence; his success in controlling the borders has increased his international economic connections. As a prosperous local businessman, he entered politics. Connected to the power elites through his economic gains, he moves beyond his local relations by restructuring clan relations along economic lines. He welcomes the opportunity to be seen as a patron of a general Islamic revival, but toes the line on extremist discourse because it is threatening to his economic well-being.

Asel (Baktagul's sister) (Chapters 2, 4) is a housewife who lives in a village in the south of Kyrgyzstan. She was kidnapped for marriage (*ala kachuu*) and taken to a village where she did not have friends and where her sole responsibility is to raise her children and tend to the needs of the household. She did not want to marry her husband, but her parents refused to retrieve her after her kidnapping. She has accepted her life, though she wishes she could have finished her studies at the university and could be closer to her family and the city.

TABLE A.1. List of Interlocutors

North	South
Adilet, Jyrgal (brothers)	Azarmat
Aibek	*Baktagul, Asel, Cholpon* (sisters, mother, daughter)
Aidar	**Baktyor**
Begaim	*Bakyt*
Dimira, Mairam (mother, daughter)	*Erkin, Nurbek* (brothers)
Kanibek	**Farhod**, **Rustan** (classmates)
Kubat	**Iqbol**
Tolkun	**Ismoiljon**
	Kadirbek
	Kuban
	Muktar
	Murat
	Nargiza
	Nurdeen
	Toliq
	Zafar

Note: **Bold** indicates that a person is an ethnic Uzbek; *italics* indicate that a person lives in a community bordering a mountain/valley.

Azarmat (Chapters 1, 2, 3, 5, Conclusion) is a man in his mid-thirties who wears a white skullcap and a beard that comes to his clavicle. He lives in the Ferghana Valley of Osh oblast and meets three or four times a week with a missionary member of Tablighi Jama'at. Azarmat studies the Qur'an daily with his friends. He reads Arabic poorly and does not understand it, but his ability to recount stories and passages from the Qur'an garners him status in the village as someone who is knowledgeable about Islam.

Baktagul (Asel's sister) (Chapters 2, 3, 4, 5) is a Kyrgyz woman who lives in Osh and used to be a nurse. She now works as a seller in the main bazaar. Once a week, she or her husband go to the Karasuu bazaar to replenish her stock of soap and toiletries. Although she is the primary tenant of the stall, she is still responsible for cleaning the house and making meals.

Baktyor (Chapters 4, 5, Conclusion) is a member of Hizb ut-Tahrir. Almost everyone knows he is one of the leaders of the movement in his community and on juma namaz he can be found opposite the mosque entrance with three or four other members of Hizb ut-Tahrir, accepting money or covertly distributing literature. He does not have formal theological training but frequently repeats what he has read in Hizb ut-Tahrir propaganda.

Bakyt (Chapters 3, 4, Conclusion) is working to get a mosque built in the village where he lives. He was a lawyer who worked for the regional administration and retired eight years ago. He was a heavy drinker who neglected his family and treated his wife poorly. Once he retired, he realized that he had very few friends and, dissatisfied with his life, he became more interested in Islam.

Begaim (Chapters 2, 3, 4, 5, Conclusion) is a woman in her mid-forties who looks worn and prematurely old. She lives in Lahol, in Naryn oblast. Reminiscing about the Soviet period, she laments that life is better everywhere else and summarizes the situation by saying, "The problem is that we do not die."

Cholpon (Chapter 4, Conclusion) is Asel's infant daughter.

Dimira (Mairam's mother) (Chapters 3, 4, 5, Conclusion) considers herself to be a shaman. She heals and mediates with the spirit world and, according to her beliefs, practices religion as it has always been practiced in the mountains of Kyrgyzstan.

Erkin (Nurbek's older brother) (Chapter 3, Conclusion) lives down the road from Bakyt. Erkin graduated from high school and spent some time at university but returned home when his father got ill. He helped raise his four siblings and does most of the heavy labor around the house. His parents were strict and his father forbade drinking. He does not drink alcohol and while on most days he does perform namaz, he only rarely goes to mosque. He loves the mountains and does not enjoy visiting the city.

Farhod (Chapter 3), a friend and former classmate of Rustan, has not observed anything religiously in the past six years and is not devoted to anything but cheap vodka. A mechanic, he does not pray but justifies having two wives by saying that Muhammad said it was right for a Muslim to have up to four wives.

Iqbol (Chapters 3, 4, 5, Conclusion) is a young Tablighi Jama'at missionary with a long black beard who dresses in white. He prays five times a day, teaches Qur'an at the mosque, and walks around with prayer beads moving regularly between his fingers. After Kyrgyzstan gained independence he went to Pakistan and India to study Islam. He has returned to his home village to teach his fellow villagers about Islam and because of his appearance and missionary work at the mosque, he is respected by some and feared by others who refer to him as an "extremist," a "Wahhabist," and a "terrorist."

Ismoiljon (Chapters 2, 3, 4, 5, Conclusion) is an Uzbek blacksmith who works in the bazaar in Osh. He is a fourth-generation knife maker who wanted to be a taxi driver until his father maimed him to push him into taking over the family trade. Now in his fifties, he appreciates his profession and recently went on hajj with his wife.

Jyrgal (Adilet's brother) (Chapter 3, Conclusion) went to the city and became the intellectual of the family. He laments that, compared to his brother, he is lax in his religious practice. He struggles to find the place of Islam in relation to modernity and rationality.

Kadirbek (Chapter 5, Conclusion) is a member of Hizb ut-Tahrir and believes Islam should play an active role in governance.

Kanibek (Chapters 4, 5, Conclusion) is a Kyrgyz teacher in his early fifties who believes that ancestors remain a valuable part of one's life; that it is effective to tie a piece of cloth on a tree and make a wish; and that burning archa cleanses the room of unwanted spirits. He goes to mosque only on Orozo Ait (Eid al-Fitr) and Kurban Ait (Eid al-Adha) and considers himself both a Muslim and a communist.

Kuban (Chapter 5, Conclusion) considers being Muslim part of his national identity but is more concerned with making money than the religious character of his environment. He supports the government regulating religion and cracking down on Islamic groups that disrupt the state.

Kubat (Chapter 4, Conclusion) is an aksakal in his mid-sixties, and a particularly talented storyteller. He captivates everyone with stories of his childhood, his family, and the epic of his ancestors' greatness. In his stories, he conveys his views of the moral obligations that bind Kyrgyz in society.

Mairam (Chapters 3, 4, Conclusion) is Dimira's middle daughter and the only one who is really interested in learning the shamanistic skills of her mother. She lives in a village in the mountains.

Muktar (Chapters 2, 3, 4, 5, Conclusion) is a former classmate of Ismoiljon and a former engineer who lives in Osh. He is a taxi driver, an atheist, and a father. He is proud of his Uzbek lineage and the land his family once owned in the center of the city.

Murat (Introduction, Chapter 2, 3, Conclusion) is a Kyrgyz man in his mid-twenties who lives in the south of the country and considered himself wayward before he became more serious about religion. He talks about his new responsibilities with the birth of his son and is committed to becoming a better father. He attempts to make sense of his religious self in relation to the presence of Islamic groups such as the Islamic Movement of Uzbekistan and Hizb ut-Tahrir.

Nargiza (Chapter 4, Conclusion) is an Uzbek woman in her late forties who wears a headscarf against the wishes of her husband, lives in the south of the country, and is more conciliatory toward Christians when she talks with people from the West. Overhearing her conversations with locals, however, reveals that her feelings are more negative. She is a theologically conservative Muslim who is supportive of the efforts of Iqbol and Baktyor, but claims to be unwilling to take money from them to open an Islamic educational center. In reality, what she wants is an Islamic school that teaches regular school subjects as part of a strict Islamic education. She complains that the madrassas do not teach education beyond Islam and students need a more rounded education so that they can go on to be qualified for a variety of jobs and remain rooted in Islam.

Nurbek (Erkin's brother) (Chapters 2, 3, 4, Conclusion) is a man in his mid-twenties from a village near Nookat. He has a university education and now lives and works in Osh. When he is visiting his family, he goes to pray at the mosque and visits the chaikhana (teahouse) to meet with a number of aksakals (elders) happy to see him back in the village. The aksakals are proud of Nurbek and want him to have the right wife, to raise a family, and to teach his children the traditions of their heritage. They know he has *new* knowledge, because he works with computers and speaks a little English. Most of his life has been in post-Soviet Kyrgyzstan.

Nurdeen (Chapter 5, Conclusion) sees himself as a traditionalist, arguing that ancestors and sacred sites are an active part of what it means to be Kyrgyz and Muslim, for it connects Kyrgyz to their past and the land and serves as a fitting guide for the present and future.

Rustan (Chapter 3, Conclusion) is an ethnic Uzbek who traces his lineage back to the Prophet Muhammad. Nonetheless, he is a frequent drinker and socialite who has not visited mosque in years. He is proud of his Muslim heritage but admits to not being a serious practitioner. He does believe, however, that there is something for him to gain from his ancestors having been serious practitioners.

Toliq (Chapters 2, 3, 4, 5, Conclusion) is also a former classmate of Ismoiljon and Muktar. He became a taxi driver right out of high school and recently took out a loan to upgrade his old car to a Mercedes-Benz. He presents himself as a devout Muslim and ambitious businessman who can make a respectable living with his car. He says it is not the profession he would have chosen, but it is the only one that was readily available to him. Since getting his Mercedes, he has become more arrogant and elitist in his interactions with his fellow taxi drivers, and also more desperate for money.

Tolkun (Chapters 1, 2, 3, 4, 5, Conclusion) is a woman in her mid-fifties who lives in a remote mountain village in Naryn oblast. She frequents mazars, especially on Thursday. She knows some prayers from the Qur'an though she has no formal religious schooling. She prays to Allah, calls on the spirits for help, and regards what she does as the way one should practice Islam.

Zafar (Chapter 4, Conclusion) owns a small shop that sells household accessories in the village where he lives. For the past six years, he has been meeting with four of his friends on an almost daily basis to study the Qur'an. He has also been learning Arabic and now has a better command of the language than the imam of the local mosque. He has begun to challenge some of the interpretations of the imam and because of that has been labeled a member of Hizb ut-Tahrir despite his denial of association with the organization.

Appendix B

Methodology and Description of the Field

As described in the Introduction (see "Explaining 'the Field'"), the vast majority of material used here draws upon long-term ethnographic engagement in 1999–2001, 2004–05, 2006, 2008, 2012, and 2013. In the summer of 2005, to complement my ongoing qualitative research, I carried out a survey of religious practice (Montgomery 2007b, 279–99) in two oblasts (Osh and Naryn) of Kyrgyzstan where I had focused the bulk of my ethnographic work. In Osh oblast, it was administered in Osh city and four *raions* (districts) (Aravan, Kara-suu, Nookat, and Uzgen). In Naryn oblast, it was administered in three raions (At-Bashi, Kochkor, and Naryn). The survey sample size consisted of 869 total respondents (263 in Naryn and 536 in Osh).

The survey of religious practice consisted of 43 percent men and 57 percent women respondents (47.9 percent men, 51.3 percent women, and 0.8 percent no response in Naryn; 40.2 percent men, 59.5 percent women, and 0.3 percent no response in Osh). According to the 1999 census produced by the National Statistics Office (NSO), the population of Naryn oblast consists of 50.5 percent men and 49.5 percent women, and Osh oblast, 49.6 percent men and 50.4 percent women. The gender breakdown in Naryn closely approximates the results of the 1999 census. Figures for Osh, however, include more women. This is likely due to the fact that the survey was conducted during the summer, when residents of Osh—where land is more arable than in Naryn—are working in the fields. Labor migration may also play a factor in the discrepancy. Overrepresentation of women in survey work in Central Asia is extremely common, especially during the summer.

The ethnic breakdown of respondents for the survey of religious practice included 528 Kyrgyz, 218 Uzbek, and 53 of other ethnicities. In Naryn oblast, 94 percent of respondents were Kyrgyz and 2 percent were Uzbek; in Osh, 52 percent were Kyrgyz and 41 percent were Uzbek. The 1999 census produced by the NSO puts the ethnic breakdown in Naryn oblast as 98.7 percent Kyrgyz and 0.3 percent Uzbek. In Osh oblast the figures are 63.8 percent Kyrgyz and 31.1 percent Uzbek. The ethnic breakdown in Naryn closely approximates the results of the 1999 census. While the survey figures for Osh appear to suggest an undersample of Kyrgyz and an oversample of Uzbeks, the figures are a much closer approximation of the 1999 census results for the actual locations in which the survey was administered.

The combined age breakdown for Naryn and Osh oblasts was: respondents aged sixteen to nineteen, 5 percent; twenty to twenty-nine, 29 percent; thirty to thirty-nine, 23 percent; forty to forty-nine, 23 percent; fifty to fifty-nine, 11 percent; sixty and over, 9 percent. According to the NSO, the age breakdown for Naryn oblast was: respondents aged sixteen to nineteen, 7.6 percent; twenty to twenty-nine, 15.4 percent; thirty to thirty-nine, 13.0 percent; forty to forty-nine, 9.0 percent; fifty to fifty-nine, 4.3 percent; sixty and over, 8.0 percent. For Osh oblast, it was: respondents aged sixteen to nineteen, 8.4 percent; twenty to twenty-nine, 16.6 percent; thirty to thirty-nine, 13.8 percent; forty to forty-nine, 8.2 percent; fifty to fifty-nine, 3.6 percent; sixty and over, 6.1 percent. The survey figures approximate the 1999 census data.

The survey data were collected by thirty-two enumerators, students and faculty at local universities. The survey was piloted prior to the administration of the survey. After the pilot field test, revisions were made to ensure clarity of the survey. I trained the enumerators during a two-day training session and accompanied them to field sites to ensure quality control.

In terms of the balance between the use of qualitative and quantitative data, the interlocutors who drive the narrative of the book are all people I knew with the varying degrees of closeness all relationships have. The survey data gives a broader sense of what the various aspects of my ethnographic site looked like relative to discussions of an anthropology of knowledge, but it makes most sense when informed by the ethnographic experience. Here, I give an overview of how the data characterizes the environment of my research relative to: (1) the general demographics of the field; (2) the social organization of knowledge; (3) the corpus of knowledge; (4) the medium of knowledge; and (5) the relationship between religious practice and belief.

DEMOGRAPHICS OF THE FIELD

The vast majority of those surveyed self-identified as Muslim (98 percent), and this was true along administrative (Naryn and Osh oblast), ethnic (Kyrgyz, Uzbek, and other), and geographic (mountain, valley, in-between community) groupings, with the exception of 18 percent of other ethnic groups identifying as Orthodox Christian (14 percent), Protestant (2 percent), and atheist (2 percent). As noted above, more women participated in the survey (57 percent women to 43 percent men) and three-quarters of respondents were between twenty and forty-nine (30 percent were twenty to twenty-nine, 24 percent were thirty to thirty-nine, and 22 percent were forty to forty-nine). Twice as many respondents were married than were single (42 percent and 21 percent respectively) but nearly a quarter identified as being in a cohabitational relationship (24 percent). Six percent were divorced, 5 percent widowed, and 3 percent identified as nonmonogamous: being married with a lover (2 percent) or having multiple spouses (1 percent). In terms of material wealth, 35 percent owned a car, 54 percent a telephone, 94 percent a television, 77 percent a radio, and 74 percent had running water. The majority worked in education

(21 percent), as housewives (15 percent), or in agriculture and the small-scale economic market (9 percent); 16 percent were unemployed. In terms of education, 28 percent completed university, 23 percent technical school, and 23 percent finished secondary school; 16 percent did not finish secondary school and 8 percent did not finish university. A quarter of the respondents did not have children while nearly half had two to four children (9 percent had one child, 19 percent had two children, 15 percent had three, 14 percent had four). Two-thirds of households had four to seven residents (10 percent had three, 20 percent had four, 19 percent had five, 15 percent had six, and 13 percent had seven).

SOCIAL ORGANIZATION OF KNOWLEDGE

The social organizational characteristics of knowledge were explored along the lines of the influence of religion and tradition and how it played out in the public sphere. Eighty-eight percent claimed that religion influenced their behavior (31 percent somewhat; 57 percent a lot) and 91 percent claimed tradition was important (50 percent somewhat; 41 percent a lot). Three-quarters believe there is a relation between religion and tradition; a comparable percentage (76 percent) see an increased religiosity in the country since independence. 58 percent believe strong religious beliefs make good politicians (14 percent were neutral and 27 percent disagreed) and 53 percent believe that tradition should guide contemporary leaders. There is a general sense that religion can contribute positively to state affairs: 59 percent believe religious people are more trustworthy (18 percent are neutral and 21 percent disagree); 50 percent believe the state should control religious affairs (19 percent are neutral and 21 percent disagree); and 47 percent believe religious observance increases one's potential for economic success (23 percent are neutral and 25 percent disagree). Sixty-three percent see that shared religious belief makes ethnic difference irrelevant and in relation to significant life events such as marriage and death, the majority see religion as more important than tradition (46 percent consider a religious wedding more important than a traditional ceremony whereas 60 percent view a religious funeral as more important than a traditional one).

CORPUS OF KNOWLEDGE

In terms of the general body of religious knowledge people profess to have, it relates both to how they identify and its importance to them. The vast majority of respondents identify as practicing their religion (51 percent) or somewhat practicing (34 percent) with only 14 percent identifying as non-practicing. Likewise, the majority see religion as being important to their lives: 62 percent as very important, 31 percent as somewhat important, and only 7 percent as unimportant. Despite the importance religion plays in people's self-image, 70 percent see themselves as having average or below average knowledge about religion relative to others in their community (51 percent average, 29 percent below average, and 20 percent above average). These figures are comparable to people's perception of knowledge about tradition relative to others in their community (54 percent average, 20 percent below average, and 26 percent above average). Very few are familiar with either international or contemporary regional Islamic scholars and the majority see themselves as unfamiliar with differences between Sunni and Shi'ia (74 percent unfamiliar), the schools of Sunni Islam (84 percent unfamiliar), or Sufi practice (88 percent unfamiliar). Forty-six percent believe that Muslims worship one God and others worship a different God whereas 22 percent believe that Jews, Christians, and Muslims worship the same God. There is a low belief in magic (63 percent do not believe, 13 percent do, 24 percent are unsure) and a moderate belief in both miracles (41 percent believe, 28 percent do not, 30 percent unsure) and superstition (32 percent believe, 41 percent do not, 27 percent are unsure). Fifty-four percent can name their seven forefathers, 53 percent see tribe membership as important, and 43 percent see clan membership as important.

MEDIUM OF KNOWLEDGE

A good deal of the medium of knowledge relates to the frequency of particular modes. Nearly a quarter talk with their friends about religion on a regular basis (9 percent daily, 15 percent weekly) and only 15 percent never talk with their friends about religion (37 percent talk on special occasions, 13 percent monthly, and 11 percent less than once a month). Twenty-eight percent never study religious texts and only 18 percent do so regularly (5 percent daily, 13 percent weekly) though over half of those surveyed pray regularly (30 percent pray five times a day, 13 percent daily, and 9 percent at least once a week). Nearly one-third never visit sacred sites whereas over half (53 percent) do so on special occasions.

RELATIONSHIP BETWEEN RELIGIOUS PRACTICE AND BELIEF

There is a general sense that expression of religiosity has either increased or remained unchanged during the period of independence and the administration of the survey (1991–2005): 45 percent claim prayer frequency has increased whereas 52 percent claim there has been no change; 35 percent claim the frequency of visits to places of worship have increased while 62 percent see it as unchanged; 26 percent see an increase in the frequency of visits to sacred sites whereas 69 percent see it as unchanged; and 47 percent see religion as having an increased influence on their behavior since independence (51 percent see no change). Despite the general perception of rising orthodoxy, accessing fortunetellers, reading horoscopes, belief in magic, and belief in miracles has decreased only negligibly (10 percent, 5 percent, 8 percent, and 6 percent respectively). Fifteen percent visit fortunetellers more frequently (74 percent no change); 26 percent read horoscopes more often (69 percent no change); 8 percent believe more in magic (83 percent no change); and 19 percent believe more in miracles (75 percent no change).

It is, of course, little surprise that the more people pray and visit places of worship or sacred sites, the more they see religion influencing their behavior. Of those who pray five times a day, 91 percent claim that religion influences their behavior somewhat or a lot. But even among those who never pray or visit places of worship, the degree to which religion influences their behavior is still very high: 81 percent and 83 percent respectively. At one level, such would seem a discrepancy but in talking with my interlocutors in how they conceive themselves as struggling to enact their religious selves alongside the competing demands and ideals of their lives, it makes sense. In getting at what it means to be Muslim or to have religion influence one's life, we need the stories to supplement the quantitative. There is a general atmosphere in which people function, but all are living their own stories, with new chapters written—and rewritten—all the time.

Notes

Book epigraphs: Tolstoy (1994, 1368); Berlin (1990, xi). Epigraph attributed to Kant (1784), "Idee zu einer allgemeinen Geschichte in welbürgerlicher Absicht," though the translation is unique to Berlin.

PREFACE

Epigraphs: Borges (1967, 92); Durkheim (1995, 2).

1. For more on the importance of difference, see Seligman, Wasserfall, and Montgomery (2015).

2. "Social navigation" is a term that I began using in the early 2000s. Certainly antecedents of the idea come from the pragmatist philosophy of John Dewey, though I do not know if he uses the term. Much later, the essence of social navigation can be found in the work of the existential anthropologist Michael Jackson; it was likely used in conversations with him years ago, when I first started work on this project. While so many ideas emerge out of a multitude of influences, I trace the origin of my usage of the term (roughly) to Dewey and Jackson.

INTRODUCTION: AN ANTHROPOLOGY OF KNOWLEDGE AND LIFE "IN THE FIELD"

Epigraphs: Plato (1991, book VII, 515a. 193); James (1982, 488).

1. For more on how Islam is represented in practice and anthropology, see Montgomery (2015b).

2. The official name of the country is the Kyrgyz Republic, but Kyrgyzstan is more frequently used in the colloquial, and here the terms are used interchangeably.

3. The framework of an anthropology of knowledge pursued here builds upon the work of Fredrik Barth (1975, 1987, 1989, 2002).

4. See Dewey (1916).

5. There are, of course, philosophical frameworks that some will claim are universal and transcend all cultures, but culture itself can be used to explain why one community adopts one ethical system, for example, over another ethical system.

6. Culture in this respect is a bit like the terms *nation* and *society*, which have come to imply particular groupings and to reify particular orderings that lead to the term being something that not only defines but also creates. There are certain characteris-

tics of a nation, and the leaders of nations wanting to be considered legitimate try to conform themselves accordingly (Wolf 1997, 3, 6, 387).

7. There is a move within cognitive science to try and explain the acquisition of religious knowledge in scientific terms with flowcharts resembling models used to design artificial intelligence (see Whitehouse 2004). While there is some utility to these attempts, they tend to create the impression that we have a greater scientific understanding of how the mind works than we actually do. For example, we do not yet understand the full complexity of the brain nor are we able to artificially simulate object recognition in a three-dimensional space, let alone the processes behind complex behaviors like those associated with religion.

8. For an evaluation of the "island of democracy" discussion, see Laruelle and Engvall (2015).

9. For an overview of country demographics, see Central Intelligence Agency (2013b).

10. For a good discussion of how Uzbeks in Kyrgyzstan see themselves in relation to their titular country and the one in which they live, see Liu (2002, 2012).

11. The scene during the 2010 putsch, however, was more violent (see International Crisis Group 2010).

12. The populations of Rishton and Sokh are predominately Tajik, even though they are part of Uzbekistan.

13. It is always difficult to know if an answer given can be interpreted with certainty, that it accurately corresponded to the question I intended to ask. That being said, answers to some questions can be viewed with greater certainty than others. For example, a question asking who people view as the most influential Islamic scholar was most frequently answered as Ibn Sina (Avicenna). Ibn Sina was certainly one of the most familiar names on the list to Central Asians, but the interpretation of what that answer means is complicated as most people know Ibn Sina from his influential medical treatises and not necessarily from his religious writings. I have relied largely on my ethnographic work to make sense of the data for purposes of interpretation as well as the contextualization of what can be considered both accurate and useful.

While the number of surveys administered allows for statistical significance, the statistical aspects of the survey were not my focus. For me, the issue of representativeness involved a greater number of surveys than what was statistically required, based on how I viewed the variables I would be analyzing. In the end, the data is representative of the population with which I was working.

14. Though not *Wahhabis*, in common usage Wahhabi is a pejorative label applied to people viewed as extreme in the strictures of their practice and open to the use of violence to attain a particular end (see Rasanayagam 2006b).

15. For an expanded account of this story and its implications, see Montgomery (2015a).

16. Out of respect to my interlocutors, all names are pseudonyms and in some instances, the exact village names are not given. If one village name is substituted for another, it is within the categorizations as described above.

17. For two relevant studies on the role of social memory, see Privratsky (2001) and Paxson (2005).

Chapter 1: Learning Everyday (Islam)

Epigraphs: Bandura (1977, 27); Goethe (1989, 86).

1. The descriptive terms "orthodox" and "heterodox" are, of course, mine. Azarmat and Tolkun use the terms "good" and "bad," respectively.

2. Some very good scholarship on Central Asia addresses the complexity of everyday life, including Borbieva (2012); Hilgers (2009); Kehl-Bodrogi (2008); Liu (2012); Louw (2007); McBrien (2006); Pelkmans (2007); Rasanayagam (2011); Schwab (2011); Zanca (2011). The absence to which I refer is not a lacuna in scholarship so much as a general understanding outside small academic circles.

3. For an overview of country demographics, see Central Intelligence Agency (2013a).

4. I certainly do not want to claim that statistics are without value. They can be very important. One need only think of the first British census in India: for the first time people perceived that Muslims were a minority religion in the country, even though they were the majority in the north. That statistic changed the way people saw themselves as Muslims (see Eaton 1993).

5. For more on ethnicity, see Brubaker (2004).

6. "*On ne nastoiashchii Kyrgyz*"—Russian: "He is not a genuine Kyrgyz."

7. For a critique of this, see Montgomery and Heathershaw (2016).

8. See, for example, Winnicott (1971) on the issue of the transitional object.

9. This is what Berger and Luckmann (1966) refer to as primary socialization. See *The Social Construction of Reality*, especially chapter 3.

10. Talking about the "Great Game" of Central Asia emphasizes the role of outsiders trying to manipulate the region rather than a focus on the region from the view of those who lived there.

11. For energy production figures compiled from Asian Development Bank figures, see Olcott (2005, 269).

12. The role of cotton in Uzbekistan is a very interesting story connected to the United States Civil War and the desire of imperial Russia to free itself of dependence on United States cotton. The problems of cotton were exacerbated by the Soviet planned economies and continued under the Uzbek government. For more on the cotton economy, see, for example: Environmental Justice Foundation (2005); Lipovsky (1995); and Rumer (1990).

13. For more on the Kyrgyz protests, see Collins (2011); Hanks (2011); Heathershaw (2007b); Radnitz (2010); Reeves (2011a); Temirkulov (2010).

14. While the 2010 violence in Osh came on the heels of an increase in Kyrgyz nationalism under the Bakiyev presidency, the dynamics out of which it evolved remains unclear. While many Osh Uzbek residents did not want to get involved, as in 2005, once violence began targeting the different ethnic groups it became an ethnic conflict even as it is unlikely to have begun that way (Reeves 2011a).

15. The protests in Kokand were in November 2004 and resulted in a change of tax policy.

16. Uzbekistan evicted the United States from the Karshi-Khanabad air base in July 2005 in a move that was seen as in response to the United States' call for an international investigation into the Andijan protests.

17. *Omen* (amen) is said at the end of a blessing or prayer that is accompanied by moving one's hands in a downward brushing motion over the face.

18. There is a danger of the everyday being used to discount what people do; that is, that by referring to something as part of the everyday it is relativized and any sense of being critical is lost. The everyday is perhaps the most difficult to articulate because so much of it is hidden. Nonetheless, the term is intended to guide analysis by bringing the overlooked into the foreground.

19. In the late nineteenth century, adherents of Reform Judaism, to show their "progressiveness," ignored kashrut and served shellfish at a dinner of the Central Conference of American Rabbis.

20. Such as: William James: "Religion . . . shall mean for us *the feelings, acts, and experiences of individual men in their solitude, so far as they apprehend themselves to stand in relation to whatever they may consider the divine* [original emphasis]. Since the relation may be either moral, physical, or ritual, it is evident that out of religion in the sense in which we take it, theologies, philosophies, and ecclesiastical organizations may secondarily grow" (1982, 31).

Emile Durkheim: *"A religion is a unified system of beliefs and practices relative to sacred things, that is to say, things set apart and forbidden—beliefs and practices which unite into one single moral community called a Church, all those who adhere to them"* [original emphasis] (1995, 44).

Clifford Geertz: "A religion is: (1) a system of symbols which acts to (2) establish powerful, pervasive, and long-lasting moods and motivations in men by (3) formulating conceptions of a general order of existence and (4) clothing these conceptions with such an aura of factuality that (5) the moods and motivations seem uniquely realistic" (1973, 90).

21. *The Fundamentals* were a series of twelve volumes published between 1910 to 1914 that were written in reaction to late-nineteenth-century liberal Protestantism. *The Fundamentals* advocated a return to what conservative Evangelicals saw as the five fundamentals of Christian belief: the Bible's literal inerrancy; Christ's divine virgin birth, atonement, and His physical resurrection and bodily return.

22. See Almond, Appleby, and Sivan (2003, esp. 14–17) on the problems of the term. See also the five-volume *Fundamentalism Project* edited by Marty and Appleby (1991, 1993a, 1993b, 1994, 1995).

23. In 328 BCE, Alexandria Eschate, "Alexandria the Furthest," was founded in what is present-day Khojand (Soucek 2000, 13).

24. For a good engagement with the problems of the "Great Game," see Morrison (2014).

25. The term in its current meaning came into use after the Second World War, though is often attributed to Rudyard Kipling's use of the phrase in his novel *Kim* (1995). See Hopkirk (1992); Meyer and Brysac (1999); and Yapp (2001).

The ceding of the Wakhan Corridor to Afghanistan in 1907 effectively ended the Great Game. To the outside world at least, the Russians, and later the Soviets, had secured their position over their Central Asian territories. The war in Afghanistan, however, saw Central Asia again become an area over which outside powers struggled for influence and control. With the Soviet invasion of Afghanistan in 1979, the United States saw an opportunity to play out the aggressions of the Cold War and support-ed the *mujahedeen*, the resistance forces fighting the Soviet-supported communist troops. The war dragged on for ten years, ending with the Soviet withdrawal in 1989. The United States failed to follow through on its promises of support and left the re-gion, marking the end of what some have seen as the second great game (see Bradsher 1999; Roy 1990).

26. The reason to include these as part of Central Asia is largely on grounds of ethnic and cultural similarities. However, there are also reasons that these countries can be considered to be outside of the region—Azerbaijan is on the other side of the Caspian; Afghanistan is sometimes linked to the Middle East, sometimes to the Indi-an subcontinent; and Mongolia and Xinjiang both had different histories than Soviet Muslim Central Asia.

27. On the issue of borders in this region, see Megoran (2002); Reeves (2007, 2011c, 2014).

28. A number of good histories exist on Central Asia. See Barthold (1992); Beck-with (2009); Crews (2006); Frye (1996); Geiss (2003); Golden (2011); Grousset (1970); Soucek (2000).

29. Al-Bukhari and Ibn Sina were the best-known historical Islamic scholars, ac-cording to data from the survey I conducted.

30. A caravanserai was a place for travelers to find food, shelter, and protection along their journey. Because of its remoteness, Tash Rabat was forgotten about after the Silk Road ceased to be important and remained largely intact when it was "redis-covered" during the Soviet period.

31. Tash Rabat is also near Koshoy Korgon, the ruins of a tenth–twelfth-century CE citadel that is tied to Kyrgyz mythology as the place where Manas buried his friend Koshoy.

32. These percentages are unofficial estimates provided by Kyrgyz nationals that worked with the October 2000 presidential election commission. The Vice-Governor of Naryn oblast requested this information on my behalf, but was told that statistical information about Osh oblast was secretive and required a written request and min-istry approval. Such secrecy did not apply to other regions of the Kyrgyz Republic and suggested a heightened awareness and fear of renewed fighting in the Osh area.

Violence did ensue in 2010, but seemingly for different reasons than what was feared in 2000 (see Reeves 2011a).

33. The enclaves were results of land swaps between collective farms (see Reeves 2014).

34. For more on the "colonization of consciousness" as exemplified by this, see Comaroff and Comaroff (1991).

35. Poliakov (1992) speaks about parallel Islam and traditional society, typical of Soviet ethnographers whose analytical slant was meant to fit Soviet policy. See Privratsky (2001) for examples of how religious aspects of wedding and funeral rituals were moved from public view to private domain, but kept alive and communicated as tradition.

36. It was the case in the late 1990s and early 2000s that Uzbek men living in Osh viewed Uzbekistan as a state of greater authority and functionality than Kyrgyzstan (Liu 2002). Since the mid-2000s, however, Uzbeks in Osh have seen the path of Uzbekistan as a government in decline and are thus more inclined to speak favorably of their opportunities as citizens of Kyrgyzstan (Liu 2012).

37. Geertz writes, in supposed agreement "with Max Weber, that man is an animal suspended in webs of significance he himself has spun, I take culture to be those webs, and the analysis of it to be therefore not an experimental science in search of law but an interpretive one in search of meaning" (1973, 5). Deweyian pragmatism also supports the idea that man makes meaning (see McDermott 1981).

38. "Seventy-five percent Muslim" is a figure commonly referenced by the CIA World Factbook and therefore replicated as a standard descriptor of religious demographics in Kyrgyzstan (Central Intelligence Agency 2013a).

Chapter 2: "Muslim by Birth, Atheist by Belief"

Epigraphs: Aristotle (1999, 4); Pascal (1995, 464).

1. For Aristotle, *phronesis* is used to connote a soundness of judgment in the realm of practical issues. It is a companion to *sophia*, the theoretical contributor to one's success in attempting to live a good life (Aristotle 1999). For a good discussion of Aristotle's approach to practical knowledge, see Dunne (1997).

2. The number of classes formed depends on the size of the school and number of students. As students advance, the year changes but the class they are in stays the same. For example, first-year students considered the smartest are in 1A and in ninth grade they would be the 9A class. If the school offers a curriculum in Russian, the best class is generally 1A and the best Kyrgyz-language class is 1B. The numbering of classes proceeds in line with the Russian alphabet.

3. This continues through university, where bribery and purchasing of grades commonly subsidizes the incomes of faculty members.

4. For statistics on gender in Kyrgyz schools, see Tiuliundieva (2006).

5. It is often wrongly assumed that only men can pray in mosques in Kyrgyzstan and that women do not study in madrassas. Women can pray in mosques; unfortunately most mosques do not have a separate room for them to pray, but the main mosque in Bishkek does.

Also, in Batken, there is an all-girl madrassa. This was a conscious decision of the local imam, who had only enough money for either a boys' or a girls' madrassa. He opted for a girls' madrassa because, he said, girls will become mothers and spend much more time with their children than their husbands and thus would have a more significant impact in making the community more Islamic. Many of the girls who attended did so because their parents could not afford to send them to school, but some went because they wanted to study only Islam.

6. On the construction of social memories, see Connerton (1989) and Paxson (2005).

7. *Aksakal* (Kyrgyz), "white beard," a term of respect. Traditionally, to grow facial hair, a man must either be the oldest in his immediate family or get permission from his father to grow a beard or moustache. Thus, having a white beard is a marker of age and status in a family.

8. For more on the aksakal councils, see the work of Judith Beyer (2007, 2013, 2015).

9. Turkestan is where the mausoleum of Khodja Akhmed Yassawi is located. Yassawi was a famous poet, philosopher, and preacher whose teachings founded one of the main Sufi orders of Central Asia, which bears his name. Turkestan is located in current-day Kazakhstan. For an excellent ethnography on Turkestan, see Privratsky (2001).

10. For wonderful ethnography on collective farms, albeit in Buryat Republic, see Humphrey (1998).

11. For more on how this can be contextualized, see Montgomery (2013a).

12. An example of how knowledge at this level becomes intensely shared (and at times radicalized) is that of Hizb ut-Tahrir members who meet in prison. As will be discussed later, many accused of being members of Hizb ut-Tahrir are farmers with limited formal Islamic education who want to be better Muslims and perceive in Hizb ut-Tahrir a more serious and pious devotion to Islam. While in prison, however, they discover something about the threat and power in their adherence to religion.

13. The khanate of Kokand, located in the Ferghana Valley, was abolished in the 1870s and incorporated into the governorate-general of Turkestan.

14. For more on this, see Allworth (1973, esp. chaps. 11–13); Roy (2000, 3).

15. For more on the idea of Soviet nationalism, see Fragner (2001).

16. For more on this, see Cornell (1999).

17. Based on research conducted on visits to Uzbekistan, June 2000, and March 2001.

18. For a discussion on the evolution of nationalism in Kazakhstan, see Sarsembayev (1999).

19. There can be seen differences between the traditional roles of sedentary agrarian Uzbeks and nomadic shepherding Kyrgyz, but in the plains of the Ferghana Valley these distinctions are less significant.

20. To further complicate matters, the Osh province of 1990 has, since independence, been divided into three separate oblasts: Osh, Jalal-Abad, and Batken. When I refer to Osh province, I am referring to the region as a whole.

21. While the roots of the 1990 Osh conflict appeared to outside observers to be largely about a dispute over land claims—even today there are over 100 separate land disputes resulting from the arbitrary borders that separate ethnicities and ethnic claims (Grebenshchikov 2000)—the conflict was also influenced by the Uzbek percep-

tion of being underrepresented in Kyrgyz government and the Kyrgyz perception of Uzbek dominance in retail and trade (Anderson 1997, 68).

22. The ritual and community structures of the Uzbek-Kyrgyzstani and Kyrgyz are similar. Outside the Osh region, mixed marriages between the two ethnic groups are common. In the Osh region of the Ferghana Valley, however, there is little intermarriage and people intermingle only as necessary (Zaharova and Megoran 2000).

23. In Russian *yurta*—a round felt structure housing nomads during summer migrations in the upper pastures.

24. For a critical inquiry into this, see Laruelle and Engvall (2015).

25. For Uzbek clans historically, see Ilkhamov (2002); for Kyrgyz clans, see Abramzon (1990 [1971]). For more on the basics of clan and tribal organization, see Krader (1963, 1971); Hudson (1964). For contemporary works on clans in Central Asia, see Collins (2004); Gullette (2010); Schatz (2004, 2005); Vaisman (1995).

26. On nomadism and nomadic societies see Barfield (1981, 1993); Krader (1963).

27. In Kyrgyzstan, very few, if any, Kyrgyz still migrate year-round. More migrate in Naryn oblast than other parts of the country; they generally leave in mid-April or May and return in mid-September or October. For the winter months, they live in more sedentary settlements, many of which were built during the Soviet period.

28. The idea of social navigation can be seen clearly in Bourdieu (2000); Vigh (2006).

29. At the time, the exchange rate was 42 Kyrgyz som to the U.S. dollar.

CHAPTER 3: "OUR ANCESTORS ALSO LIVE HERE"

Epigraphs: Shils (1981, 41); Russell (1992, 9).

1. The axial age is a construct that helps us understand and explain change that took place in the period between 500 BCE and 600 CE when the great religious traditions of the world evolved. It is during this period that soteriological concerns developed: a split between transcendence and the world in which we live. Thus, when the gods move from the tangible, lived-in world of pharaoh-gods or the Greek pantheon to gods located outside, beyond the lived world, in a transcendent world accessible only by the bridge of salvation, the existing social order can be questioned. Kings no longer have the authority of gods but are held accountable by gods. Elites who may also serve as gatekeepers to the soteriological bridge can question this accountability. Populations now organize themselves along faith communities rather than just by ethnicity or location, and new types of conflicts—over ultimate meanings—can develop. See Eisenstadt (1982, 1985, 1986); Bellah (2011); Bellah and Joas (2012).

2. While neither Gorbunova (1986) nor Zadneprovskij (2000) focuses on religion in these works, they do discuss the archeological finds during this period. Gorbunova, for example, discusses funerary rites and notes that a particular placement of the corpse appears to have been strictly followed; that pottery found in the graves was always on the right of the body; and that mutton bones were found in a number of the graves (36–39). This suggests an otherworldly purpose in people's lives that can be seen by the presence and placement of artifacts near the grave.

3. For a discussion of the nomadic life, see Barfield (1993, esp. chap 5).

4. On the utility of animism, see Harvey (2006); Horton (1968); Nida and Smalley (1959); Willerslev (2007).

5. Whereas a shaman is generally seen as a voice for spirit world, a priest is an intermediary. Evans-Pritchard, in speaking about the Nuer in Sudan, characterized the difference between shaman and priest as such: "Whereas in the priest man speaks to God, in the prophet [shaman] . . . God speaks to man" (Lessa and Vogt 1979, 302).

6. The term shamanism comes from Siberia, the homeland of many who migrated from Central Asia. For more on shamanism, see Baldick (2012); Balzer (1990, 1997); Eliade (1964); Emmons (2000); Halifax (1979); Halemba (2003); Hoppál (1984); Reid (2002).

It is important to note, as Pedersen does, that we may overlook many shamanistic elements if we are only focusing on shamans as we conceive them. There are many more shamanistic elements that people in Kyrgyzstan draw upon than there are shamans, as well as those who are "not quite shamans" who use various shamanistic elements to advance the image of their connectedness to the spirits (Pedersen 2011).

7. *Archa* (Kyrgyz: juniper).

8. For a good historical discussion of household rites, the domestic cult, and the hearth fire, see DeWeese (1994, 40 ff.). For more on Zoroastrianism, see Boyce (2001); Nigosian (1993).

9. There are some claims that secret Zoroastrian communities exist in Uzbekistan and Tajikistan.

10. It is not uncommon that various people go to a religious site with different purposes; this can be seen at both mazars and mosques. See Saroyan (1997).

11. Soucek (2000, 117 ff.). For an impressive discussion of conversion narratives in Central Asia, see DeWeese (1994). In addition to Muslim missionaries, there were also Christians trying to convert the area in the thirteenth and fourteenth centuries. DeWeese (1994, 135).

12. Soucek (2000, 37). Eaton (1993) gives a description of the way Sufi missionaries worked on the Indian subcontinent. On shrines, see McChesney (1991).

13. DeWeese does a nice job responding to biases against claims of the lax adoption of Islam among Kyrgyz in his discussion of Manas and oral traditions (1994, 59–69).

14. It is worth noting that not all members of the Soviet government working in Central Asia were supportive of the national-territorial delimitation plan. For example, Georgiy Chicherin, People's Commissar for Foreign Affairs of the USSR from 1923 to 1930 tried to convince Stalin not to make any radical changes to the boundaries of Central Asia. In a letter to Stalin, Chicherin described the redrawing of boundaries as putting "Bukhara, Khiva, and Turkestan into a big cauldron and to divide them according to the nationalities principle, thus creating new republics" (5 April 1924). In later letters to Stalin, Chicherin said that "it has been absolutely clear to me from the latest reports . . . that the issue of national delimitation has not been thought out enough" (22 May 1924) and that continuing such a path would lead to "a Pandora's box . . . being created, where all will be fighting against all" (6 June 1924). See Karasar (2002).

15. For an excellent essay on the use of law as a tool to influence change in Central Asia, see Massell (1968).

16. Saroyan (1997). See especially his essay "The Islamic Clergy and Community in the Soviet Union," pp. 43–56, and "The Reinterpretation and Adaptation of Soviet Islam," pp. 57–87.

17. See Roy (2000).

18. The Central Asian republics actually supported signing the New Union Treaty (prior to the August coup, which led to the dissolution of the Soviet Union) because they needed the economic support and Soviet-established common markets.

19. For an example of how such categories are used, see Bennigsen and Wimbush (1985); Poliakov (1992). For a good discussion of this problem, see Rasanayagam (2006a).

20. There are also calls to reassess *ijtihad*. I spoke with some people in the months prior to the 2005 Andijan events who argued that Akramiya represented a new Islamic school. After Andijan, people were less open to discussing this, though at all times very few took this claim seriously.

21. It is interesting to note that both Soviet-influenced and Western-inspired philosophies of rationality occasionally differ from what may be understood as rational to Kyrgyz who have been less persuaded by Soviet and Western ways of thought. So too is the case with authority.

22. There are women with small businesses, but they seemed not to be as focused on using Islam for social advancement, whereas successful businessmen might use Islam to advance their status and political reach.

23. For more on the mazars in Kyrgyzstan, see Aitpaeva (2013); Aitpaeva and Egemberdieva (2009); Aitpaeva, Egemberidieva, and Toktogulova (2007).

24. Qutb was the founder of the Muslim Brotherhood. For more on Qutb, see Lee (1997); Mitchell (1993).

25. Naqshband was a fourteenth-century founder of a Sufi order near Bukhara. For more on Naqshband, see Gaborieau, Popovic, and Zarcone (1990); Özdalga (1999); Trimingham (1998).

26. Interestingly, in the survey of religious practice that I conducted in Kyrgyzstan in 2005, Kyrgyz and Uzbeks tend to list Arabs as the most religious ethnic group, suggesting that Arabs practice Islam more correctly. The foundation of this assumption involves an importation of cultural practices that are often foreign to the Central Asian context.

27. For more on Hizb ut-Tahrir in Kyrgyzstan and the IMU, see Heyat (2004); Karagiannis (2005, 2010); McGlinchey (2005, 2011); Naumkin (2003).

28. Charisma concerns itself with ultimate meanings. There is charisma in ordering, regardless of the order, for the ability to impose order is the ability to invoke meaning. And any order is a more palatable option than complete chaos. The paradox of charisma is that at the same time it creates and legitimates order, its institutionalization in the postaxial period allows the questioning of charismatic order by those claiming to interpret the soteriological. These are the elites and these are the ones with whom we as academics generally concern ourselves. See Eisenstadt (1968); Jaspers (1953); Shils (1975).

29. On the utility of conflict to define the group, see Coser (1956).

30. While most of the discussion and concerns of boundary maintenance are connected to the group, boundary maintenance begins with the individual's ability to recognize and demarcate boundaries. Freud, for example, saw the failure to distinguish the ego from the external world as a sign of pathology; see Freud (1989).

31. Olufsen (1911) and Canfield (1973) both speak of a geographical layering that places the minority group—the one seen as the most heterodox—at elevations the more orthodox groups do not want to live. In Canfield's study of the Hindu Kush, for example, the Sunnis are in the valley, with Shi'ia living higher up, and Ismailis living higher yet.

32. As I have suggested earlier, all religions draw from earlier sources and thus to a certain extent the term *syncretism* can be problematic unless it is acknowledged that the results of syncretism can be either heterodox or orthodox. For more on syncretism, see Leopold and Jensen (2004); Matory (1994); Stewart and Shaw (1994).

33. *Isrik* (*Peganum harmala*) is a plant that is burned to rid an area of bad spirits, much like archa.

CHAPTER 4: "LISTEN AND WATCH!"

Epigraphs: Rousseau (1966, 11); Kearney (2002, 3).

1. Generally a ritual interjection, *omen* (pronounced o-men) means "amen, let it be so"; in Kyrgyz, амин, омийин, оомийн, оомийин; in Uzbek, омин, овмин, овмийн.

Muslim prayers can be divided into *salaah* (canonical prayers), *du'aa* (supplication), and *dhikr* (remembrance). See Fakir (1978, 32–34).

Omen is *du'aa*. The act of prayer, a blessing or benediction, and the first sura of the Qur'an (*Fatiah* in Arabic) is called *bata* (бата) in Kyrgyz and *fotiha* (фотиха) in Uzbek.

2. *Plov*, a traditional rice dish, is one of the few dishes, along with *shashlik*—grilled meat—that a male will assume an "expertise" in cooking.

3. Postmodernists argue that the text itself is really quite malleable, rewritten in a sense by each reader. I do not disagree with this; theoretically it is true. But this assumes a level of critical thinking that is not always found in the villages and among those trained more in a system of memorization than critical interpretation of the text. Regardless, I do not take issue with the malleability of the text but rather suggest that though many often perceive the text as nonmalleable, the degree to which each individual is able to understand the text makes its message malleable. The problem lies in the translation of meaning.

4. A cloth placed on the floor on which food is placed. There will always be some bread on the *dosterkan* for the guests, along with whatever other food can be provided.

5. The girls are often busy helping the women prepare the meal or clean after the meal.

6. The centerpiece of Kyrgyz literature, "Manas" was not written down until the late nineteenth century (and even then, only part of it) though it was mentioned as early as the fifteenth century. See *Manas* (1999); Prior (1995); and van der Heide (2008).

7. There is generally some variation in the recitation of Manas, with manaschis incorporating differences in setting and their own learning of Manas. For an example of how epics are reinterpreted and retold with variation in context and location, see Aitpaeva (2006).

8. One version is that Almambet was born circumcised; another suggests that he was wet-nursed by a Dungan (Chinese Muslim) and thereafter refused his infidel mother. See DeWeese (1994, 59–66).

9. Luria's research looked at perception, generalization and abstraction, deduction and inference, reasoning and problem solving, imagination, and self-analysis and self-awareness among the changing population. An example of his research follows.

Subject: Mirzanb, age thirty-three, uneducated; works in a village; has been in Fergana once, never in any other city. Is shown drawings of: *glass-saucepan-spectacles-bottle*.

"I don't know which of the things doesn't fit here. Maybe it's the bottle? You can drink tea out of the glass—that's useful. The spectacles are also useful. But there's vodka in the bottle—that's bad."

Uses principle of "utility" to classify objects.

Could you say that the spectacles don't belong in this group?

"No, spectacles are also a useful thing."

Subject is given a complete examination of how three of the objects refer to the category of "cooking vessels."

So wouldn't it be right to say the spectacles don't fit in this group?

"No, I think the bottle doesn't belong here. It's harmful!"

But you can use one word—vessels—for these three, right?

"I think there's vodka in the bottle, that's why I didn't take it. . . . Still, if you want me to. . . . But, you know, the fourth thing [spectacles] is also useful."

Disregards generic term.

"If you're cooking something you have to see what you're doing, and if a person's eyes are bothering him, he's got to wear a pair of glasses."

But you can't call spectacles a vessel, can you?

"If you're cooking something on fire, you've got to use the eyeglasses or you just won't be able to cook" (Luria 1976, 57–58).

10. Naryn had a military base that served to protect the border area with China. An old Russian woman with whom I spoke many times was one of the first Russians to arrive in Naryn in the early 1930s. She was eight years old when she came with her parents—her father worked at the military base—and she praised the reforms of the Soviet Union, which she referred to as "giving civilization to the illiterate Kyrgyz."

11. This process was phased in, with standards increasing each year. See Grant (1964); Kamalov (1975, 43–57); Kolmakova (1957, 597 ff.).

12. It is of course the case that knowledge of the text does not preclude serious discussions over ideas. But when that knowledge is limited, the discussion also becomes limited, generally centered on arguments of behavior that is nontextual.

13. Referring back to the Old Testament, for example, Mormons or Anabaptists legitimate polygyny, which is a position that runs contrary to prevailing cultural norms (Goody 2000, 10).

14. On the value of secretive knowledge, see Barth (1975, 1987, 1989).

15. The serial was produced in Brazil between 2001 and 2002 though it was aired on Kyrgyz television in 2004–05. The story features a Brazilian woman of Moroccan descent wanting to pursue her love for a man her family does not approve. The story addressed the issue of human cloning, but its resonance for many of my interlocutors was more centered on the tensions between living in the Islamic and Western worlds. See also McBrien (2012).

16. Some Christian groups are gaining popularity and creating an environment that sets up tension in a place with little plurality. In general, the relationship had been one where Russians were Orthodox Christians and everyone else was Muslim. Many of the new Christian groups, however, are trying to offer a new life, free of many restrictions of the existing social structure. This represents a new push to try to come to terms with a different corpus and how it fits within a revised social structure of knowledge. For more, see Montgomery (2007a).

17. The Reformation can be seen as one such period. See Voegelin (1952).

18. *Tushoo kesuu* means "cutting the way." *Toi* [Kyrgyz] is a general word for celebration or party.

19. The Basmala is the first verse of the Qur'an and is translated from Arabic as: "In the name of Allah, most Gracious, most Compassionate. . . ."

20. *Ak jol* [Kyrgyz] (literally, white road), often said to someone traveling so that the journey will be safe.

21. This raises the problem of definitions and what I actually mean by ritual. Defining a term can at its base serve as a point of discounting and closing the discussion of an argument. For my purposes, it is enough to borrow a definition from Roy Rappaport, who sees ritual as "*the performance of more or less invariant sequences of formal acts and utterances not entirely encoded by the performers*" (original emphasis), Rappaport (1999, 24).

For more on key discussions of ritual, see also Bell (1992, 1997); Turner (1995); Seligman et al. (2008); Seligman and Weller (2012).

22. Arabic: partial ablutions done prior to salat.

23. For more on the development of craft, see Bensman and Lilienfeld (1991); Langer (1953).

Chapter 5: Framing Politics, Morality, and a Practice of Understanding

Epigraphs: Dewey (1991 [1910], 11); Asad (1986, 17).

1. My use of the term "frames" is not intended to imply that I situate my critique within a schema of frame analysis per se (see, e.g., Goffman 1974). I accept the basic idea that there are distinctions of frames in thought and frames in communication (Druckman 2001a, 2001b), but use the term colloquially to imply a way of seeing, understanding, and interacting with information and events. Thus I interchangeably discuss frame, view, and perspective to argue that a particular vision implies a certain bias about which we would benefit from self-reflection.

2. See Bennigsen and Wimbush (1986); Gross (1992); Hann and Pelkmans (2009); Ro'i (1995); Shahrani (1994).

3. While some may be critical of the discussion to use "good" and "bad" as analytical categories, it is a reflection of how Central Asians talk about each other and even many outside of academic concerns do find utility in these terms. See Mamdani (2002); Rasanayagam (2011, esp. chap. 3).

4. For an excellent discussion of the subjunctive use in imagining community connections, though in a different sense, through ritual, see Seligman et al. (2008).

5. For more on the idea of developing a theory of the rough ground, see Montgomery (2014). This chapter is adapted from that article.

6. Examples include: International Crisis Group (2009); Kamalov (2010); Levy (2009); Pannier (2011). See also Heathershaw and Megoran (2011); Reeves (2005); Thompson and Heathershaw (2005).

7. It is remarkable, of course, that commonness carries an air of being unremarkable and that the voice of the majority comes to be silenced in its majority.

8. Throughout this chapter, I am largely talking about policy and ethnographic frames from a Western perspective (Western governments, academics, advisory circles), but I believe the process describes the role of bias and agenda more generally. Local Islamophobia, for example, is generated not only by Western policy discourse but also by Soviet policy that saw religion as a threat to the state (Froese 2008).

9. Marx said in the first chapter of *The Eighteenth Brumaire of Louis Napoleon*, "Man makes his own history, but he does not make it out of the whole cloth; he does not make it out of conditions chosen by himself, but out of such as he finds close at hand" (Marx 2004, 3).

10. This includes orientalist critiques, such as Said (1994, 1997); Varisco (2007).

11. See, for example, Devji (2008). The social origins of various movements are often seen locally as just (see Mitchell 1993; Norton 2007).

12. There is a growing sense of the importance of public or engaged anthropology; see, for example, Besteman and Gusterson (2005).

13. For an excellent engagement with practical knowledge, from whence originates the idea of a theory of the rough ground, see Dunne (1997).

14. Lakoff's (1987) comparison of "women, fire, and dangerous things" is illustrative of the influence of categories of danger.

15. Such realities become clear when, for example, talking about Jehovah's Witnesses refusing life-saving blood transfusions to avoid eternal damnation. The calculus of the refusing makes sense to the Jehovah's Witness and not someone else precisely because they do not categorize danger in the same way.

16. While the War in Afghanistan diminished its presence in Central Asia, some intelligence reporting suggests that the IMU was still active, at least in Afghanistan and Pakistan, ten years after being folded into the international "War on Terror." See Roggio (2011).

17. This includes reporters like Alisher Saipov, editor-in-chief of *Siyosat*, the Uzbek-language paper in Kyrgyzstan, who was assassinated in Osh, Kyrgyzstan, in October 2007 for being outspoken on human rights abuses in Uzbekistan.

18. The author's own experience on this includes conversations with reporters from some of the leading news outlets in the West and Russia.

19. Examples include: BBC (2009a, 2009b, 2009c, 2009d, 2010a, 2010b); Times of Oman/Reuters (2010).

20. In the mid- to late-1990s there was an emphasis on Kyrgyz as identity. By the mid-2000s, economic realities precipitated a recognition in some villages that had dropped Russian-language education from their schools of a need to reinstate Russian as an actively taught language, especially in light of labor migration that makes Russian a practical necessity to minimize abuses of migrants. As well, competency in Kyrgyz language during the early 2000s became a political tool to regulate those who could run for public office.

21. By 2000, this was already appearing in schools in Naryn Oblast (personal observation). See Akayev (2003); van der Heide (2008).

"Literally translated, the Seven Principles are as follows:

1. The undividable unity of all the people, its head in one collar, its arm in one sleeve.
2. Accord, friendship, and cooperation between nationalities.
3. Ethnic pride and clear conscience.
4. Through relentless work and advanced industry and science, well-being and prosperity are aspired.
5. Humanism, nobility, and forgiveness.
6. Having a sweet relation with nature.
7. Strengthening the Kyrgyz government and guarding her like an eye's pupil." (van der Heide 2008, 274)

22. See Akayev (2003, chap. 3: "Religious Revival and Local Tradition"); Omuraly uulu (1994); Sarygulov (2005).

23. For more on these types of ritual practices, see Aitpaeva et al. (2007); Aitpaeva and Egemberdieva (2009); Aitpaeva (2013).

24. Similarly, Uzbekistan supported Sufism and the rejuvenation of various Sufi sites to foster a type of Islam seen as compatible with the state. See, for example, Louw (2007).

25. In Kyrgyzstan, the State Agency for Religious Affairs works on behalf of the state to foster a version of Islam compatible with the state. And while such agencies come with the authority of the state, it also works with the state agenda. There have been ongoing attempts to standardize and locally accredit Islamic education and worship. This seeks to create an environment where Kyrgyz see the state as authoritative in shaping the development of a Muslim public. The state gets involved in pushing a particular vision of Islam not because of a sense of moral obligation in fostering religious development, but because of the practicality of having the population view the state as religious partner rather than adversary. This, it is hoped, would curb public support for antigovernment enthusiasm.

26. See, among others, Borbieva (2012); Louw (2007); McBrien (2006); Pelkmans (2007); Rasanayagam (2011); Schwab (2011).

27. See notes 18 and 19 above.

28. Fortunately, there are some ethnographers working on Islam in Central Asia whose work is both thoughtful and informative (such as Borbieva 2012; Hilgers 2009; Kehl-Bodrogi 2008; Liu 2012; Louw 2007; McBrien 2006; Pelkmans 2007; Rasanayagam 2011; Schwab 2011; Zanca 2011) and others working within the ethnographic frame (such as Igmen 2012; Kamp 2006; Khalid 2007; Northrop 2004). Unfortunately, the nuanced message of their work seems not to be the dominant message heard in popular media.

29. Stories are significant because the stories we tell impact our framing of moral truths. For a discussion of this around three heroic figures—a Muslim saint, tribal chief, and king—and international actors, see Edwards (1996).

30. This is higher than the national average because the survey did not include areas like Bishkek and Chui oblast, where one would find more ethnic Russians identifying with Orthodox Christianity. The percentages, however, do not vary significantly and in both cases reflect the sense that the country is overwhelmingly Muslim by self-identification, even if the corollary stereotyping is "Muslim, but less so by practice."

There has also been a state survey/census that had questions about religion. I, of course, give preference to my own data as I was better able to control the collection environment and had more of a sense that people were more willing to talk about religion with me, an ethnographer of religion, than with the state, which is not neutral in regard to religion and public life.

31. For more on the role of sound in Islam, see Hirschkind (2006).

32. Varisco (2005) goes even further than Asad (1986), attacking the representation of Islam by Ahmed (2002), Geertz (1968), Gellner (1981), and Mernissi (1987).

33. For more on such constructions of morality and wellness, see Beyer (2013); Borbieva (2013); Botoeva and Spector (2013); Féaux de la Croix (2013); Louw (2013); Montgomery (2013b); Mostowlansky (2013); Rasanayagam (2011); Werner, Barcus, and Brede (2013).

34. As Schielke is right to remind us, sometimes "there is too much Islam in the anthropology of Islam" (2010, 1) and we need to pay more attention to how people construct their everyday lives.

CONCLUSION

Epigraphs: Tolstoy (1994, 1366); dictum attributed to Hume, see Seligman and Weller (2012, 204).

Bibliography

Abramzon, S. M. 1990 [1971]. *Kirgizy i ikh etnogeneticheskie i istoriko-kulturnye sviazi.* Frunze: Nauka [in Russian].

Ahmad, Mumtaz. 1991. "Islamic Fundamentalism in South Asia: The Jamaat-i-Islami and the Tablighi Jamaat." In *Fundamentalisms Observed.* Edited by M. E. Marty and R. S. Appleby. Chicago: University of Chicago Press. 457–530.

Ahmed, Akbar. 2002. *Discovering Islam: Making Sense of Muslim History and Society.* Revised ed. London: Routledge.

Aitpaeva, Gulnara. 2006. "The Triad of Crime, Punishment, and Forgiveness in the Kyrgyz Epic *Kojojash.*" *Journal of Folklore Research* 43, no. 2: 109–28.

Aitpaeva, Gulnara, ed. 2013. *Sacred Sites of the Southern Kyrgyzstan: Nature, Manas, Islam.* Bishkek: Aigine Research Center.

Aitpaeva, Gulnara, and Aida Egemberdieva, eds. 2009. *Sacred Sites of Ysyk-Köl: Spiritual Power, Pilgrimage, and Art.* Bishkek: Aigine Research Center.

Aitpaeva, Gulnara, Aida Egemberidieva, and Mukaram Toktogulova, eds. 2007. *Mazar Worship in Kyrgyzstan: Rituals and Practitioners in Talas.* Bishkek: Aigine Research Center.

Akayev, Askar. 2003. *Kyrgyz Statehood and the National Epos "Manas."* New York: Global Scholarly Publications.

Alger, Horatio, Jr. 1990. *Ragged Dick or, Street Life in New York with the Boot Blacks.* New York: Signet Classic.

Allworth, Edward, ed. 1973. *The Nationality Question in Soviet Central Asia.* New York: Praeger.

Allworth, Edward. 1990. *The Modern Uzbeks: From the Fourteenth Century to the Present.* Stanford: Hoover Institution Press.

Allworth, Edward, ed. 1994. *Central Asia: 130 Years of Russian Dominance, A Historical Overview.* 3rd ed. Durham: Duke University Press.

Almond, Gabriel A., R. Scott Appleby, and Emmanuel Sivan. 2003. *Strong Religion: The Rise of Fundamentalisms Around the World.* Chicago: University of Chicago Press.

Anderson, Benedict. 1991. *Imagined Communities: Reflections on the Origin and Spread of Nationalism.* Revised ed. London: Verso.

Anderson, John. 1997. *The International Politics of Central Asia.* Manchester: Manchester University Press.

Aristotle. 1999. *Nicomachean Ethics*. Translated by Terence Irwin. 2nd ed. Indianapolis: Hackett Publishing Company.

Asad, Talal. 1986. "The Idea of an Anthropology of Islam." Washington, DC: Center for Contemporary Arab Studies, Georgetown University.

Auerbach, Erich. 2003. *Mimesis: The Representation of Reality in Western Literature*. Translated by W. R. Trask. Princeton: Princeton University Press.

Babur, Emperor of Hindustan. 2002. *The Baburnama: Memoirs of Babur, Prince and Emperor*. Translated by W. M. Thackston. New York: Modern Library.

Bacon, Elizabeth E. 1980. *Central Asians Under Russian Rule: A Study in Culture Change*. Ithaca: Cornell University Press.

Balci, Bayram. 2003. "Fethullah Gülen's Missionary Schools in Central Asia and Their Role in the Spreading of Turkism and Islam." *Religion, State & Society* 31, no. 2: 151–77.

Balci, Bayram. 2012. "The Rise of the Jama'at al Tabligh in Kyrgyzstan: The Revival of Islamic Ties between the Indian Subcontinent and Central Asia?" *Central Asian Survey* 31, no. 1: 61–76.

Baldick, Julian. 2012. *Animal and Shaman: Ancient Religions of Central Asia*. New York: New York University Press.

Balzer, Marjorie Mandelstam, ed. 1990. *Shamanism: Soviet Studies of Traditional Religion in Siberia and Central Asia*. Armonk: M. E. Sharpe.

Balzer, Marjorie Mandelstam, ed. 1997. *Shamanic Worlds: Rituals and Lore of Siberia and Central Asia*. Armonk: North Castle Books.

Bandura, Alfred. 1977. *Social Learning Theory*. Englewood Cliffs: Prentice-Hall.

Baran, Zeyno, S. Frederick Starr, and Svante E. Cornell. 2006. "Islamic Radicalism in Central Asia and the Caucasus: Implications for the EU." Silk Road Papers Series. Central Asia-Caucasus Institute, Washington and Uppsala (July).

Barfield, Thomas J. 1981. *The Central Asian Arabs of Afghanistan: Pastoral Nomadism in Transition*. Austin: University of Texas Press.

Barfield, Thomas J. 1989. *The Perilous Frontier: Nomadic Empires and China, 221 BC to AD 1757*. Cambridge: Blackwell.

Barfield, Thomas J. 1993. *The Nomadic Alternative*. Upper Saddle River: Prentice-Hall.

Barro, Robert, and Joshua Mitchell. 2004. "Religious Faith and Economic Growth: What Matters Most—Belief or Belonging?" Heritage Foundation Lecture no. 841. Washington, DC.

Barth, Fredrik, ed. 1969. *Ethnic Groups and Boundaries: The Social Organization of Culture Difference*. Prospect Heights: Waveland Press.

Barth, Fredrik. 1975. *Ritual and Knowledge Among the Baktaman of New Guinea*. Oslo: Universitetsforlaget.

Barth, Fredrik. 1987. *Cosmologies in the Making: A Generative Approach to Cultural Variation in Inner New Guinea*. Cambridge: Cambridge University Press.

Barth, Fredrik. 1989. "The Guru and the Conjurer: Transactions in Knowledge and the Shaping of Culture in Southeast Asia and Melanesia." *Man* 25: 640–53.

Barth, Fredrik. 2002. "An Anthropology of Knowledge." *Current Anthropology* 43, no. 1: 1–18.

Barthold, W. 1992. *Turkestan: Down to the Mongol Invasion.* Translated by T. Minorsky. 3rd ed. New Delhi: Munshiram Manoharlal.

BBC. 2009a. "Kyrgyz Expert Wary of Widespread Radical Islam in Country," *BBC Monitoring Central Asia Unit* (5 April) [24.kg, 3 April, in Russian]. http://go.galegroup .com/ps/i.do?id=GALE%7CA197229182&v=2.1&u=upitt_main&it=r&p=AONE &sw=w&asid=52b7678024878045264bd3c71b90a6d9. Accessed 30 October 2013.

BBC. 2009b. "Kyrgyz Imams Blamed for Increase in Followers of Radical Teachings." *BBC Monitoring Central Asia Unit* (21 August) [Interfax, in Russian, 19 August]. http://go.galegroup.com/ps/i.do?id=GALE%7CA206382251&v=2.1&u=upitt_ main&it=r&p=AONE&sw=w&asid=b0f9acad71c5edb849c8a32defa28bf1. Accessed 30 October 2013.

BBC. 2009c. "Kyrgyz Religious Watchdog Says Salafism Threat to Country." *BBC Monitoring Central Asia Unit* (2 December) [Channel 5 TV, Bishkek, in Russian, 1 December]. http://go.galegroup.com/ps/i.do?id=GALE% 7CA213375837&v=2.1&u=upitt_main&it=r&p=AONE&sw=w&asid=db 9b2905937aa4d566600e426e1858ac. Accessed 30 October 2013.

BBC. 2009d. "Kyrgyzstan Tightening Screw on Islam Under Cover of Fighting Terror— Clergyman." *BBC Monitoring Central Asia Unit* (30 October) [Kyrgyz Television 1, Bishkek, in Russian, 29 October]. http://go.galegroup.com/ps/i.do?id=GALE% 7CA210901107&v=2.1&u=upitt_main&it=r&p=AONE&sw=w&asid=bfbf 114653c61e56852194bbea8da2af. Accessed 30 October 2013.

BBC. 2010a. "Kyrgyz Pundit Says Radical Islam Threatening Central Asian 'Secular Regimes.'" *BBC Monitoring Central Asia Unit* (9 December) [*Delo No*, Bishkek, in Russian, 1 December]. http://go.galegroup.com/ps/i.do?id=GALE% 7CA243946686&v=2.1&u=upitt_main&it=r&p=AONE&sw=w&asid=c19e3f72c 9462b5ec4c86b1e47f62695. Accessed 30 October 2013.

BBC. 2010b. "Pundit Predicts 'Second Palestine' in Kyrgyz South." *BBC Monitoring Central Asia Unit* [*24.KG*, Bishkek, in Russian, 16 August]. http://go.galegroup .com/ps/i.do?id=GALE%7CA234694469&v=2.1&u=upitt_main&it=r&p=A ONE&sw=w&asid=8a24349fe8cfa27547ea06f883798e57. Accessed 30 October 2013.

Becker, Seymour. 1968. *Russia's Protectorates in Central Asia: Bukhara and Khiva, 1865–1924.* Cambridge: Harvard University Press.

Beckwith, Christopher I. 2009. *Empires of the Silk Road: A History of Central Eurasia from the Bronze Age to the Present.* Princeton: Princeton University Press.

Bell, Catherine. 1992. *Ritual Theory, Ritual Practice.* Oxford: Oxford University Press.

Bell, Catherine. 1997. *Ritual: Perspectives and Dimensions.* Oxford: Oxford University Press.

Bellah, Robert N. 2011. *Religion in Human Evolution: From the Paleolithic to the Axial Age.* Cambridge: Belknap Press.

Bellah, Robert N., and Hans Joas, eds. 2012. *The Axial Age and Its Consequences.* Cambridge: Belknap Press.

Bellér-Hann, Ildikó. 2000. *The Written and the Spoken. Literacy and Oral Transmission Among the Uyghur.* Berlin: Das Arabische Buch.

Bennigsen, Alexandre, and Chantal Quelquejay. 1961. *The Evolution of the Muslim Nationalities of the USSR and Their Linguistic Problems.* Translated by G. Wheeler. London: Central Asian Research Centre.

Bennigsen, Alexandre, and S. Enders Wimbush. 1985. *Mystics and Commissars: Sufism in the Soviet Union.* Berkeley: University of California Press.

Bennigsen, Alexandre, and S. Enders Wimbush. 1986. *Muslims of the Soviet Empire: A Guide.* Bloomington: Indiana University Press.

Bensman, Joseph, and Robert Lilienfeld. 1991. *Craft and Consciousness: Occupational Technique and the Development of World Images.* New York: Aldine de Gruyter.

Berger, Peter L., and Thomas Luckmann. 1966. *The Social Construction of Reality: A Treatise in the Sociology of Knowledge.* New York: Anchor Books.

Berkey, Jonathan P. 2003. *The Formation of Islam: Religion and Society in the Near East, 600–1800.* Cambridge: Cambridge University Press.

Berlin, Isaiah. 1990. *The Crooked Timber of Humanity: Chapters in the History of Ideas.* New York: Vintage Books.

Berman, Morris. 2000. *Wandering God: A Study in Nomadic Spirituality.* Albany: State University of New York Press.

Besteman, Catherine, and Hugh Gusterson, eds. 2005. *Why America's Top Pundits Are Wrong: Anthropologists Talk Back.* Berkeley: University of California Press.

Beyer, Judith. 2007. "Imagining the State in Rural Kyrgyzstan: How Perceptions of the State Create Customary Law in the Kyrgyz *Aksakal* Courts." *Max Planck Institute for Social Anthropology Working Papers* no. 95.

Beyer, Judith. 2013. "Ordering Ideals: Accomplishing Well-Being in a Kyrgyz Cooperative of Elders." *Central Asian Survey* 32, no. 4: 432–47.

Beyer, Judith. 2015. "Customizations of Law: Courts of Elders (*Aksakal* Courts) in Rural and Urban Kyrgyzstan." *Political and Legal Anthropology Review* 38, no. 1: 53–71.

Borbieva, Noor O'Neill. 2012. "Kidnapping Women: Function, Symbol, and Power in Central Asian Marriage." *Anthropological Quarterly* 85, no. 1: 141–70.

Borbieva, Noor O'Neill. 2013. "Anxiety, Order and the Other: Well-Being among Ethnic Kyrgyz and Uzbeks." *Central Asian Survey* 32, no. 4: 501–13.

Borges, Jorge Luis. 1967. *A Personal Anthology.* Translated and edited by Anthony Kerrigan. New York: Grove Press.

Botoeva, Aisalkyn, and Regine A. Spector. 2013. "Sewing to Satisfaction: Craft-Based Entrepreneurs in Contemporary Kyrgyzstan." *Central Asian Survey* 32, no. 4: 487–500.

Bourdieu, Pierre. 1977. *Outline of a Theory of Practice.* Translated by R. Nice. Cambridge: Cambridge University Press.

Bourdieu, Pierre. 2000. *Pascalian Meditations.* Translated by R. Nice. Stanford: Stanford University Press.

Boyce, Mary. 2001. *Zoroastrians: Their Beliefs and Practices.* London: Routledge.

Bradsher, Henry S. 1999. *Afghan Communism and Soviet Intervention.* Oxford: Oxford University Press.

Brubaker, Rogers. 2004. *Ethnicity Without Groups.* Cambridge: Harvard University Press.

Canfield, Robert Leroy. 1973. *Faction and Conversion in a Plural Society: Religious Alignments in the Hindu Kush*. Vol. 50. Ann Arbor: Museum of Anthropology, University of Michigan.

Central Intelligence Agency. 2013a. *The World Fact Book: Kyrgyzstan*. https://www.cia.gov/library/publications/the-world-factbook/geos/kg.html. Last accessed 28 October 2013.

Central Intelligence Agency. 2013b. *The World Fact Book: Uzbekistan*. https://www.cia.gov/library/publications/the-world-factbook/geos/uz.html. Accessed 28 October 2013.

Collins, Kathleen. 2002. "Clans, Pacts, and Politics in Central Asia." *Journal of Democracy* 13, no. 3: 137–52.

Collins, Kathleen. 2004. "The Logic of Clan Politics: Evidence from the Central Asian Trajectories." *World Politics* 56: 224–61.

Collins, Kathleen. 2011. "Kyrgyzstan's Latest Revolution." *Journal of Democracy*. 22, no. 3: 150–64.

Comaroff, John L., and Jean Comaroff. 1991. *Of Revelation and Revolution*. Vol. 1: *Christianity, Colonialism, and Consciousness in South Africa*. Chicago: University of Chicago Press.

Connerton, Paul. 1989. *How Societies Remember*. Cambridge: Cambridge University Press.

Cornell, Svante E. 1999. "The Devaluation of the Concept of Autonomy: National Minorities in the Former Soviet Union." *Central Asian Survey* 18, no. 2: 185–96.

Coser, Lewis. 1956. *The Functions of Social Conflict*. New York: Free Press.

Crews, Robert D. 2006. *For Prophet and Tsar: Islam and Empire in Russian and Central Asia*. Cambridge: Harvard University Press.

de Certeau, Michel. 1984. *The Practice of Everyday Life*. Translated by Stephen Rendall. Berkeley: University of California Press.

Devji, Faisal. 2008. *The Terrorist in Search of Humanity: Militant Islam and Global Politics*. New York: Columbia University Press.

DeWeese, Devin. 1994. *Islamization and Native Religion in the Golden Horde: Baba Tükles and Conversion to Islam in Historical and Epic Tradition*. University Park: Pennsylvania State University Press.

Dewey, John. 1910. "A Short Catechism Concerning Truth." In *The Influence of Darwin on Philosophy and Other Essays*, 154–68. New York: Henry Holt.

Dewey, John. 1916. "The Control of Ideas by Facts." In *Essays in Experimental Logic*, 230–249. Chicago: University of Chicago Press.

Dewey, John. 1991 [1910]. *How We Think*. New York: Prometheus.

Druckman, James N. 2001a. "On the Limits of Framing Effects: Who Can Frame?" *The Journal of Politics* 63, no. 4: 1041–66.

Druckman, James N. 2001b. "The Implications of Framing Effects for Citizen Competence." *Political Behavior* 23, no. 3: 225–56.

Dunne, Joseph. 1997. *Back to the Rough Ground: Practical Judgment and the Lure of Technique*. Notre Dame: University of Notre Dame Press.

Durkheim, Emile. 1995. *The Elementary Forms of Religious Life*. Translated by Karen E. Fields. New York: Free Press.

Eaton, Richard M. 1993. *The Rise of Islam and the Bengal Frontier: 1204-1760*. Berkeley: University of California Press.

Edwards, David B. 1996. *Heroes of the Age: Moral Fault Lines on the Afghan Frontier.* Berkeley: University of California Press.

Eickelman, Dale F. 1984. "The Study of Islam in Local Contexts." *Contributions to Asian Studies* no. 17: 1-16.

Eisenstadt, S. N. 1968. "Introduction." In *Max Weber on Charisma and Institution Building*. Chicago: University of Chicago Press. ix-lvi.

Eisenstadt, S. N. 1982. "The Axial Age: The Emergence of Transcendental Visions and the Rise of Clerics." *European Journal of Sociology* 23: 294-314.

Eisenstadt, S. N. 1985. "Civilizational Formations and Political Dynamics." *Scandinavian Political Studies* 8, no. 4: 231-51.

Eisenstadt, S. N., ed. 1986. *The Origins and Diversity of Axial Age Civilizations*. Albany: State University of New York Press.

Eliade, Mircea. 1964. *Shamanism: Archaic Techniques of Ecstasy*. New York: Penguin Books.

Emmons, Charles F. 2000. "On Becoming a Spirit Medium in a 'Rational Society.'" *Anthropology of Consciousness* 12, no. 1-2: 71-82.

Environmental Justice Foundation. 2005. *White Gold: The True Cost of Cotton*. London: Environmental Justice Foundation.

Esenova, Saulesh. 2002. "Soviet Nationality, Identity, and Ethnicity in Central Asia: Historic Narratives and Kazakh Ethnic Identity." *Journal of Muslim Minority Affairs* 22, no. 1: 11-38.

Fakir, Abu Bakr. 1978. *A Manual of Prayer and Fasting*. Ndabeni, Western Cape: Rustica Press.

Féaux de la Croix, Jeanne. 2013. "How to Build a Better Future. Kyrgyzstani Development Workers and the 'Knowledge Transfer' Strategy." *Central Asian Survey* 32, no. 4: 448-61.

Foltz, Richard. 2010. *Religions of the Silk Road: Premodern Patterns of Globalization.* 2nd ed. New York: Palgrave.

Fragner, Bert G. 2001. "'Soviet Nationalism': An Ideological Legacy to the Independent Republics of Central Asia." In *Identity Politics in Central Asia and the Muslim World: Nationalism, Ethnicity and Labour in the Twentieth Century*. Edited by W. van Schendel and E. J. Zürcher. London: I. B. Tauris. 13-34.

Freud, Sigmund. 1989. *Civilization and Its Discontents*. New York: W. W. Norton.

Friedman, D. 1990. "Mass Rallies Broken Up in Kirghizia; Death Toll Now 115" (10 June). Associated Press. http://lexis-nexis.com.

Froese, Paul. 2008. *The Plot to Kill God: Findings from the Soviet Experiment in Secularization*. Berkeley: University of California Press.

Frye, Richard N. 1996. *The Heritage of Central Asia: From Antiquity to the Turkish Expansion*. Princeton: Markus Wiener.

Gaborieau, Marc, Alexandre Popovic, and Thierry Zarcone, eds. 1990. *Naqshbandis: Historical Developments and Present Situation of a Muslim Mystical Order*. Istanbul: l'Institut Français d'Études Anatoliennes d'Istanbul.

Geertz, Clifford. 1968. *Islam Observed: Religious Development in Morocco and Indonesia*. Chicago: University of Chicago Press.

Geertz, Clifford. 1973. *The Interpretation of Cultures*. New York: Basic Books.

Geiss, Paul Georg. 2001. "Mahalla and Kinship Relations. A Study of Residential Communal Commitment Structures in Central Asia of the 19th Century." *Central Asian Survey* 20, no. 1: 97–106.

Geiss, Paul Georg. 2003. *Pre-Tsarist and Tsarist Central Asia: Communal Commitment and Political Order in Change*. New York: RoutledgeCurzon.

Gellner, Ernest. 1981. *Muslim Society*. Cambridge: Cambridge University Press.

Giustozzi, Antonio, and Dominique Orsini. 2009. "Centre-Periphery Relations in Afghanistan: Badakhshan between Patrimonialism and Institution-Building." *Central Asian Survey* 28, no. 1: 1–16.

Goethe, Johann Wolfgang von. 1989. *The Sorrows of Young Werther*. Translated by Michael Huse. New York: Penguin Books.

Goffman, Erving. 1974. *Frame Analysis: An Essay on the Organization of Experience*. Boston: Northeastern University Press.

Golden, Peter B. 2011. *Central Asia in World History*. Oxford: Oxford University Press.

Goody, Jack. 2000. *The Power of the Written Tradition*. Washington, DC: Smithsonian Institution Press.

Gorbunova, N. G. 1986. *The Culture of Ancient Ferghana: VI century B.C.–VI century A.D.* Oxford: B.A.R.

Grant, Nigel. 1964. *Soviet Education*. Baltimore: Penguin Books.

Grebenshchikov, Igor. 2000. "Central Asian Pawn: Kyrgyzstan—A Vulnerable Pawn in the Central Asian Chess Game" (17 November). www.iwpr.net.

Gross, Jo-Ann, ed. 1992. *Muslims in Central Asia: Expressions of Identity and Change*. Durham: Duke University Press.

Grousset, René. 1970. *The Empire of the Steppes: A History of Central Asia*. Translated by N. Walford. New Brunswick: Rutgers University Press.

Gullette, David. 2010. *The Genealogical Construction of the Kyrgyz Republic: Kinship, State and 'Tribalism.'* Leiden: Global Orient.

Haghayeghi, Mehrdad. 1996. *Islam and Politics in Central Asia*. New York: St. Martin's Press.

Halemba, Agnieszka. 2003. "Contemporary Religious Life in the Republic of Altai: The Interaction of Buddhism and Shamanism." *Sibirica* 3, no. 2: 165–82.

Halifax, Joan. 1979. *Shamanic Voices: A Survey of Visionary Narratives*. New York: Penguin Books.

Hanks, Reuel R. 2011. "Crisis in Kyrgyzstan: Conundrums of Ethnic Conflict, National Identity and State Cohesion." *Journal of Balkan and Near Eastern Studies* 13, no. 2: 177–87.

Hann, Chris, and Mathijs Pelkmans. 2009. "Realigning Religion and Power in Central Asia: Islam, Nation-State and (Post)Socialism." *Europe-Asia Studies* 61, no. 9: 1517–41. doi: 10.1080/09668130903209111.

Hansen, Valerié. 2012. *The Silk Road: A New History*. New York: Oxford University Press.

Harvey, Graham. 2006. *Animism: Respecting the Living World*. New York: Columbia University Press.

Heathershaw, John. 2007a. "Peace as Complex Legitimacy: Politics, Space and Discourse in Tajikistan's Peacebuilding Process, 2000–2005." Ph.D. diss., London School of Economics.

Heathershaw, John. 2007b. "The Tulip Fades: 'Revolution' and Repercussions in Kyrgyzstan." *Perspective* 17, no. 2: 2–6.

Heathershaw, John. 2009. *Post-Conflict Tajikistan: The Politics of Peacebuilding and the Emergence of Legitimate Order*. London: Routledge.

Heathershaw, John, and David W. Montgomery. 2014. "The Myth of Post-Soviet Muslim Radicalization." *Chatham House Research Paper*. November.

Heathershaw, John, and Nick Megoran. 2011. "Contesting Danger: A New Agenda for Policy and Scholarship in Central Asia." *International Affairs* 87, no. 3: 589–612.

Hefner, Robert W. 2000. *Civil Islam: Muslims and Democratization in Indonesia*. Princeton: Princeton University Press.

Henderson, John B. 1998. *The Construction of Orthodoxy and Heresy: Neo-Confucian, Islamic, Jewish, and Early Christian Patterns*. Albany: State University of New York Press.

Heyat, Farideh. 2004. "Re-Islamisation in Kyrgyzstan: Gender, New Poverty and the Moral Dimension." *Central Asian Survey* 23, no. 3–4: 275–87.

Hilgers, Irene. 2009. *Why Do Uzbeks Have to Be Muslims? Exploring Religiosity in the Ferghana Valley*. Berlin: Lit Verlag.

Hirsch, Edward. 2002. *The Demon and the Angel: Searching for the Source of Artistic Inspiration*. San Diego: Harvest Book.

Hirschkind, Charles. 2006. *The Ethical Soundscape: Cassette Sermons and Islamic Counterpublics*. New York: Columbia University Press.

Hopkirk, Peter. 1992. *The Great Game: The Struggle for Empire in Central Asia*. New York: Kodansha International.

Hoppál, Mihály, ed. 1984. *Shamanism in Eurasia*. Göttingen: Edition Herodot.

Horton, Robin. 1968. "Neo-Tylorianism: Sound Sense of Sinister Prejudice?" *Man* 3, no. 4: 625–34.

Hudson, Alfred E. 1964. *Kazak Social Structure*. New Haven: Yale University Publications in Anthropology.

Human Rights Watch. 2004. "Creating Enemies of the State: Religious Persecution in Uzbekistan." Human Rights Watch Report. http://hrw.org/reports/2004/uzbekistan0304/. Accessed 28 October 2013.

Human Rights Watch. 2007. "Nowhere to Turn: Torture and Ill-treatment in Uzbekistan." Human Rights Watch Report. http://www.hrw.org/reports/2007/11/05/nowhere-turn. Accessed 28 October 2013.

Human Rights Watch. 2011. "'No One Left to Witness': Torture, the Failure of Habeas Corpus, and the Silencing of Lawyers in Uzbekistan." Human Rights Watch Report. http://www.hrw.org/reports/2011/12/13/no-one-left-witness-0. Accessed 28 October 2013.

Humphrey, Caroline. 1998. *Marx Went Away—But Karl Stayed Behind*. Updated ed. Ann Arbor: University of Michigan Press.

İğmen, Ali. 2012. *Speaking Soviet with an Accent: Culture and Power in Kyrgyzstan.* Pittsburgh: University of Pittsburgh Press.

Ilkhamov, A. 2002. *Etnicheskii Atlas Uzbekistana.* Tashkent: R. Elinina [in Russian].

International Crisis Group. 2005a. "Kyrgyzstan: After the Revolution." Brussels: International Crisis Group. http://www.crisisgroup.org/en/regions/asia/central-asia/kyrgyzstan/097-kyrgyzstan-after-the-revolution.aspx. Accessed 15 June 2013.

International Crisis Group. 2005b. "Uzbekistan: The Andijon Uprising." Brussels: International Crisis Group. http://www.crisisgroup.org/en/regions/asia/central-asia/uzbekistan/B038-uzbekistan-the-andijon-uprising.aspx. Accessed 15 June 2013.

International Crisis Group. 2009. "Women and Radicalisation in Kyrgyzstan." Asia Report 176 (3 September). http://www.crisisgroup.org/en/regions/asia/central-asia/kyrgyzstan/176-women-and-radicalisation-in-kyrgyzstan.aspx. Accessed 22 August 2011.

International Crisis Group. 2010. "The Pogroms in Kyrgyzstan." Brussels: International Crisis Group. http://www.crisisgroup.org/en/regions/asia/central-asia/kyrgyzstan/193-the-pogroms-in-kyrgyzstan.aspx. Accessed 15 June 2013.

International Crisis Group. 2011. "Central Asia: Decay and Decline." Brussels: International Crisis Group. http://www.crisisgroup.org/en/regions/asia/central-asia/201-central-asia-decay-and-decline.aspx. Accessed 22 August 2011.

Jackson, Michael. 2005. *Existential Anthropology: Events, Exigencies and Effects.* New York: Berghahn Books.

Jackson, Michael. 2007. *Excursions.* Durham: Duke University Press.

James, William. 1982 [1902]. *The Varieties of Religious Experience: A Study in Human Nature.* New York: Penguin Books.

Jaspers, Karl. 1953. *The Origin and Goal of History.* London: Routledge.

Kamalov, Erkin. 2010. "Terrorism Feared Possible in Southern Kyrgyzstan," *Central Asia Online* (26 October). http://www.centralasiaonline.com/cocoon/caii/xhtml/en_GB/features/caii/features/main/2010/10/26/feature-01. Accessed 22 August 2011.

Kamalov, U. 1975. *Velikii Oktiabr i prosveshchenie mass.* Tashkent: Uzbekistan [in Russian].

Kamp, Marianne. 2006. *The New Woman in Uzbekistan: Islam, Modernity, and Unveiling Under Communism.* Seattle: University of Washington Press.

Karagiannis, Emmanuel. 2005. "Political Islam and Social Movement Theory: The Case of Hizb ut-Tahrir in Kyrgyzstan." *Religion, State & Society* 33, no. 2: 137–50.

Karagiannis, Emmanuel. 2010. *Political Islam in Central Asia: The Challenge of Hizb ut-Tahrir.* London: Routledge.

Karasar, Hasan Ali. 2002. "Chicherin on the Delimitation of Turkestan: Native Bolsheviks Versus Soviet Foreign Policy. Seven Letters from the Russian Archives on Razmezhevanie." *Central Asian Survey* 21, no. 2: 199–209.

Kearney, Richard. 2002. *On Stories.* New York: Routledge.

Kehl-Bodrogi, Krisztina. 2008. *"Religion Is Not So Strong Here": Muslim Religious Life in Khorezm after Socialism.* Berlin: Lit Verlag,

Keller, Shoshana. 2001. *To Moscow, Not Mecca: The Soviet Campaign Against Islam in Central Asia, 1917–1941.* Westport: Praeger.

Kendzior, Sarah. 2007. "Poetry of Witness: Uzbek Identity and the Response to Andijon." *Central Asian Survey* 26, no. 3: 317–34.

Khalid, Adeeb. 1999. *The Politics of Muslim Cultural Reform: Jadidism in Central Asia.* Berkeley: University of California Press.

Khalid, Adeeb. 2003. "A Secular Islam: Nation, State, and Religion in Uzbekistan." *International Journal of Middle East Studies* 35, no. 4: 573–98.

Khalid, Adeeb. 2007. *Islam after Communism: Religion and Politics in Central Asia.* Berkeley: University of California Press.

Khazanov, Anatoly M. 1995. *After the USSR: Ethnicity, Nationalism, and Politics in the Commonwealth of Independent States.* Madison: University of Wisconsin Press.

Kipling, Rudyard. 1995. *Kim.* Calcutta: Rupa.

Kleinbach, Russell, Mehrigiul Ablezova, and Medina Aitieva. 2005. "Kidnapping for Marriage (*ala kachuu*) in a Kyrgyz Village." *Central Asian Survey* 24, no. 2: 191–202.

Kleveman, Lutz. 2004. *The New Great Game: Blood and Oil in Central Asia.* New York: Grove Press.

Kolmakova, M. N., ed. 1957. *Narodnoe Obrazovanie v SSSR.* Moscow: Akademiia Pedagogicheskikh Nauk [in Russian].

Krader, Lawrence. 1963. *Social Organization of the Mongol-Turkic Pastoral Nomads.* The Hague: Mouton.

Krader, Lawrence. 1971. *Peoples of Central Asia.* 3rd ed. Bloomington: Indiana University Press.

Kurzman, Charles. 2011. *The Missing Martyrs: Why There Are So Few Muslim Terrorists.* New York: Oxford University Press.

Lakoff, George. 1987. *Women, Fire, and Dangerous Things: What Categories Reveal about the Mind.* Chicago: University of Chicago Press.

Langer, Susanne K. 1953. *Feeling and Form: A Theory of Art.* New York: Charles Scribner's Sons.

Laruelle, Marlène. 2012. "The Paradigm of Nationalism in Kyrgyzstan: Evolving Narrative, the Sovereignty Issue, and Political Agenda." *Communist and Post-Communist Studies* 45, no. 1–2: 39–49.

Laruelle, Marlène, and Johan Engvall, eds. 2015. *Kyrgyzstan beyond "Democracy Island" and "Failing State": Social and Political Changes in a Post-Soviet Society.* Lanham: Lexington Books.

Lee, Robert D. 1997. *Overcoming Tradition and Modernity: The Search for Islamic Authenticity.* Boulder: Westview Press.

Leopold, Anita Maria, and Jeppe Sinding Jensen, eds. 2004. *Syncretism in Religion: A Reader.* London: Routledge.

Lessa, William A., and Evon Z. Vogt, eds. 1979. *Reader in Comparative Religion: An Anthropological Approach.* 4th ed. New York: HarperCollins.

Levi, Scott C. 2007. "The Ferghana Valley at the Crossroads of World History: The Rise of Khoqand, 1790–1822." *Journal of Global History* 2, no. 2: 213–32.

Levi, Scott C., and Ron Sela, eds. 2010. *Islamic Central Asia: An Anthology of Historical Sources.* Bloomington: Indiana University Press.

Levy, C. J. 2009. "Central Asia Sounds Alarm on Islamic Radicalism." *The New York Times,* 18 August.

Lewis, David. 2008. *The Temptations of Tyranny in Central Asia.* New York: Columbia University Press.

Lipovsky, Igor. 1995. "The Central Asian Cotton Epic." *Central Asian Survey* 14, no. 4: 529–42.

Liu, Morgan Y. 2002. "Recognizing the Khan: Authority, Space, and Political Imagination Among Uzbek Men in Post-Soviet Osh, Kyrgyzstan." Ph.D. diss., University of Michigan, Ann Arbor.

Liu, Morgan Y. 2012. *Under Solomon's Throne: Uzbek Visions of Renewal in Osh.* Pittsburgh: University of Pittsburgh Press.

Louw, Maria Elisabeth. 2007. *Everyday Islam in Post-Soviet Central Asia.* London: Routledge.

Louw, Maria Elisabeth. 2013. "Even Honey May Become Bitter When There Is Too Much of It: Islam and the Struggle for a Balanced Existence in Post-Soviet Kyrgyzstan." *Central Asian Survey* 32, no. 4: 514–26.

Löwith, Karl. 1993. *Max Weber and Karl Marx.* Translated by H. Fantel. London: Routledge.

Lubin, Nancy, Barnett R. Rubin, and Keith Martin. 1999. *Calming the Ferghana Valley: Development and Dialogue in the Heart of Central Asia.* New York: Century Foundation Press.

Luckmann, Thomas. 1967. *The Invisible Religion: The Problem of Religion in Modern Society.* New York: Macmillan.

Luria, A. R. 1976. *Cognitive Development: Its Cultural and Social Foundations.* Translated by M. Lopez-Morillas and L. Solotaroff. Cambridge: Harvard University Press.

Mamdani, Mahmood. 2002. "Good Muslim, Bad Muslim: A Political Perspective on Culture and Terrorism." *American Anthropologist* 104, no. 3: 766–75.

Mamdani, Mahmood. 2004. *Good Muslim, Bad Muslim: America, the Cold War, and the Roots of Terror.* New York: Three Leaves Press.

Manas: The Great Campaign: Kirghiz Heroic Epics. 1999. Bishkek: Kyrgyz Printing Plant.

Manz, Beatrice Forbes. 1989. *The Rise and Rule of Tamerlane.* Cambridge: Cambridge University Press.

Marozzi, Justin. 2004. *Tamerlane: Sword of Islam, Conqueror of the World.* Cambridge: De Capo Press.

Marshall, David F. 1996. "A Politics of Language: Language as a Symbol in the Dissolution of the Soviet Union and Its Aftermath." *International Journal of the Sociology of Language* 118: 7–41.

Martin, Richard C., and Abbas Barzegar, eds. 2010. *Islamism: Contested Perspectives on Political Islam.* Stanford: Stanford University Press.

Marty, Martin E., and R. Scott Appleby, eds. 1991. *Fundamentalisms Observed.* 5 vols. Vol. 1, *The Fundamentalism Project.* Chicago: University of Chicago Press.

Marty, Martin E., and R. Scott Appleby, eds. 1993a. *Fundamentalisms and Society: Reclaiming the Sciences, the Family, and Education.* 5 vols. Vol. 2, *The Fundamentalism Project.* Chicago: University of Chicago Press.

Marty, Martin E., and R. Scott Appleby, eds. 1993b. *Fundamentalisms and the State: Remaking Polities, Economies, and Militance.* 5 vols. Vol. 3, *The Fundamentalism Project.* Chicago: University of Chicago Press.

Marty, Martin E., and R. Scott Appleby, eds. 1994. *Accounting for Fundamentalisms: The Dynamic Character of Movements.* 5 vols. Vol. 4, *The Fundamentalism Project.* Chicago: University of Chicago Press.

Marty, Martin E., and R. Scott Appleby, eds. 1995. *Fundamentalisms Comprehended.* 5 vols. Vol. 5, *The Fundamentalism Project.* Chicago: University of Chicago Press.

Marx, Karl. 2004 [1852]. *The Eighteenth Brumaire of Louis Bonaparte.* Whitefish, MT: Kessinger.

Massell, Gregory J. 1968. "Law as an Instrument of Revolutionary Change in a Traditional Millieu: The Case of Soviet Central Asia." *Law and Society Review* 2, no. 2: 179–228.

Masters, Edgar Lee. 1992. *Spoon River Anthology.* New York: Signet Classic.

Masud, Muhammad Khalid, ed. 2000. *Travellers in Faith: Studies of the Tablighi Jama'at as a Transnational Islamic Movement for Faith Renewal.* Leiden: E. J. Brill.

Matory, J. Lorand. 1994. "Rival Empires: Islam and the Religions of Spirit Possession Among the Oyo-Yoruba." *American Ethnologist* 21, no. 3: 495–515.

Maynayev, B. 1990. "State of Emergency Declared in South Kirghizia" (6 June). BBC Summary of World Broadcasts. http://lexis-nexis.com.

McBrien, Julie. 2006. "Listening to the Wedding Speaker: Discussing Religion and Culture in Southern Kyrgyzstan." *Central Asian Survey* 25, no. 3: 341–57.

McBrien, Julie. 2012. "Watching Clone: Brazilian Soap Operas and Muslimness in Kyrgyzstan." *Material Religion* 8, no. 3: 374–97.

McChesney, R. D. 1991. *Waqf in Central Asia: Four Hundred Years in the History of a Muslim Shrine, 1480–1889.* Princeton: Princeton University Press.

McDermott, John J., ed. 1981. *The Philosophy of John Dewey.* Chicago: University of Chicago Press.

McGlinchey, Eric. 2000. "Contours of Discontent? Demographics and Perceptions of Governance in Kazakhstan and Kyrgyzstan." *Journal of Central Asian Studies* 5, no. 1: 14–30.

McGlinchey, Eric. 2005. "Autocrats, Islamists, and the Rise of Radicalism in Central Asia." *Current History* 104, no. 684: 336–42.

McGlinchey, Eric. 2011. *Chaos, Violence, Dynasty: Politics and Islam in Central Asia.* Pittsburgh: University of Pittsburgh Press.

Megoran, Nick. 2002. "The Borders of Eternal Friendship? The Politics and Pain of Nationalism and Identity Along the Uzbekistan-Kyrgyzstan Ferghana Valley Boundary, 1999–2000." Ph.D. diss., Cambridge University.

Megoran, Nick. 2012. "Averting Violence in Kyrgyzstan: Understanding and Responding to Nationalism." London: *Chatham House, Russia and Eurasia Programme Paper* 2012/03.

Mernissi, Fatima. 1987. *Beyond the Veil: Male-Female Dynamics in Modern Muslim Society.* Revised ed. Bloomington: Indiana University Press.

Meyer, Karl E., and Shareen Blair Brysac. 1999. *Tournament of Shadows: The Great Game and the Race for Empire in Central Asia.* Washington, DC: Counterpoint Press.

Michaels, Paula A. 2003. *Curative Powers: Medicine and Empire in Stalin's Central Asia.* Pittsburgh: University of Pittsburgh Press.

Mitchell, Richard P. 1993. *The Society of the Muslim Brothers.* Oxford: Oxford University Press.

Montgomery, David W. 2004. "Suicide Bombings in Uzbekistan; Human Rights and Elections in Kazakhstan." *NIS Observed: An Analytical Review* 9, no. 12. http://web.bu.edu/iscip/digest/vol9/ed0912.html#centasia/.

Montgomery, David W. 2007a. "*Namaz*, Wishing Trees, and Vodka: The Diversity of Everyday Religious Life in Central Asia." In *Everyday Life in Central Asia, Past and Present.* Edited by R. Zanca and J. Sahaedo, 355–70. Bloomington: Indiana University Press.

Montgomery, David W. 2007b. "The Transmission of Religious and Cultural Knowledge and Potentiality in Practice: An Anthropology of Social Navigation in the Kyrgyz Republic." Ph.D. diss., Boston University, Boston.

Montgomery, David W. 2013a. "Introduction: Negotiating Well-being in Central Asia." *Central Asian Survey* 32, no. 4: 423–31.

Montgomery, David W. 2013b. "Relations Made Over Tea: Friendship and Contentedness in Reflection on a Meaningful Life in Central Asia." *Central Asian Survey* 32, no. 4: 475–86.

Montgomery, David W. 2014. "Towards a Theory of the Rough Ground: Merging the Policy and Ethnographic Frames of Religion in the Kyrgyz Republic." *Religion, State, & Society* 42, no. 1: 23–45.

Montgomery, David W. 2015a. "Islam beyond Democracy and State in Kyrgyzstan." *Central Asian Affairs* 2, no. 1: 35–50.

Montgomery, David W. 2015b. "On Muslims and the Navigation of Religiosity: Notes on the Anthropology of Islam." In *The Ashgate Research Companion to Anthropology.* Edited by Pamela J. Stewart and Andrew J. Strathern. Aldershot: Ashgate. 227–53.

Montgomery, David W., and John Heathershaw. 2016. "Islam and Danger: A Reconsideration of the Link between Religiosity, Radicalism, and Rebellion in Central Asia." *Religion, State, & Society* 44, no. 3. DOI: 10.1080/09637494.2016.1220177.

Morrison, Alexander. 2014. "Introduction: Killing the Cotton Canard and Getting Rid of the Great Game: Rewriting the Russian Conquest of Central Asia, 1814–1895." *Central Asian Survey* 33, no. 2: 131–42.

Mostowlansky, Till. 2013. "'The State Starts from the Family': Peace and Harmony in Tajikistan's Eastern Pamirs." *Central Asian Survey* 32, no. 4: 462–74.

Myles, John F. 2004. "From Doxa to Experience: Issues in Bourdieu's Adoption of Husserlian Phenomenology." *Theory, Culture & Society* 21, no. 2: 91–107.

Naumkin, Vitaly V. 2003. *Militant Islam in Central Asia: The Case of the Islamic Movement of Uzbekistan.* Berkeley: University of California.

Nida, Eugene A., and William A. Smalley. 1959. *Introducing Animism*. New York: Friendship Press.

Nigosian, S. A. 1993. *The Zoroastrian Faith: Tradition and Modern Research*. Montreal: McGill-Queen's University Press.

Northrop, Douglas. 2004. *Veiled Empire: Gender and Power in Stalinist Central Asia*. Ithaca: Cornell University Press.

Norton, Augustus Richard. 2007. *Hezbollah: A Short History*. Princeton: Princeton University Press.

Olcott, Martha Brill. 2005. *Central Asia's Second Chance*. Washington, DC: Brookings Institution Press.

Olcott, Martha Brill. 2007. "Roots of Radical Islam in Central Asia." Carnegie Endowment for International Peace Paper, Washington, DC. www.carnegieendowment .org/files/olcottroots.pdf.

Olufsen, Ole. 1911. *The Emir of Bokhara and His Country: Journeys and Studies in Bokhara*. London: William Heinemann.

Omuraly uulu, Choiun. 1994. *Tengirchilik: uluttuk filosofiianyn unggusuna chalgyn*. Bishkek: KRON firmasy [in Kyrgyz].

Ong, Walter J. 1982. *Orality and Literacy: The Technologizing of the Word*. New York: Routledge.

Özdalga, Elisabeth, ed. 1999. *Naqshbandis in Western and Central Asia: Change and Continuity*. Istanbul: Swedish Research Institute in Istanbul.

Pannier, Bruce. 1999. "Central Asia: Conflict in Kyrgyzstan Threatens Fergana Valley" (September 1). Radio Free Europe/Radio Liberty. www.rferl.org.

Pannier, Bruce. 2011. "The Growing Thread of Militants in a Corner of Central Asia." *RFE/RL* (23 April). http://www.rferl.org/content/militants_growing_threat_is _corner_of_central_asia/9503283.html. Accessed 22 August 2011.

Pascal, Blaise. 1995. *Pensées*. New York: Penguin Books.

Paxson, Margaret. 2005. *Solovyovo: The Story of Memory in a Russian Village*. Bloomington: Indiana University Press.

Pedersen, Morten Axel. 2011. *Not Quite Shamans: Spirit Worlds and Political Lives in Northern Mongolia*. Ithaca: Cornell University Press.

Pelkmans, Mathijs. 2007. "'Culture' as a Tool and an Obstacle: Missionary Encounters in Post-Soviet Kyrgyzstan." *Journal of the Royal Anthropological Institute* N.S. 13: 881–99.

Plato. 1991. *The Republic of Plato*. Translated by A. Bloom. 2nd ed. New York: Basic Books.

Poliakov, Sergei P. 1992. *Everyday Islam: Religion and Tradition in Rural Central Asia*. Translated and edited by A. Olcott. Armonk: M. E. Sharpe.

Polo, Marco. 1958. *The Travels*. Translated by R. E. Latham. New York: Penguin Books.

Pouillon, Jean. 1982. "Remarks on the Verb 'To Believe.'" In *Between Belief and Transgression: Structuralist Essays in Religion, History, and Myth*. Edited by Michel Izard and Pierre Smith. Chicago: University of Chicago Press. 1–8.

Prior, Daniel, ed. 1995. *Manas: The Epic Vision of Theodor Herzen*. Bishkek: Far Flung Press.

Privratsky, Bruce G. 2001. *Muslim Turkistan: Kazak Religion and Collective Memory.* Richmond, Surrey: Curzon Press.

Rabinow, Paul. 2007. *Reflections on Fieldwork in Morocco.* Berkeley: University of California Press.

Radnitz, Scott. 2010. *Weapons of the Wealthy: Predatory Regimes and Elite-Led Protests in Central Asia.* Ithaca: Cornell University Press.

Rappaport, Roy A. 1999. *Ritual and Religion in the Making of Humanity.* Cambridge: Cambridge University Press.

Rasanayagam, Johan. 2006a. "Introduction." *Central Asian Survey* 25, no. 3: 1–15.

Rasanayagam, Johan. 2006b. "'I'm Not a Wahhabi': State Power and Muslim Orthodoxy in Uzbekistan." In *The Post-Socialist Religious Question: Faith and Power in Central Asia and East-Central Europe.* Munich: Lit Verlag. 99–124.

Rasanayagam, Johan. 2011. *Islam in Post-Soviet Uzbekistan: The Morality of Experience.* Cambridge: Cambridge University Press.

Rashid, Ahmed. 2002. *Jihad: The Rise of Militant Islam in Central Asia.* New York: Penguin Books.

Reeves, Madeleine. 2005. "Locating Danger: *Konfliktologiia* and the Search for Fixity in the Ferghana Valley Borderlands." *Central Asian Survey* 24, no. 1: 67–81.

Reeves, Madeleine. 2007. "Travels in the Margins of the State: Everyday Geography in the Ferghana Valley Borderlands." In *Everyday Life in Central Asia: Past and Present.* Edited by J. Sahadeo and R. Zanca. Bloomington: Indiana University Press. 281–300.

Reeves, Madeleine. 2010. "A Weekend in Osh." *London Review of Books* 32, no. 13: 17–18.

Reeves, Madeleine. 2011a. "After Internationalism? The Unmaking of Osh." *NewsNet: News of the Association of Slavic, East European, and Eurasian Studies* 51, no. 5: 1–4.

Reeves, Madeleine. 2011b. "Staying Put? Towards a Relational Politics of Mobility at a Time of Migration." *Central Asian Survey* 30, no. 3/4: 555–76.

Reeves, Madeleine. 2011c. "Introduction: Contested Trajectories and a Dynamic Approach to Place." *Central Asian Survey* 30, no. 3/4: 307–30.

Reeves, Madeleine. 2012. "Black Work, Green Money: Remittances, Ritual, and Domestic Economies in Southern Kyrgyzstan." *Slavic Review* 71, no. 1: 108–34.

Reeves, Madeleine. 2014. *Border Work: An Ethnography of the State at Its Limits in Central Asia.* Ithaca: Cornell University Press.

Reid, Anna. 2002. *The Shaman's Coat: A Native History of Siberia.* New York: Walker

Rochat, Philippe. 2009. *Others in Mind: Social Origins of Self-Consciousness.* Cambridge: Cambridge University Press.

Roggio, Bill. 2011. "ISAF Captures IMUs Top Afghan Commander." *Long War Journal* (21 April). http://www.military.com/news/article/isaf-captures-imus-top-afghan-commander.html. Accessed 22 August 2011.

Ro'i, Yaacov, ed. 1995. *Muslim Eurasia: Conflicting Legacies.* London: Frank Cass.

Ro'i, Yaacov. 2000. *Islam in the Soviet Union: From the Second World War to Gorbachev.* New York: Columbia University Press.

Rousseau, Jean-Jacques. 1966. "Essay on the Origin of Languages Which Treats of Melody and Musical Imitation." In *On the Origin of Language*. Jean-Jacques Rousseau and Johann Gottfried Herder. Translated by J. H. Moran and A. Gode. Chicago: University of Chicago Press.

Roy, Olivier. 1990. *Islam and Resistance in Afghanistan*. 2nd ed. Cambridge: Cambridge University Press.

Roy, Olivier. 2000. *The New Central Asia: The Creation of Nations*. New York: New York University Press.

Ruel, Malcolm. 1997. "Christians as Believers." In *Belief, Ritual and the Securing of Life: Reflexive Essays on a Bantu Religion*. Leiden: E. J. Brill. 36–59.

Rumer, Boris. 1990. *Soviet Central Asia: A Tragic Experiment*. New York: Routledge Press.

Russell, Bertrand. 1992. *Human Knowledge: Its Scope and Limits*. New York: Routledge.

Rywkin, Michael, ed. 1988. *Russian Colonial Expansion to 1917*. London: Mansell.

Sacks, Harvey. 1984. "On Doing 'Being Ordinary.'" In *Structures of Social Action: Studies in Conversation Analysis*. Edited by J. M. Atkinson and J. Heritage. Cambridge: Cambridge University Press. 413–29.

Said, Edward W. 1994. *Orientalism*. New York: Vintage.

Said, Edward W. 1997. *Covering Islam: How the Media and the Experts Determine How We See the Rest of the World*. Revised ed. New York: Vintage.

Saroyan, Mark. 1997. *Minorities, Mullahs, and Modernity: Reshaping Community in the Former Soviet Union*. Edited by E. W. Walker. Berkeley: International and Area Studies.

Sarsembayev, Azamat. 1999. "Imagined Communities: Kazak Nationalism and Kazakification in the 1990s." *Central Asian Survey* 18, no. 3: 319–46.

Sarygulov, Dastan. 2005. *Kirgizy: proshloe, nastoiashchee i budushchee*. Bishkek: Fond Tengir-Ordo [in Russian].

Schatz, Edward. 2004. *Modern Clan Politics: The Power of "Blood" in Kazakhstan and Beyond*. Seattle: University of Washington Press.

Schatz, Edward. 2005. "Reconceptualizing Clans: Kinship Networks and Statehood in Kazakhstan." *Nationalities Papers* 33, no. 2: 231–54.

Schielke, Samuli. 2010. "Second Thoughts about the Anthropology of Islam, or How to Make Sense of Grand Schemes in Everyday Life." *Working Papers*. Berlin: Zentrum Moderner Orient.

Schutz, Alfred. 1970. *On Phenomenology and Social Relations*. Chicago: University of Chicago Press.

Schwab, Wendell. 2011. "Islam in Print: The Diversity of Islamic Literature and Interpretation in Post-Soviet Kazakhstan." Ph.d. diss., Indiana University, Bloomington.

Seligman, Adam B. 1999. "Toleration and Religious Tradition." *Society* 36, no. 5: 47–53.

Seligman, Adam B. 1997. *The Problem of Trust*. Princeton: Princeton University Press.

Seligman, Adam B. 2000. *Modernity's Wager: Authority, the Self, and Transcendence*. Princeton: Princeton University Press.

Seligman, Adam B., Rahel R. Wasserfall, and David W. Montgomery. 2015. *Living with Difference: How to Build Community in a Divided World.* Berkeley: University of California Press.

Seligman, Adam B., and Robert P. Weller. 2012. *Rethinking Pluralism: Ritual, Experience, and Ambiguity.* Oxford: Oxford University Press.

Seligman, Adam B., Robert P. Weller, Michael J. Puett, and Bennett Simon. 2008. *Ritual and Its Consequences: An Essay on the Limits of Sincerity.* Oxford: Oxford University Press.

Shahrani, M. Nazif. 1994. "Muslim Central Asia: Soviet Development Legacies and Future Challenges." In *Central Asia and the Caucasus after the Soviet Union: Domestic and International Dynamics.* Edited by M. Mesbahi. Gainesville: University Press of Florida. 56–71.

Shils, Edward. 1975. *Center and Periphery: Essays in Macrosociology.* Chicago: University of Chicago Press.

Shils, Edward. 1981. *Tradition.* Chicago: University of Chicago Press.

Sievers, Eric W. 2002. "Uzbekistan's Mahalla: From Soviet to Absolutist Residential Community Associations." *Journal of International and Comparative Law at Chicago-Kent* 2: 91–158.

Silverstein, Brian. 2002. "Discipline, Knowledge, and Imperial Power in Central Asia: 19th Century Notes for a Genealogy of Social Forms." *Central Asian Survey* 21, no. 1: 91–105.

Soucek, Svat. 2000. *A History of Inner Asia.* Cambridge: Cambridge University Press.

Stalin, Joseph. 1913. "Marxism and the National Question." *Prosveshchenie*, nos. 3–5 (March–May).

"State of Emergency Declared in South Kirghizia." 1990 (5 June). ITAR-TASS. http://lexis-nexis.com.

Stewart, Charles, and Rosalind Shaw, eds. 1994. *Syncretism/Anti-Syncretism: The Politics of Religious Synthesis.* London: Routledge.

Street, Brian V. 1999. *Literacy and Theory in Practice.* Cambridge: Cambridge University Press.

Temirkulov, Azamat. 2010. "Kyrgyz 'Revolutions' in 2005 and 2010: Comparative Analysis of Mass Mobilization." *Nationalities Papers* 38, no. 5: 589–600.

Thompson, Chad D., and John Heathershaw. 2005. "Discourses of Danger in Central Asia: Introduction." *Central Asian Survey* 24, no. 1: 1–4.

Times of Oman/Reuters. 2010. "Kyrgyzstan 'Weak Link' for Extremists: Security Chief." *Times of Oman/Reuters* (27 June). LexisNexis Academic. http://rt4rf9qn2y.search.serialssolutions.com/?ctx_ver=Z39.88-2004&ctx_enc=info%3Aofi%2Fenc%3AUTF-8&rfr_id=info:sid/summon.serialssolutions.com&rft_val_fmt=info:ofi/fmt:kev:mtx:journal&rft.genre=article&rft.atitle=Kyrgyzstan+%22weak+link%22+for+extremists%3A+security+chief&rft.jtitle=Times+of+Oman&rft.date=2010-06-27&rft.pub=Al+Bawaba+%28Middle+East%29+Ltd&rft.externalDocID=2067641081&paramdict=en-US. Accessed 30 October 2013.

Tishkov, Valery. 1995. "'Don't Kill Me, I'm a Kyrgyz!': An Anthropological Analysis of Violence in the Osh Ethnic Conflict." *Journal of Peace Research* 32, no. 2: 133–49.

Tishkov, Valery. 2004. *Chechnya: Life in a War-Torn Society.* Berkeley: University of California Press.

Tiuliundieva, N. 2006. "The Accommodation of Children and Young People in Kyrgyzstan by the System of Education, and the Problem of Gender Inequality." *Russian Education and Society* 48, no. 1: 72–87.

Tolstoy, Leo. 1994. *War and Peace.* Translated by C. Garnett. New York: Modern Library.

Trimingham, J. Spencer. 1998. *The Sufi Orders in Islam.* Oxford: Oxford University Press.

Turner, Victor. 1995. *The Ritual Process: Structure and Anti-Structure.* Hawthorne, NY: Aldine de Gruyter.

Vaisman, Demian. 1995. "Regionalism and Clan Loyalty in the Political Life of Uzbekistan." In *Muslim Eurasia: Conflicting Legacies.* Edited by Y. Ro'i. London: Frank Cass. 105–22.

van der Heide, Nienke. 2008. "Spirited Performance: The Manas Epic and Society in Kyrgyzstan." Ph.D. diss., Tilburg University, Tilburg.

Varisco, Daniel Martin. 2005. *Islam Obscured: The Rhetoric of Anthropological Representation.* New York: Palgrave Macmillan.

Varisco, Daniel Martin. 2007. *Reading Orientalism: Said and the Unsaid.* Seattle: University of Washington Press.

Vigh, Henrik. 2006. *Navigating Terrains of War: Youth and Soldiering in Guinea-Bissau.* New York: Berghahn Books.

Voegelin, Eric. 1952. *The New Science of Politics: An Introduction.* Chicago: University of Chicago Press.

Wachtel, Andrew Baruch. 2013. "Kyrgyzstan between Democratization and Ethnic Intolerance." *Nationalities Papers.* 41, no. 6: 971–86.

Waldron, Jeremy. 1988. "Locke: Toleration and the Rationality of Persecution." In *Justifying Toleration: Conceptual and Historical Perspectives.* Edited by S. Mendus. Cambridge: Cambridge University Press. 61–86.

Weatherford, Jack. 2005. *Genghis Khan and the Making of the Modern World.* New York: Three Rivers Press.

Werner, Cynthia. 1998. "Household Networks and the Security of Mutual Indebtedness in Rural Kazakstan." *Central Asian Survey* 17, no. 4: 597–612.

Werner, Cynthia. 2009. "Bride Abduction in Post-Soviet Central Asia: Marking a Shift Towards Patriarchy through Local Discourses of Shame and Tradition." *Journal of the Royal Anthropological Institute* 15: 314–31.

Werner, Cynthia, Holly Barcus, and Namara Brede. 2013. "Discovering a Sense of Well-Being through the Revival of Islam: Profiles of Kazakh Imams in Western Mongolia." *Central Asian Survey* 32, no. 4: 527–41.

Westermarck, Edward. 1933. *Pagan Survivals in Mohammedan Civilization: Lectures on the Traces of Pagan Beliefs, Customs, Folklore, Practises and Rituals Surviving in the Popular Religion and Magic of Islamic Peoples.* Amsterdam: Philo Press.

Whitehouse, Harvey. 2004. *Modes of Religiosity: A Cognitive Theory of Religious Transmission*. Walnut Creek, CA: Alta Mira Press.

Whitfield, Susan. 1999. *Life Along the Silk Road*. Berkeley: University of California Press.

Willerslev, Rane. 2007. *Soul Hunters: Hunting, Animism, and Personhood among the Siberian Yukaghirs*. Berkeley: University of California Press.

Winnicott, D. W. 1971. *Playing and Reality*. New York: Routledge.

Wolf, Eric R. 1997. *Europe and the People Without History*. Berkeley: University of California Press.

Wood, Frances. 2002. *The Silk Road: Two Thousand Years in the Heart of Asia*. Berkeley: University of California Press.

Wuthnow, Robert. 2001. *Creative Spirituality: The Way of the Artist*. Berkeley: University of California Press.

Yapp, Malcolm. 2001. "The Legend of the Great Game." *Proceedings of the British Academy* 111: 179–98.

Yurchak, Alexei. 2006. *Everything Was Forever, Until It Was No More: The Last Soviet Generation*. Princeton: Princeton University Press.

Zadneprovskij, J. A. 2000. *The Osh Settlement: On the History of Ferghana in the Late Bronze Age*. Bishkek: Kvazar-Service.

Zaharova, Antonina, and Nick Megoran. 2000. "Osh Ten Years On: Positive Developments in Ethnic Relations" (September 19). *EurasiaNet*. www.eurasianet.org/departments/insight/articles/eav091800.shtml.

Zanca, Russell. 2011. *Life in a Muslim Uzbek Village: Cotton Farming After Communism*. Belmont, CA: Wadsworth.

Zverev, B. 1990. "Ethnic Clashes in Southern Kirghizia" (5 June). ITAR-TASS. http://lexis-nexis.com.

Index

Solomon's Mountain (*Solomon Too*), 41, 59, 86, 111, 158

spirits, 22, 52, 82–85, 94, 122; ancestral, 41, 88, 95, 103, 110, 158

storytelling, 18, 20, 24, 107, 109–11, 119, 134

Sufism, 87, 179,

syncretism, 10, 26, 35, 81–83, 94, 98–99, 101–4, 143, 161

Tablighi Jama'at, 16, 22, 28, 91, 95–96, 134, 144

Tamerlange (Timur), 40–41, 43

Taoism, 41

Tash Rabat, 41–42

Tengrism, 95, 144

traditionalism, xii, 10, 23, 26–27, 35, 90, 98, 103; re-traditionalism, 26–27, 38

Tulip Revolution. *See* putsch: 2005 Kyrgyz

Turkestan: mausoleum, 59, 187n9; region, 64, 67

Turkey, 40, 81, 83, 91 95, 122, 123, 125, 134, 157, 158

tushoo kesuu, 126–30,134, 162

Wahhabi, 16, 95

water, 31, 77, 83, 84, 85; irrigation, 9, 44, 71, 104

Zoroastrian, 41, 81, 86